Reading Lives

Reconstructing Childhood, Books, and Schools in Britain, 1870–1920

Gretchen R. Galbraith

St. Martin's Press
New York

ISBN 0-312-12143-1

Library of Congress Cataloging-in-Publication Data

Galbraith, Gretchen R., 1963–
    Reading lives : reconstructing childhood,
books, and schools in Britain, 1870–1920 / by Gretchen R. Galbraith.
        p.   cm.
    Includes bibliographical references (p.) and index.
    ISBN 0-312-12143-1
    1. Children—Great Britain—Books and reading—History—
19th century.   2. Children—Great Britain—Books and reading—
History—20th century.   3. Education, Elementary—Great Britain—
History—19th century.   4. Education, Elementary—Great Britain—
History—20th century.   I. Title.
Z1037.A1G35   1997
028.5'5'0941—dc21   97-11631
                                                                                CIP

Internal design and typesetting by Letra Libre

First edition: September, 1997
10   9   8   7   6   5   4   3   2   1

This book is dedicated to Deborah and Peter Galbraith

Contents

Acknowledgements

I have been looking forward to writing this page for a long time. I want first to thank John Gillis, a wonderfully generous advisor from beginning to end. Thanks also to the people who took the time to read portions of my work and to help me to clarify my ideas: Tammy Proctor, Carolyn Shapiro, Fran Kelleher, Claudia Klaver, Ellen Ross, Peter Galbraith, Kevin Galbraith, Pamela Walker, Judith Walkowitz, Kay Vandergrift, Harold Poor, Tori Smith, Joy Dixon, Erika Rappaport, and Bonnie Smith.

Thanks as well to the people whose friendship and hospitality have kept me going over the years: Linda Hughes (also a wonderful reader), Jan and Charlie Sherman, Elizabeth MacCarthy, Sandy and Kelly Parker, the book coven, Socrates' Newsstand, Greg Sumner, Ellen Blaschinski, Susan Amussen, Michelle Duram, Jim Smither and Janet Coryell, Gertrude and Bruce Butterfield, Joyce and Whit Butterfield, and Michael Galbraith. I can only begin to thank Carolyn and Harvey Butterfield and Deborah and Peter Galbraith for their love and example.

Thanks to the librarians and archivists at Grand Valley State University, Rutgers University, the New York Public Library, the British Library, Brunel University, the Greater London Record Office, and the Wellcome Institute. These are the people who worked their magic to make the materials for this study appear when I needed them. Finally, this project could not have been completed without the financial support of Grand Valley State University, the National Academy of Education, the Spencer Foundation, and Rutgers University.

Introduction

The Victorian and Edwardian British cared deeply about what their nation's children read. While some pessimistically warned that unsuitable literature would ruin both children and the nation, others saw the power of reading as a key to boundless imaginative and intellectual opportunities. Preoccupation with middle-class children's leisure reading in their homes resonated with debates over what and how working-class children were reading in new publicly funded elementary Board schools. This concern with children's reading habits grew out of an understanding of reading as consumption: you were what you read. It was fueled by a sense of cultural crisis related to a perceived jump in mass literacy at a time when cheap literature was more abundant than ever. Integral to the reconstruction of middle and working-class childhoods, this vigilance toward children's reading was also a vehicle for negotiating the social, economic, and political transformations that defined British history between 1870 and 1914.

Heightened international competition in the late nineteenth century gave middle-class "discoveries" of poverty greater significance, raising questions about the nation's ability to reproduce a healthy population, produce wealth, and defend its empire. Class and gender boundaries were also being redrawn, as evidenced by the growth of the labor and women's suffrage movements. The erosion of Britain's industrial and imperial preeminence and the disruption of political stability by feminists and the organized working-class contributed to a series of crises of liberalism beginning in the 1880s.[1] Challenging existing boundaries between the state, the individual, and society, these crises forced reexamination of assumptions about the inviolability of parental authority and about what role the state should play in the lives of the nation's poorest children. Children, their books, and schools were never far removed from these political, class, and gender struggles.

This study of the politics of child literacy brings together the usually discrete histories of childhood, education, literacy, and children's literature. Given the elusiveness of children's lives in historical records, historians have followed Philippe Aries in exploring how conceptions of childhood have changed over time.[2] Carolyn Steedman and other scholars have provided nuanced readings of the beliefs and desires that adults have invested in the concept of childhood.[3] Historians have also revisited the century-old narrative of how enlightened middle-class reformers extended to poor children the comfort, safety, and innocence considered the birthright of nineteenth-century middle-class children. Exploring the linkages among child-saving efforts and the histories of public health and the medical profession, scholars have also shown that growing public concern for the bodies of poor children was partly the product of media-savvy philanthropic and medical campaigns. As Hugh Cunningham points out, the middle classes' child-saving impulse was always a complex mixture of fear and empathy toward poor children.[4]

Anna Davin's study of growing up in working-class London reminds us that the changing ideology of childhood wrought class and gender-specific changes in the experiences of children.[5] Davin and other historians also make it clear that the redefinition of childhood was inseparable from changes in adulthood, parenthood, and family life. Parental roles gained new meanings and became more rigidly gender-specific over the course of the nineteenth century. In the twentieth century, mothers came under increasing scrutiny from government and philanthropists, and their abilities were measured against the new standards of mothercraft and psychoanalysis.[6]

The forging of a modern working-class childhood has been linked to the Education Act of 1870, which created state-run elementary Board schools. The very process of bringing large numbers of children into classrooms heightened awareness of their physical conditions. In formulating and revising the curriculum for these new Board schools, educators and politicians articulated their conceptions of the purpose of elementary education and, implicitly, defined working-class childhood. Fights over how extensive and book-oriented the curriculum should be intersected with struggles over whether the government should provide this education free of charge and take a more active role in protecting students' physical well-being. Dina Copelman's study of London's women teachers recasts the debate over whether the 1870 Education Act marked the beginning of improved conditions for poor children or created a new means by which the upper classes could dominate the lower classes. Describing Board schools as "contested spaces," Copelman argues that elementary education in London was marked by constant negotiations involving parents, educators, and philanthropists.[7] The history of Board school education contains a number of moments of contestation among groups with conflicting and shifting agendas. This study focuses particularly on those moments when educators' understandings of, and goals for, children's reading were shaped by social and political pressures from inside and outside the classroom.

Demand for textbooks for new elementary Board schools contributed to the enormous growth in the market for children's literature in the late nineteenth century. Authors, publishers, and magazine editors also scrambled to keep up with demands for children's literature destined for middle- and upper-class nurseries at a time when gift-giving was being made an ever larger part of birthday and holiday celebrations.[8] Both contemporaries and historians have celebrated these decades as the "golden age" of children's literature, marked by greater imaginative freedom and devotion to portraying and appealing to "real" children.

Moving beyond earlier assumptions about the desires of Victorian and Edwardian child readers, scholars have more recently conceptualized an ideal reader's response to children's literature. These studies demonstrate that reading is a process to which readers bring experiences shaped by individual, familial, and national histories.[9] Yet an ideal reader response cannot be made to stand in for children's actual reading experiences that are irrecoverable from history by means of current linguistic and psychological theories. The history of children's literature must be linked to the history of the literary industry and to the agendas of the adults who wrote, produced, and bought it.[10] It is, finally, records of adult memories and interpretations of children and their literature with which we must work.

Concern for children's reading practices was never far removed from that of popular literacy as a whole. Late Victorian and Edwardian periodicals were filled with pronouncements about the reading habits of the lower classes. Typically, these articles warned that the lower classes were being demoralized by a diet of cheap, sensational literature.[11] A few writers dissented, playfully suggesting that middle-class reading habits were not terribly highbrow either and that a little escapist fiction never harmed anyone.[12]

Controversies over the meaning of literacy continue, in new guises, into the present. Some scholars sharply distinguish literacy from orality. They argue that orality is associated with communality and formulaic, conservative thinking, while literacy fosters self-awareness, a sense of individual isolation, and analytic, linear thought.[13] Others take a more skeptical view of the equation between literacy and objectivity and argue that the separation between orality and literacy is seldom clear-cut or complete. Certainly, in late nineteenth-century Britain there was no clean break between orality and literacy, but instead a mix of the two within individual life cycles and in families and communities. Nor can attainment of literacy be straightforwardly equated with social and economic advancement, given that many factors—including class, gender, and education—structure an individual's access to power. Ultimately, literacy must be placed in historical context and viewed as a social practice connected to other social practices, institutions, and power structures.[14]

Part One of this study is devoted to autobiographical memories of British childhoods lived between 1860 and 1914. Chapter One explores how men and women from across Britain's class spectrum reconstructed memories of family, education, and childhood's end, in order to evaluate their own lives and the social and political transformations through which they lived. Chapter Two examines the place of reading in memories of childhood, as components of private and social moments and as symbols of imagination and aspiration. Divided by class, gender, and time, memories of reading were crucial to autobiographers' reconstructions of childhood as explorations of identity and historical change.

Part Two examines the role children's literature played in forging a middle-class consensus that childhood was a uniquely innocent, imaginative stage of life. Chapter Three addresses how literary critics and reformers defined and defended the boundaries of appropriate children's literature, a process that incorporated tensions over whether childhood should be unified or divided by class and gender. Chapter Four is devoted to the history of the children's magazine *Little Folks*. Begun in 1871, this popular magazine periodically revised its editorial persona and opportunities for reader participation in step with the increasing commercialization of children's literature. Chapter Five deals with how Andrew Lang, a literary critic and anthropologist, and Edith Nesbit, a writer and Fabian socialist, found in children's literature both commercial success and an outlet for beliefs and social visions no longer accepted in the adult literary market. While sharing a common vision of childhood, the two authors' careers diverged sharply in an increasingly professional and gender-divided publishing world.

Part Three is devoted to elementary education in London. Situated in the nation's capital, and required to deal with a large, concentrated population of poor children, London's Board schools became lightning rods for controversies over the content of their curriculums and the physical conditions of their students. Chapter Six provides an overview of the social, political, and educational history of the School Board for London and the Board schools it oversaw. The overpressure crisis of 1884 is the subject of Chapter Seven. Riveting the attention of Parliament and the press, this controversy over whether working-class children were dying from educational stress became an opportunity for the nation's leaders to reexamine and articulate their beliefs about the purpose of elementary education and the role the state should play in caring for poor children. These chapters precede Chapter Eight's examination of reading in Board schools because educators' evaluations of children's literacy are inseparable from the political and social battles waged over Board schooling. In assessing children's reading, educators were engaging contemporary theories about children's cognitive development and about the power of books to shape readers' minds. They were also taking up questions about whether elementary education should be basic and terminal, perpetuating class and gender divisions, or provide a ladder to higher education and social mobility.

The issue of the power of reading, far from trivial, is a key means by which a society defines itself. At the end of the twentieth century, childhood is again a touchstone of political debate, the image of the innocent child providing a vocabulary for talking about social ills even as services to poor children are cut. At a time when children's book sales are booming, child illiteracy can still raise the specter of a nation's economic and cultural decline. By studying the social and political importance afforded children's reading a century ago, perhaps we can think more clearly about the meaning of child literacy at a time when both Britain and the United States are again reworking the state's role in children's lives and the content and structure of public education.[15]

Part One

British Childhoods Remembered

Chapter One

"As through a Telescope Reversed": British Childhoods, 1860–1914

The generations of British men and women born between 1860 and 1914 have left behind a particularly rich store of autobiographies. Well-known middle- and upper-class men, men and women of working-class origins whose lives shaped—and were shaped by—the growth of trade unionism and the Labour Party, and women's suffrage activists from all classes recorded their life stories. The less famous wrote unpublished autobiographies for themselves, their families, and friends. Recent oral history projects have preserved the life stories of men and women who might never have dared to write them.[1] Almost universally, these men and women employed their childhood memories to explore questions of identity and historical change. The ways in which autobiographers reconstructed those childhood memories were in turn an amalgam of class, gender, time and place of birth, and their perspectives at the time of writing.[2]

These generations of autobiographers wrote for various, often complex reasons: to entertain, to instruct, to make money, to record their roles in political and social changes, out of nostalgia for a bygone era, and to make sense of their lives.[3] The sociologist and Fabian socialist Beatrice Webb, born in 1858, declared that she was documenting the early environment of a sociologist and her search for a creed. J. R. Clynes, born in 1869, explained that he wrote for the silent of the working class and that his story merged with theirs. Another Labour politician, Margaret Bondfield, born in 1873, recorded her story of becoming Britain's first woman cabinet minister. The author Graham Greene, born in the early 1900s, explained that he wrote his autobiography for the same reasons he wrote novels: to reduce the chaos of experience to some kind of order. Dora Russell, born in the 1890s, wrote partly to correct her former husband Bertrand Russell's account of their marriage, and also to record her role in the political events in which they jointly participated.[4]

Some people felt more entitled to write autobiographies than others. Well-known upper-class autobiographers like Margot Tennant Asquith (a member of the London intellectual circle of "Souls" in her youth and later the wife of Prime Minister H. H. Asquith) took it for granted that their reminiscences would have an audience. Working-class Labour politicians wrote with a sense that they had a duty to record their memories, but like less well-known autobiographers, they often began by justifying their boldness in writing or with the disclaimer that they were writing only at the urging of others.[5]

Autobiographers, like theorists, disagree about the reliability of memory.[6] Arthur Ransome reminded readers that memory picks and chooses. Annie Kenney claimed only to be writing her own truth—not anyone else's—about the suffrage movement. Eleanor Acland argued that she could clearly see her childhood, but that her memories of adolescence were overlaid "with an accretion of adult ideas" about herself. Like other autobiographers, she claimed an objectivity regarding childhood, but not for later years. Margaret Bondfield presented her autobiography as a record of "hard facts and strong convictions. It is a fragment of real life."[7]

In organizing and narrating their unique life stories, people drew upon other autobiographies, fiction, oral traditions, and shared cultural myths.[8] For readers and writers alike, autobiographical patterns and narrative frameworks are particularly clear in accounts of childhood. Autobiographers generally gave ample space to childhood memories both because they considered them sources of insight into later character and success and because they often felt it safer, or more appropriate, to talk about their private lives and emotions in a distant childhood than in the present.[9] Most British autobiographers organized their childhood recollections around a common set of themes that included their earliest memories, family, home, education, and the transition into adulthood.[10] There is also a pattern to the silences: few wrote about sexuality or bodily functions, the exceptions being those who wrote with a psychoanalytic lens, including Helen Corke, who explained that hers was the record of "the awakening of an individual consciousness, and its subsequent expansion."[11]

Autobiographers foregrounded certain memories in presenting their child selves as signposts pointing toward the adults they had become. Leah Manning linked her childhood love of parades and processions to her adult work for suffrage, antifascism, and the peace movement. Ben Turner, like other Labour leaders, characterized himself as a rebel from childhood.[12] Margot Asquith, known for a spirit and outspokenness made possible by upper-class privilege, recalled that she and her siblings were allowed to run wild as children and that she had been the wildest of all. Like other women who described themselves as young rebels and tomboys, she had found a way to say that she had not readily conformed to authority or to rules of feminine decorum. Emmeline Pethick-Lawrence and Clara Grant had directed their rebelliousness against school rules they found intolerable. For Pethick-Lawrence, these stories foreshadowed her militant suffrage activism in the Women's Social and Political Union. Grant, a teacher and settlement worker in London's East End for over three decades, had to question many rules in order to effect the social and educational reforms she sought. "I was six when I committed my first act of rebellion against the established order of things," she wrote, in describing her refusal to follow what she considered to be stupid instructions for filling in her copybook.[13] These autobiographers made sense of who they had become by looking back into their early years.

A strong sense of what childhood should be also informed autobiographers' memories. By the 1880s, the experience of at least a few years of formal schooling was increasingly shared across class and gender lines as more middle-class girls and working-class children entered schools. The ideal of childhood as a protected stage of life, although still unattainable for most below the middle class, was becoming more pervasive in social policy and literary depictions of children. Having grown up while the meaning and circumstances of childhood were being redefined, autobiographers worked with a shared vocabulary of childhood to reconstruct divergent childhood experiences.[14]

Autobiographers of all classes associated childhood with imaginative play. Others, though, remembered a mixture of pleasure and terror or recalled childhoods dominated by fear.[15] These earliest memories were strongly colored by class and material circumstances. Born in 1904, middle-class Graham Greene's first memory at age four was of being pushed in his pram with a dead dog lying at his feet. Food ranked high in some working-class writers' hierarchy of memories. Trade unionist Ben Turner, born in 1863, remembered being frightened with tales of "Breakfast Mary," who stole uneaten food. George Baldry, son of a farm laborer and born in the late 1880s, wrote that his early memories had to do with "summat to put in my mouth."[16]

Determining the environment and material circumstances of childhood, class was also a subjectively important source of identity and differentiation. Graham Greene remembered having learned class consciousness as a child. Leah Manning, another middle-class child born at the turn of the century, recounted the time that she met up with girls in tattered petticoats while wandering the streets: "slum kids, I thought bitterly with deep class consciousness."[17] For Eleanor Acland, being the granddaughter of a mill owner and daughter of a Liberal Member of Parliament (MP) meant segregation from the community "which surrounded us and provided us with the where-withal of life." It was "borne in on us, perhaps unintentionally, that people in our position were not expected" to interact with those who were considered "the 'lower orders,' unless, owing to illness or poverty, ignorance or wickedness, they needed a helping hand extended to them."[18] During Dora Russell's childhood, her family's status and income rose as her father worked his way up in the civil service. Like Acland, she learned about class through charity. She and her siblings "learned to think of the poor as people we ought to be sorry for." They joined the Children's League of Pity and took flowers to school each week for local hospitals.[19]

Working-class autobiographers suggested that they, too, developed a strong sense of class early in life. Rose Kerrigan learned the difference between "haves" and "have nots" because her father chose a working-class synagogue over a "very middle class" one. J. H. Howard learned—and resented—the lessons of deference to squire and parson taught in a workhouse school.[20] Both Frank Benson and William Bowyer knew as children that they were of the "respectable" working class, Bowyer because he lived in a Battersea slum in south-west London, but at the end of the street that claimed the right to call itself respectable.[21] Angela Rodaway, born three decades after Bowyer, in 1918, grew up in a family whose sense of "superiority" demanded a way of living that was "almost monastic in its strictness." It meant that they struggled to keep up appearances in their Islington neighborhood after her father lost his business and remained unemployed as the Depression deepened. It also meant that the children did not learn for years of their father's unemployment—he stayed away from home all day to preserve what he and his wife considered a shameful secret. The toll of such "superiority" was heavy. Rodaway described her mother as having had "an unremitting lifeless energy. She had a thin mouth and tired eyes, like dents in a tin."[22]

As important as the respectability of Benson, Bowyer, and Rodaway was the fine line separating lower middle-class families from the working class. Helen Corke, whose father's business declined while she was growing up, remembered that a move to a house without a yard meant that her parents could no longer enforce their rule against playing in the street—a protection against consorting with children of lesser status. Frederick Willis, whose childhood was steeped in memories of middle-class comfort, remembered that his family sent him to Board school (considered working class) only under compulsion; Willis himself considered this a renunciation of his birthright. Whatever one's class origins, they were explained early in the autobiography to establish the author's identity, often in a shorthand that readers were expected to understand.[23]

Family members and servants in well-off homes played large roles in most autobiographers' childhood stories. Siblings entered into recollections of play, nursery, and school, while descriptions of parents and grandparents gave emotional substance to writers' memories. Many middle- and upper-class children spent their time in nurseries with nurses and governesses, only interacting with parents at set times of day. This regimen translated into memories of parents as either distant and reserved or as adored objects of worship. Reflecting on the differences between child rearing in the 1950s and the late nineteenth century, Winifred Peck thought that "[i]n nearly every way the closer intercourse between parents and children must be to the good," but that the former distinction between child and adult spaces had "invested a parent with the mystery and enchantment of a certain distance."[24] Working-class children, on the other hand, were cared for by, and shared meals and bedrooms with, parents and siblings. While a number of upper-class writers described achieving emotional intimacy with parents only as teens or young adults, working-class children usually had strong emotional ties to parents, whether of love or resentment, from an early age.

While some writers remembered fathers who were accessible and fun playmates,[25] most fathers figured more remotely in childhood memories than mothers who had day-to-day responsibility for home and childcare. Robert Roberts recorded the one occasion when his working-class father walked with him in public (clearly an event). For some working- and middle-class children, this remoteness reinforced the sense that their father was the ultimate authority, although Dorothy Scannell remembered her father as merely a "Paper Tiger" in her mother's home. Howard Spring, born in the late 1880s, remembered an exceptionally inaccessible father whose only intimate moments with his family occurred when he read to them.[26]

Like many writers, Spring presented his mother as the emotional center of his childhood. As historian Ellen Ross has shown, mothers were of central importance in working-class children's lives, as providers of comfort that was both material and emotional—in fact, it would be hard to separate the two. Across several generations, autobiographers took pride in recounting their working-class mothers' ability to care for their families. Philip Ballard remembered that his family survived without much money because his mother "ruled our little household with a genial despotism. . . . Her vision was so clear, and there was so much unselfishness in her nature, and such deep wells of tenderness that we all adored her."[27] Minnie Bowles, born thirty-eight years after Ballard in 1903, described her mother as "the strong base on which all else depended."[28] Philip Inman proudly remembered the first time he was able to do the accounts for his mother's laundry business; others had similar memories of the day they handed their first earnings over to their mothers.[29]

Although critical of his father's inability to provide for his family, Howard Spring remembered his father's aloofness with a degree of bemusement—

after all, fathers often had little to do with children's daily existence. Because working-class mothers were supposed to be emotionally central to their children's lives, the pain and resentment of adults like Emma Smith and George Meek who remembered shadowy or harsh mothers were much stronger.[30] Kathleen Woodward, born in 1896 into a London working-class family, wrote that her mother "reluctantly bore" six children and had to support them and her invalid husband by doing laundry and cleaning and negotiating with the Guardians of the Parish. Woodward's painful awareness of having been unwanted was mixed with sympathy for the burdens her angry, hopeless mother had borne.[31]

Children of wealthier families were more matter-of-fact about the distance from their mothers that was structured into family life. Margot Asquith simply commented that she had seen little of her mother when she was young.[32] Beatrice Webb remembered her mother as a source of arbitrary authority "whose rare interventions in my life I silently resented." Her father, in contrast, was the "central figure of the family life—the light and warmth of the home."[33] For Webb and other middle-class children, nannies often filled the role of comforter, and nurseries became places of refuge: Sonia Keppel's nursery was her fortress, her nanny the garrison commander. Emmeline Pethick-Lawrence, though, remembered her nursemaids as tyrants against whom there was no recourse. She called her nursery a prison that prepared her for her stays in Holloway Jail as a suffragette.[34]

Descriptions of family also enabled autobiographers to explain their heritages of class, values, and beliefs, sometimes in elaboration of themes presented in introductory genealogies.[35] Helen Corke vividly remembered her lower middle-class parents' shock at her wild sobs in reaction to neighborhood boys' torturing of a frog: "Then comes the realisation, slow but abiding, that to them, my loss of self-control is a worse matter" than the boys' cruelty. Like many other autobiographers' descriptions of working-class parents, John Fraser's conveyed a sense of dignity and wisdom that, for him, outweighed their lack of education. Nicknamed "Prince of Scabs," William Collison, a working-class "Free Labour" opponent of trade unions, remembered his policeman father's resoluteness in the face of neighbors' hostility, and this strengthened his own sense of righteous isolation when he faced "a hostile mob."[36]

Several women born between 1876 and 1895, who were political activists as adults, considered their fathers their greatest influences. Emmeline Pethick-Lawrence believed that she had inherited her love of justice from her father. After her first arrest as a suffragette, he was "proud that a child of his had not hesitated to make a stand for the extension of democratic liberty."[37] In Margaret Rhondda's family, "it was almost the done thing" to go to prison during suffrage protests before World War I. Her father, a former Liberal

MP, did not stand in the way of the suffrage activities of his wife and daughter. He also took Rhondda, newly married, into his coal business, at her mother's suggestion. Reflecting on her unconventional life, she wrote that if she had been born twenty years earlier, or with a less understanding family or "modern-minded father," it was doubtful she would have done anything outside of the home.[38] Dora Russell wrote of her closeness to her father: he talked to her often "and was ambitious about my education." He also gave Russell her first political experience, taking her to Trafalgar Square to see the 1906 election results being flashed on a screen above St. Martin's Church. "For the first time I was carried away by mass emotion, utterly intoxicated with it all."[39] Understanding the psychological, social, and financial barriers to independence that most girls of their generation faced, these women saw their fathers' (or in Rhondda's case, familial) support as crucial to their own ability to scale those barriers. On the other side were women like Helena Swanwick and Hannah Mitchell, who achieved their dreams of education or political activism despite parental indifference.

Other women noted how gender was interwoven with class and family histories. Eleanor Acland counted as pivotal in both her own and her daughter Ellen's childhoods the years that their brothers had gone off to boarding school, leaving them at home to continue studying with governesses. Beryl Lee Booker, born in 1888, remembered wishing to be a boy and her sense of loss when her brother returned home from boarding school full of disdain for girls. Another middle-class woman, Katherine Chorley, born in 1897, looked back on a childhood marked by separate spheres: her father was out in the "big world" and her mother was at home providing tranquility and comfort. She remembered that after the 9:18 train had taken all the men off to work, a town of women was left behind.[40] Both men and women remembered having understood as children how household tasks were gendered. Helen Corke and Rose Gibbs recorded their childhood dislike of the needlework lessons considered integral to girls' educations. Thomas Morgan, a "street arab" as a child, remembered his resentment at being taught "girls' work" like knitting. Girls were often assigned the bulk of the housework, but in many working-class households boys were also expected to do their share of childcare and errands. As Ben Turner explained though, these were not activities that *men* normally did. He was glad to have learned household chores as a boy so that he could now help his wife in emergencies.[41]

Across class lines, women remembered having connected and resented the imbalance between their own household obligations and their brothers' educational opportunities. Helena Swanwick, born in 1864, wrote of "the intense desire which possessed me all my youth, for more opportunities for concentration and continuity." She "resented the assumption that whereas education was of importance for my brothers, it was of no account for me. I resented also that I was required to render them personal services which they need not reciprocate."[42] A number of working-class men born between 1852 and 1885 remembered that their sisters' educations had been cut short when their labor was needed at home. A sense of regret for a sister's self-sacrifice became resentment when women themselves spoke. A suffrage and labor activist, and then a magistrate for twenty years, Hannah Mitchell, born in 1871, remembered a mother who had kept her home to work while her brothers and sister got the schooling she desired. "At eight years old my weekly task was to darn my brothers' stockings while they read or played cards or dominoes."[43] Such memories must have gained retrospective importance for Mitchell and Swanwick in light of their suffrage work as adults.

In addition to gender, familial circumstances and attitudes toward learning, class, and the era in which they were born determined children's educational histories. Arthur Ransome, born in 1884, experienced the range of schooling available to middle-class boys. He began with lessons in the nursery with a governess, moved on to a tutor, then attended day school before leaving for boarding school, the event often seen as a decisive break from childhood family life. Crucibles of middle- and upper-class masculinity, private boarding schools ("public schools") prepared boys for leadership roles in the state and empire. But the emphasis on team sports could be painful for unathletic boys like Ransome. He remembered being jeered by fellow students and having his "muscular Christian" headmaster call him a coward for his ineptitude on the playing field.[44]

Francis Power Cobbe, born in 1822, and Beatrice Webb, born in 1858, were critical of the limited educations available to middle- and upper-class girls during their lives, and both considered themselves self-educated. By the 1880s, some girls' schools offered more rigorous curriculums, but many Edwardian girls were still educated at home or were sent to academies and finishing schools to learn "feminine" accomplishments—an experience Jane Poynder remembered as painful.[45] Winifred Peck, born in the 1880s, believed that she had experienced the range of schooling available to middle-class girls in the nineteenth century. She had passed from a governess to a day school to Miss Quill's Young Ladies' Academy, which "had never changed" in thirty years. Finally, she ended up at a new girls' public school, Wycombe Abbey, "which was at least twenty years ahead of its time." Unlike Ransome, she found the school's emphasis on athleticism a joy because she was no longer scolded for being a tomboy.[46]

While Emmeline Pethick-Lawrence had known no girls who had gone on to college, Vera Brittain, Helena Swanwick, Dora Russell and Winifred Peck could see a path, albeit rocky, to university. Russell's father helped her to prepare for her university entrance examinations by studying Latin and Greek with her.[47] Vera Brittain had to overcome her parents' opposition to her dream of attending Oxford before she settled down to study for the entrance exam, impeded by confusion about the rules and by the lack of books in her provincial town. A scholarship and aid from a godmother enabled Helena Swanwick to attend Girton despite her parents' indifference. She and Winifred Peck described the joys of that first year at university: the new social freedom and, for Swanwick, precious privacy.[48]

Before the advent of government-sponsored Board schools and effective child labor laws, working-class children could patch together educations in Sunday schools, church schools, and dame schools.[49] Former Socialist and Secular Sunday school scholars enthusiastically remembered the hours each Sunday when they heard new ideas and learned reading and speaking skills.[50] As public education became more widely available after the 1870 Education Act, children began to attend school for more days each year and for more years. But whether their education consisted of a few weeks in a local working-class school, a few months each year in a church-sponsored school, or seven solid years in Board school, many autobiographers' memories of schooling were negative (imagine the memories of the majority who did not write autobiographies!). Some recalled schools as scary places where masters readily used their canes. Others remembered the monotony and the wasted time that could have been spent earning money for their families, or looked back on their lessons as symbols of a class system they despised. Those few who had enjoyed school credited a kind or inspiring teacher.[51]

Into the twentieth century, working-class children's educations were cut short by work. As George Hodgkinson put it, a strained household economy "was the first threat to our educational opportunities."[52] Many autobiographers had clear memories of that last day of school, normally followed by a first job the next day or week.[53] Sometimes, though, the transition from school to work was less decisive. As half-timers in the 1870s and 1880s, J. R. Clynes and Annie Kenney split their days between school and mill work; during World War I, eleven-year-old Clifford Hills was one of the children exempted from school to fill gaps in the agricultural labor force.[54] The end of education prompted varied, sometimes shifting, emotions. Fred Kitchen was glad that he could begin to help his struggling, widowed mother. Patrick MacGill was anxious to grow up at age twelve, but once he was out on his own, he came to resent his parents' demands that his wages be sent back to Ireland to feed his growing family. Many were glad to be done with an education they hated. Others regretted the end of structured learning. Having snatched her learning in spare moments, Hannah Mitchell considered schooling the key to a treasure house.[55]

In the 1900s, scholarships enabled a minority of working-class children to attend high school. Born in 1903, A. L. Rowse received a high school scholarship that paved the way to an Oxford scholarship and out of the world of rural poverty from which he felt alienated. For Angela Rodaway, born in 1918, a scholarship to high school had even more complicated significance. As a child, she aspired to something beyond her family's grinding poverty: "There was only one way; I must work hard to get a scholarship. After that I might work in an office, perhaps even the Civil Service, like my uncle, and then all things would be open to me." Her mother coached her in sums and sent notes to school requesting that Angela be exempted from needlework, art, and games to have extra time for English and arithmetic. Once in high school on a scholarship, she grappled with being poorer than her peers. After Rodaway had been in high school five years, her mother decided that it was time for her daughter to take the civil service exam and enter a clerical job. Once a symbol of limitless possibilities, this job soon became unbearable to her; she left it and drifted from job to job, finally leaving home as well. Rodaway ended *A London Childhood* with a description of her new life: she now devoted her days to reading and writing and hung out with artists. Unable to secure a job, she went on the dole, an act which symbolized to her that she had put her family's concern about appearances behind her.[56]

In reconstructing their childhoods, autobiographers were also evaluating the passage of time and historical change. While some viewed the past with nostalgia, others viewed it with regret and anger. Some middle-class writers criticized their childhoods in terms of the rigidity and repressiveness of their parents' class and time. Eleanor Acland wrote that her elders' minds and bodies had been "lumbered with a load of upholstery: dogmas, prejudices, formulas, customs and taboos. . . ."[57] Politically active adults were the most apt to look back with a critical eye on the class and gender divisions of their early years. After years of suffrage activism, Dora Montefiore, born in 1851, wrote that in her "unconscious nursery and schoolroom days I knew nothing of the domestic machinery which kept this sort of patriarchal home going." Phyllis Bentley, Dora Russell, and Emmeline Pethick-Lawrence presented their autobiographies as records of the opening up of educational, occupational, and political opportunities for women.[58] Leah Manning experienced poverty only vicariously in her Edwardian childhood, but celebrated the contrast between the underfed, overworked children of the past and the "splendid," robust children of today, provided for by the welfare state.[59]

Working-class Labour politicians celebrated this progress on a more personal level, contrasting children's present conditions with their own and taking pride in their roles in effecting political and social reforms. Ben Turner, born in 1863, measured the difference between past and present in terms of the freedom gained for working-class children from "mill thraldom" and scholastic limitations. William Haddow, born in 1865, and writing in 1943 after years of service as a Socialist school board member, reminded readers of how terrible conditions had been before the advent of school meals and clinics: "it takes a great deal of imagination to picture child life years ago. . . ." Children of "poor, underpaid, and badly housed parents . . . grew up ill nourished, ill clad and still suffering, sometimes permanently, from some of their infantile troubles. . . ." Such memories of hardship were not confined to the politically active. Eighty-four-year-old Alice Rushmer remembered in the 1970s that her rural working-class childhood had decidedly not been the "good old days."[60]

Born in 1869, Labour MP J. R. Clynes lived through and helped to enact major changes in the educational and labor conditions of working-class children. His autobiography, published in 1937, and its condensation and revision for a "Macmillan War Pamphlet," published in 1940, illustrate how childhood could be used to make sense of historical change. From the age of ten, Clynes had worked half-time in the local mill and attended school half-time. Looking back, "as through a telescope reversed, down the vista of the years," he saw a "small boy running barefoot over dangerous oily floors, keeping pace with spinning machinery" in an Oldham cotton mill. With this description of industrial conditions in the decade of his birth, Clynes placed himself on the "world stage" as a "little piecer," sullenly eager "to escape from the brutal slavery of school to the merciless thraldom of the mill."[61] In the pamphlet version of his autobiography, the figure of the "little piecer" served as a symbol of the deprivation and harshness of former times, and as a measure of headway to the present when children received care from birth onward. Clynes used these signs of progress as a rallying cry against Hitler, urging British readers "in these days of national emergency to stand up for the privileges and rights we have won for ourselves." He made his child self into a symbol of the linkage between his own success and that of the labor movement and into a propagandistic wartime symbol of British progress.[62]

Writers who viewed their childhoods with nostalgia dwelt more on values than on material conditions. Frederick Willis, born in the 1870s into the lower middle class, recalled his childhood as part of a bygone world of safety, law, and order. Jeremy Seabrook, in his 1973 account of a hundred years of working-class family history, contrasted modern selfishness and materialism with a remembered past in which "carefully dusted rows of school prizes" were acquired through hard labor and were therefore treasured.[63] Both middle- and working-class writers regretted the end of what they saw as a simpler time when they had used their wits to enjoy their few toys. These writers believed that children of present times (stretching from 1920 to 1970), with their abundant toys, playgrounds, and movies, appreciated their possessions less and were less capable of using their imaginations.[64]

Between conservative nostalgia for an invented past and condemnations of the past by Socialists, trade unionists, and feminists, there existed a middle ground. Some writers combined nostalgia for "simpler" times, linked to happy memories of their own childhoods, with celebrations of improvements in children's conditions and education.[65] Born in the 1880s, George Baldry was particularly ambivalent. His anecdotes about rural childhood escapades were interspersed with memories of hunger and harsh punishment, which he contrasted with the better nutrition and treatment of contemporary children. The village of his remembered youth was marked by illiteracy and isolation, but he also celebrated the villagers' capacity for storytelling and broad-mindedness. His pleasure in technological advances was also muted. He marveled at the impact of the wireless but feared that man was using the "natural forces of the earth—so it seems to me, who am growing an old man—for his own destruction." Baldry spoke for many autobiographers when he wrote that "it seems another world" than in the days when he "was a little lad sitting by the same hearth as I sit now. . . ."[66]

To measure the changes that had taken place in a lifetime, autobiographers evaluated their childhoods in terms of what childhood should be. Most middle- and upper-class writers did not dwell on whether theirs had been proper childhoods. But a few, in trying to explain why their memories of childhood were happy, expressed awareness that such memories were not universally shared. Winifred Peck and Margaret Rhondda attributed their happiness to their comfortable circumstances and to parents who gave them a sense of security.[67] Dora Russell described a "very happy childhood," which she ascribed to having had many opportunities for mental and physical fulfillment and to the Edwardian age when people had cast off "straitlaced" Victorian ways and looked forward to an "ever-prosperous future."[68]

Phyllis Bentley's memories of her Edwardian childhood were less nostalgic. When she was seven, the West Riding mill in which her father was a junior partner was closed. Her family life grew unstable: her parents' tempers frayed; her favorite brother, Frank, left school to become an office boy. Looking back on this period, she saw that "every support, every framework of my previous childish life (and Frank's) had been torn away."[69] While Bentley's memories remind us that not all middle-class childhoods were stable and protected, a number of working-class writers born between 1872 and 1911 recognized their poverty in retrospect, but remembered their childhoods as happy. Albert Mansbridge's declaration that his had been the life of "a normal child in a decent working-class home" was grounded in a particularly strong sense of what childhood should be.[70]

The majority of autobiographers who felt that theirs had fallen short of what can be called a "myth" of protected, innocent childhood were members of a transitional working-class generation that left school to work at an early age, but lived to see most working-class children spend more years in elementary schools before going to work. They articulated what was wrong with their society by relating their own histories to a sense of what childhood ought to be.[71] Lord Snell, a Labour politician born in 1865, attributed his lost childhood to his class and age: others could look back on happy days, but "I have no such memories. The children of my day and status were born to work and privation." Clynes had no memory of "golden summers, no triumphs at games," but remembered instead hunger, exhaustion, and "smoke-fouled streets." Although not political, Emma Smith's autobiography also relied on assumptions about what childhood should be. Born illegitimate, she related tales of a childhood in and out of institutions and singing in the streets for money. These accounts were structured by Smith's sure sense of what her childhood lacked: comfort, safety, and love. These writers made use of well-known narratives about "proper" childhood conditions to make sense of their early years. The knowledge that they grew up in a time when the ideal of childhood and the lives of wealthier children were increasingly remote from their own experiences gave a rhetorically powerful perspective to these reconstructions of their early years.[72]

The End of Childhood

For three working-class boys born between 1869 and 1903, childhood ended decisively with the end of school. Twelve years old in 1881, Clynes was "ready to go forth, a grown man, into the world of work." For him, manhood meant full-time labor and contributing to the family coffer as his father did. Patrick MacGill also considered himself a man when he was sent out at age twelve in 1902 to find farmwork. Looking back, he reverted to calling himself a boy at the mercy of his employers, but at age twelve he had connected manhood with independence and wage earning. When Hymie Fagan began to work at age fourteen in 1917, "officially my childhood had ended."[73]

Working-class women had more trouble locating a clear end to childhood. Born in 1871, Hannah Mitchell used the year 1885 when she left an unhappy life at home to work as a maid to divide the first two sections of her book, respectively entitled "Child" and "Woman." Dorothy Scannell, born after 1910, had memories of a comfortable working-class childhood and access to more schooling. She left school to work in a factory at fourteen, but continued to live at home until she married seven years later. Subtitled "An East End Childhood," her book ends with a funny description of her honeymoon. Introduced early to adult women's domestic labor, many working-class girls had few memories of childhood play not linked to child-minding; they experienced less decisive breaks between school and waged work, often because their schooling had been sporadic to begin with, or, in Scannell's case, because she continued to live in her parents' home.

Whether or not middle- and upper-class women autobiographers found markers of childhood's end depended on when they were born. Margot Asquith, born in 1864, wrote of her "youth" as a period that stretched into the year she "came out" into society. Her activities evolved from tree climbing to philanthropy, yet she shared a night nursery with her sister Laura until Laura married. Gwen Raverat and Leah Manning, born closer to the end of the century, had a new vocabulary for discussing childhood. Manning called her first chapter "Victorian Childhood" and her second "Edwardian Adolescence." Raverat marked the year when her brother left for school and her "Nana" left because of illness as the end of childhood and the beginning of a less happy adolescence. Working within a psychoanalytic framework, Helen Corke described her twelfth year as the one when primal terrors ended and "law and order" entered her world.[74] Unless they were sent to boarding school, these women could only retrospectively impose categories on these years before "coming out" or marriage marked a break from the routines of childhood and youth. For Phyllis Bentley, a sense of full independence came with her father's death when she was thirty-two.[75]

The break from childhood routines was sharper and earlier for middle-class boys like Graham Greene and Arthur Ransome, who remembered losing the privacy and comfort of home when they entered boarding school. Looking back on his upper-class childhood, L. E. Jones saw a distinct break between childhood and boyhood taking place at about age ten. Boyhood begins

> when we cease to make-believe; . . . when we give up acting the characters taken from our storybooks; and more specifically, when we have once tasted the primeval joys of hunting wild animals.[76]

Defining childhood as a time of innocence and imagination, he distinguished it from a boyhood stage of acquiring masculinity. He also saw boyhood as environmentally determined: his own lasted until he left Eton at nineteen because, until then, he had lived an insulated life of family and school. But he felt that such an extended boyhood would have been impossible during the two world wars.

Nineteen-fourteen marked the end of childhood for two other middle-class autobiographers. Born in 1904, Anthony Powell recalled that his childhood, "with its intensity of imaginative adventure that comes to an end with school . . . had been allowed to linger on rather beyond its statutory limits." The child of an army officer, he wrote that his childhood ended the day Britain entered World War I. Born in 1897, Katherine Chorley concluded her book in 1914, the year that the certainties of Edwardian life, and the era of her childhood, ended.[77]

Attributed to Rousseau, and popularized by Romantic poets, the image of childhood as a separate world, a period of innocence and imagination, had become part of popular culture by the late nineteenth century. It had entered the rhetoric of politicians, educators, and reformers and was depicted in children's books and in plays like *Peter Pan* and *Little Lord Fauntleroy.* Confirmed by autobiographers who remembered "magical," distant childhoods,[78] it also served as the basis for critiques of social conditions that were responsible for lost or abbreviated childhoods. Alfred Coppard's autobiography linked the personal and the social in a passage mourning the end of childhood. Sent to the East End of London at age ten after his father's death: "it was there I lost childhood, innocence, schooling, and became acquainted with grief, starvation, poor clothes, and slums. . . ."[79] Here his memories of a better past combined with an adult vision of what childhood should have been. This image of childhood was fluid enough to serve as either critique or celebration of individual and social histories.

Chapter Two

Reading Lives and Lives of Reading

In her autobiography of a middle-class Edwardian childhood, Sonia Keppel described making her way to her father's sitting room for their nightly reading sessions that represented companionship and a temporary flouting of gender:

> Always he read me boys' books. . . . The world of women was left behind. Even Mamma could have no place in our crew of two. With his shirt-front as a trusty prow against sudden danger, nightly he and I set sail for the open sea.[1]

Reading was an integral part of childhood memories of family and schooling, and of more private moments of imagination and aspiration. Like education, the "situation of reading," where children read, why, and with whom, was shaped by class, gender, material, and historical circumstances.[2]

In Victorian and Edwardian Britain, there was no clear division between orality and literacy, but instead a mix of the two within individual life cycles and in families and communities. British children learned to read through listening, repetition, memorization, and recitation. Families and neighbors gathered together to hear one person read a book or newspaper aloud, and the literate and illiterate rubbed elbows into the twentieth century. The ability to read was associated with greater introspectiveness and a sense of isolation from family and community, but it was also a bridge to communication with other readers, to collective action, and to speech-making.[3]

As caregivers, women were usually responsible for teaching children to read. This might be an older sister, mother, grandmother, or nanny, depending on the family's composition and wealth. But some working-class fathers took on this task, having had more chances than their wives to develop their literacy skills. Nellie Priest was taught to read by her father and later read to a grandmother unable to read for herself. In at least a few working-class families, children brought home literacy skills, then shared them with their parents. In Winifred Peck's large, upper middle-class family, siblings taught each other to read.[4]

An "Insatiable Thirst" for Reading

His childhood job of reading books and newspapers to a millworker gave Bob Stewart a lifelong appetite for reading. Thomas Bell felt that his early contact with books "laid the foundation for that love of literature which I regard as being as important for a man's soul as meat and drink are for his body." Katherine Chorley described the excitement of reading a new book: "[c]rash went a barrier and we marched through into some new realm of the intellect." For these adults, reading was a defining element of who they had been as children, and they wrote of this early reading with emotions not expressed with regard to other subjects.[5]

Recollections of reading also provided a way to talk about imagination and emotion. Fred Kitchen, a working-class man, remembered that seafaring stories at school had made him long for adventure. Play and reading were closely linked in Beatrice Webb's and Winfred Peck's memories of their middle-class childhoods. The pictures in the *Illustrated Evening News* would come alive before Frank Steel's eyes as he pored over them in the evenings, pausing to ask his father to explain the contents.[6] Graham Greene and Dorothy Scannell both remembered reacting strongly to literary pathos. Greene dreaded having his mother read one particular story about children who died in a forest because he was afraid of weeping. Scannell, on the other hand, avidly read another story about dying children over and over, until her mother finally threw the dog-eared book away, unable to stand her daughter's sobbing. Like Peck and Webb, Scannell entered a fantasy world when she read. She would become so wrapped up in her books as she walked home from the library that she walked under horses' noses and once narrowly missed being hit by a woman falling from a window above. Finally, her family banned her from reading as she walked. From then on, she ran all the way home from the library.[7]

Autobiographers devoted page after page to the titles of the books read at different stages of childhood. Working-class writers were especially good at recalling such physical details as the colors and textures of books' bindings. Some recorded the first book they had read for themselves or favorite books they had read time after time. Children often read the books that their parents and grandparents had read as children, and poor households shared adult books across the generations. Some learned to read with the Bible and developed a love for *The Pilgrim's Progress* and Dickens—standard works in the smallest family libraries.

Books were also linked with places and moments in adult memories of childhood. William Bowyer remembered a room littered with yellow-covered books when he was ushered in to meet his aunt's employers.[8] Patrick MacGill had little time or material for reading during his years spent as a young migrant farm laborer, so his occasional chances to read stood out all the more sharply in his mind. He remembered in particular a red-covered volume titled *The History of the Heavens,* which he had found in "some rubbish in the corner of the room. . . . I liked the story of the stars, the earth, the sun and planets, and I sat by the window for three nights reading the book by the light of the moon."[9]

Physically tied to specific moments, books were also associated with gender. Picking up on the divisions being forged by critics, educators, and publishers, children learned this lesson early. Lillian Faithfull felt that the gulf between boys and girls was marked by the books they read. Uninterested in sentimental girls' fare, she had envied boys their adventure tales. "No boy would have endured our mental pabulum, and we were delighted when we could lay hands on a smuggling story." If there was any crossing of the line between girls' and boys' books, girls usually did the crossing. Reader Bullard, who would wake himself early in order "to creep out of bed and read at the window," was one of the few male autobiographers who admitted to having read his sister's books. But he distanced himself from the experience, explaining that he was put off by the "intolerable plethora of girls" in *Little Women.*[10]

For many autobiographers, reading represented private moments of entry into imaginative realms, and it may have been the first completely solitary activity for some. George Meek wrote that reading was one of the few pleasures with which he could escape from a childhood that he remembered as mostly unhappy. J. R. Clynes also remembered reading as a source of imaginative escape. He would think about poems and books he had read to forget the exhaustion and monotony of work as a "piecer."[11] For those who grew up in families that did not value or regularly practice literacy, childhood reading could represent mental isolation from family life.[12] For many others, reading was a shared experience. Reconstructing these family reading sessions enabled writers to present the emotional texture and significance of family relationships and to explain the political and religious beliefs they associated with growing up.[13]

Family reading was a ritual that marked the rhythms of the day or week. Agnes Cowper remembered as a source of pleasure the time after homework and before bed when her brother Willie would read aloud to the family. In the Bowles family, the children themselves created a ritual around a treasured illustrated journal, *The Orchid Grower.* On Sunday mornings, "when mum and dad were having a bit of a lay-in," the children would beg to be allowed to take the journal out of the big chest in the bedroom, and the oldest was put in charge of holding the pictures up and reading out the details.

The Haddow family had secular and religious reading rituals, each associated with a particular adult. On Friday evenings, the grandmother would read an exciting serial that left them all to wonder over the next installment. Then on Sunday evenings, the father would hand out copies of the Bible and read it aloud. Unlike Friday evenings, William Haddow remembered Sunday evenings as "long and dreary."[14]

For Howard Spring, memories of sitting around the fire to read on Sunday nights had particular resonance as the only times his working-class father participated in family life. He reconstructed the patterns and physical environment of these evenings in his autobiography:

> My father sat in his armchair on the right. My mother sat facing him in a low rocking chair. Between them was a long wooden backless bench on which we all sat: my sisters, my brother and I. It was cozy enough in the kitchen then. There was a lamp hanging to a nail in the wall: a tin lamp, a glass chimney with no shade, a reflection of polished tin.

They read *The Pilgrim's Progress* and *Robinson Crusoe,* and other good books, because his father "abhorred rubbish." He would read a little, then each child would take a turn. "If we mispronounced a word once, he would correct us irritably; if twice he would clout us across the head. So we became acquainted with wholesome English." In the years after his father's death, the now more relaxed Sunday evening readings represented his mother's one leisure activity and Spring's only link with the "good" literature his father had valued.[15]

Family reading rituals were enacted in different forms in middle-class families. Graham Greene, like other middle-class children, associated the hour after tea with being read to by his mother, a leisurely time unavailable to most working-class mothers.[16] For children raised in nurseries, this teatime reading was one of the few encounters with a parent structured into their day. Lillian Faithfull associated family reading with an evening routine of the past and with "classics" that would have been wearisome to read alone, but which "were pleasant enough accompaniment to sewing, knitting or drawing."[17]

Recollections of family reading also served to convey moments of intimacy between a parent and child, often one of few such moments between a child and a working-class father who labored outside the home, or between a child and either middle-class parent. Robert Blatchford retained a vivid image of his working-class mother's dramatic flare for storytelling. Arthur Ransome remembered his middle-class mother's pleasure in reading aloud to him as the source of his own love of reading. For J. M. Barrie, reading sessions with his working-class mother represented treasured intimate moments and the beginning of his own writing. Frank Steel's memories of teatime reading with his mother symbolized the safety and pleasures of childhood before his father went bankrupt and the family was torn apart.[18]

Katherine Chorley remembered reading with both of her middle-class parents. Every Sunday after tea, Chorley's father would find their place in the green moroccan Tennyson or the gold-tooled Milton. Milton was

> rather heavy going for me at ten or eleven . . . best of all Macaulay's *Lays of Ancient Rome,* read by father with a rolling lilt so that all those grand Latin names . . . carry me along like beating wings. Later, I shall have to say what poetry I have been learning . . . and show my mark book. . . .

She had "prized" the hour after tea with her father and was resentful if a visitor "became an interloper spoiling the intimacy of the room." This ritualized activity was both serious and pleasurable. Then there were the less formal times when, after an afternoon of visiting, her mother would change out of her best clothes and settle down in the nursery chair to read. "And then something real would happen. . . . [i]n five minutes we would be well away with the *Scarlet Pimpernel,* rescuing romantic aristocrats from the clutches of the guillotine."[19]

Autobiographers linked family reading with religious or political beliefs that they had learned in childhood and which had relevance to their adult understanding of themselves. Communal reading was primarily religious in many working- and middle-class homes. Fathers usually led these religious readings, although Philip Inman's widowed mother carried on the tradition of reading from the family Bible each evening, and Hannah Mitchell's mother would gather her family around the table for New Testament readings in place of Sunday school.[20] Labor leaders listed as part of their intellectual heritages their parents' reading of the radical press. Minnie Bowles, born in 1903 and a Socialist in adulthood, remembered that her father had read his children Socialist literature before bed. When his wife protested at the lateness of the hour, "I remember his reply that 'What I'm telling these children will do them as much good as sleep.'"[21] For working-class Robert Roberts and middle-class Beatrice Webb, characterizing their families as omnivorous readers stood for a heritage of intellectual curiosity that was integral to each one's sense of self. Roberts remembered that his whole family would sit together, each reading from the *Harmsworth Self-Educator* that his father bought in parts and pausing to share a particularly startling piece of information.[22] Vera Brittain made the opposite point about the role of books in her Edwardian middle-class family. Her parents' library was scanty, and "[l]est anyone should suspect the family of being literary, these volumes were concealed beneath a heavy curtain in the chill, gloomy dining-room." This attitude toward books represented to her the provincialism and narrowness of her childhood.[23]

Echoing debates of their childhood years, autobiographers noted the "quality" of their early reading.[24] Having grown up in the decades when distinctions between "high" and "low" literature were being forged, a number stressed that appreciation for "good" literature was part of their family inheritance.[25] The late nineteenth-century controversy over the allegedly demoralizing effects of "penny dreadfuls" on lower-class boys cropped up again in autobiographers' reminiscences about what had been a cheap and plentiful staple of boys' reading. After reading H. G. Wells's defense of the genre, *Tono Bungay,* George Meek still thought "penny dreadfuls" an "unmixed evil." But Frank Steel and J. H. Howard remembered them as among the few enjoyable boys' books they could afford. While living in an orphanage, Howard and his friends learned the "penny dreadful" biographies of criminals like Dick Turpin by heart. These badly printed booklets "introduced me to a romantic world when pennies were scarce, and libraries seemed far beyond my reach." Reading them even in church, "they gave us glimpses of freedom, abandon and romance, heroism and defiance of fate, whilst we chafed at restrictions and shut doors." Beryl Lee Booker, one of few middle-class girls to mention "penny dreadfuls," read them secretly in the harness room.[26]

These stories are reminders that few children had unlimited access to reading material. Access was partly determined by family and school rules about what constituted age- and gender-appropriate reading. Grace Fulford's professional Edwardian father barred her from his bookcase and newspaper reading. But she would read the papers "on the quiet. Say there was a spicy murder or something I wanted to read." Frank Benson's Edwardian working-class parents also censored their son's reading, but he would sneak second-hand copies of favorite magazines and read them in the privacy of his bedroom. When Walter Southgate's parents tried to limit his reading for fear he would damage his eyes, he got around this restriction by reading under the bedclothes with a candle at night.[27]

Middle-class girls were most apt to have their reading censored, more or less successfully, to protect their morals. Helena Swanwick puzzled over why her mother had let her read Chaucer and Shakespeare while barring her from *David Copperfield* and *The Vicar of Wakefield;* she had read the banned books anyway with attention only sharpened by the prohibition. Katherine Chorley was not allowed to contribute Kipling's *Kim* to her boarding school's library because it did not pass the censors' inspection. Leah Manning was given a steady diet of her grandmother's childhood books—moral tales that were "required reading for little Victorian girls"—until her uncle decided to rescue her with weekly presents of penny paperbacks from W. T. Stead's series of "Books for the Bairns." These were a "bottomless well of enchant-ment." Beatrice Webb's father's views on girls' reading were the exception to the rule. When she was thirteen, he informed her that "a nice-minded girl can read anything; and the more she knows about human nature the better for her and for all the men connected with her."[28]

Besides the more or less successful enforcement of rules about age- and gender-appropriate reading, access to books was even more strongly deter-mined by family resources. Growing up with nursery shelves and family li-braries full of books, middle-class children rarely lacked for reading material. By the 1890s, parents and grandparents were spending more money in an expanding market of children's books and lavishing more presents on their children at birthdays and Christmas.[29] Some families also subscribed to cir-culating libraries, although Arthur Ransome's did not because his parents feared that the books might "become omnibuses for the passage of microbes from one house to another."[30]

Finding reading material was a greater preoccupation for working-class children. The scarcity of books in most working-class homes limited readers' choices and heightened the importance of access in autobiographers' hierar-chy of memories. On those occasions when a family could afford a new book, the gendered relationship to money within the family economy be-came clear: the father usually did the buying, probably because he felt most entitled to spend "spare" money on a luxury, while many mothers would have felt obliged to buy things more basic to the family's physical needs.[31] Working-class children's search for books and magazines spiraled outward from their homes. Most began with the few books on their families' shelves, reading them repeatedly. A few writers had memories of a glorious windfall of books sent by a wealthy friend or a parent's old employer, but most had to work harder to find their next cache.[32] Hannah Mitchell's uncle supplied her with exercise books; she did her brothers' chores in exchange for books they brought home from the schoolmaster. As word of her love of books spread, neighbors offered her the use of their small libraries.[33]

Like their parents, children would pass magazines around among them-selves. The ability to buy and swap magazines depended upon pocket money that usually came with a job, but all children had one source of free books: Sunday schools and elementary schools used prize books to reward good be-havior and achievement. Whether retrospectively treasured or considered overly pious, these books were remembered as hard-won markers of achieve-ment.[34] Some children had access to school and club libraries, but commer-cial libraries were beyond the means of most nineteenth-century working-class families, and public libraries were only becoming widely ac-cessible late in the century. For two men born in the 1880s, the local public library was remembered as a new world that they entered in their teens.

Edward Browne began an "orgie" [*sic*] of reading; it became William Bowyer's haven from painful scenes at home and his entrée into education.[35]

The public library was not always a straightforwardly friendly or accessible place for a child or adolescent. Patrick MacGill remembered the humiliation of being told to wash his hands when, as a young man, he first entered a Carnegie library. For Dorothy Scannell, joining her local library (consisting of one department, with no children's books) was a "red-letter day." But she found choosing books a complicated, intimidating task, and her problems did not end once she had a book in hand. She worried about incurring library fines that would mean expulsion because no one at home would pay them. So "I read my books on a clean piece of rag and always washed my hands first." Angela Rodaway, who "could never get enough books," was warned by her mother that books from the public library would be full of bugs. "There were, but only dead ones, 'mahogany flats' pressed between the pages."[36]

Young readers too far from a local library, or too intimidated to enter one, could usually browse in a local bookstore. Too poor to buy books, J. M. Severn was lent old papers and magazines by the local news agent. Some autobiographers read entire books in "snatches" at a local bookstall and depended on the stall owner's advice on the rare occasions when they came to buy a book. As they grew older, and more interested in politics, readers depended on bookstores for access to classic texts and the latest ideas. William Collison, an anti–trade unionist, remembered a moment of "revelation" about the "true" nature of political economy during one stint of bookshop reading. More usually, bookshop shelves yielded inspiration for young trade unionists and Socialists.[37]

A number of working-class autobiographers mentioned the importance of cheap publications that were increasingly available after the 1850s.[38] By the 1900s, the working-class Fagan and Scannell households could afford boys' and girls' magazines that would have seemed extravagant a few decades before. Dorothy Scannell grew up with a few battered family children's books, received books as Christmas presents, and had access to a library. Hannah Mitchell, born forty years earlier, had to barter with her brothers and borrow from neighbors during what she called a "book-starved childhood." The contrast is even greater between William Lovett's childhood reading in the early 1800s and Hymie Fagan's in the early 1900s. There was no bookshop in Lovett's town, and he had access only to religious books and the occasional "nonsensical pamphlet" until he joined a workingmen's circulating library at age twenty-one. Fagan read comics and magazines (even the too expensive *Boys' Own Paper,* which he took from a neighbor's dustbin), could afford to pay a penny a volume for borrowing privileges at a private library, and would spend hours in the public library, poring over the latest Sherlock Holmes adventure in *Strand* magazine.[39] Growing up in the early twentieth century when there were cheaper publications and wider variety, Scannell and Fagan could at least make limited choices about their reading material. Ben Turner spoke for most working-class children of earlier decades when he described the "strange bits of reading that fell to my lot."[40]

The Search for Knowledge

For many working-class autobiographers, childhood reading was extended into a lifelong search for knowledge in which personal desires meshed with a working-class tradition of self-improvement. J. H. Howard, a Welsh Nonconformist minister and Labour politician, remembered the day he left an orphan's home at thirteen as the beginning of his "great adventure in life." His "equipment consisted of a passion for reading, an insatiate curiosity, and a grim determination to finish school. . . ." Philip Inman used books to chart his determined advancement from "humble" beginnings to a seat on the Labour Bench in the House of Lords and chairmanship of the B.B.C. In his narrative, reading was the "path to more discoveries." For Rose Kerrigan, the "search for knowledge" was a family tradition.[41] Avid reading did not lead most working-class men and women to pulpits or Parliament, and in that sense autobiographies offer a skewed picture of the relationship between reading and social mobility.[42] But the self-educated included those who joined the rank and file of political organizations, and autobiographers show glimpses of parents, siblings, and neighbors who devoted precious leisure hours to political and religious reading and to sharing that knowledge among the local community.

Philip Inman was among those whose search for knowledge began early. He joined an evening class soon after he started his first job. After leaving school to work full-time, J. R. Clynes began to study on his own in the evenings. It was hardly a world where a twelve-year-old whose "earnings were swallowed up in the family exchequer" could get his own library, and there was no public library. But he went to a bookshop and spent two weeks' pocket money on a six-pence dictionary. Up at 4:30 A.M., he would work until 6 P.M., then begin to study his dictionary. At first his siblings' shouts disturbed his concentration, "and their toys or their hurtling bodies hit me or my table with devastating effect." But as the evening drew on, he forgot his surroundings and himself.

> Merely words, and the beautiful sound of the best of them; the swinging rhythm of perfectly-balanced sentences that grew out of them; the emotions they could call forth—it was with these intangible playthings that I spent my

evenings during one of the happiest periods of my life. My days at the mill seemed dreams; only the evenings were real.

Born after the school-leaving age had been raised, Hymie Fagan had a few more years of formal education than his nineteenth-century predecessors. He left school at fourteen and went to work in a factory. There, surrounded by Socialists and atheists, his real education began: "The factory was my university."[43]

These writers took no break between schooling and self-education. For many, though, the first day of work brought a hiatus from serious reading, for which their minds and bodies were too exhausted. A period of new or renewed interest in reading often began at age seventeen or eighteen during a period of intellectual and political restlessness. George Hodgkinson, a Labour politician and mayor of Coventry, and Lord Snell, a Labour Member of Parliament, identified this "discovery" of literature and politics as turning points in their lives.

Hodgkinson made it clear that the "facts of life" had made him a Socialist. But he also identified reading as an important element in his introduction to politics at age twenty, when he began to court the daughter of a trade-unionist family. The books that his future in-laws gave him "channelled my thoughts towards the political economy of Ruskin, thus sowing the seed for a taste for literature better than the penny dreadful and the blood and thunder stuff" available then. He "became an honest seeker after truth rather than a rebel with a chip on the shoulder, and one with a growing appetite for reading" and study.[44]

After leaving home at twelve, work left Snell with little time to read. But four years later, he began to listen to speeches and sermons in the local marketplace, absorbing every word "like a sponge." Then followed a period of "mental voracity" when he read every author he could. Looking back, he associated this reading and his work experiences with a new interest in political and social questions and with a search that led him first to the Social Democratic Federation, then into the Labour Party.[45]

Autobiographers associated such reading with intensity: Patrick MacGill remembered reading "ravenously." Some also remembered this as a period of "haphazard" reading and misdirected energy. During Ben Tillet's "intellectual awakening" at seventeen, he developed a catholic taste in books. Only later, in his view, did he begin to read with method or to apply his knowledge. In these narratives of journeys toward political belief, this early period of directionless reading gave way to a solidifying of values and beliefs when contact was made with a trade union or political party.[46]

Some political autobiographers adopted the language of religious conversion to describe their political awakenings: Snell wrote of his sense of relief after making his "confession of faith" at a Social Democratic Federation meeting.[47] Political conversion stories like Snell's shared the intensity of Gipsy Smith's contemporary narrative of religious conversion. Born in 1860, Gipsy Smith had only had a few months of schooling before his conversion, which brought "the awakening" of his intellect. "Everything had a new meaning to me . . . my desire for reading was tremendously intensified. I now had something to learn for. . . ."[48] Smith's goal was to preach the gospel; as with Hodgkinson, Snell, and Tillet, his intellectual search accompanied new faith and new clarity of purpose. The political and the religious were never far apart. New political conviction often emerged from a period of religious doubt. Politics replaced religion for some: when the deacon of her church forced Margaret Bondfield to choose between the Church and her trade-union activities, she chose the latter "without hesitation." For others, the two fed each other. Labour MP James Griffiths, who first heard the Labour leader Keir Hardie speak during a Welsh Nonconformist revival in 1904, held political and religious beliefs that were both rooted in a vision of social change.[49]

While these searches for knowledge and political truths share many common features, other working-class autobiographies do not fit neatly into the same narrative structure. Some men chose more individual paths of self-improvement and social mobility. Thomas Okey's autobiography traced his "literary pilgrimage" from basket maker to a Cambridge Chair of Italian Studies. Okey saw no single defining moment in his life, but rather a series of stages of belief. He joined the Ethical Movement in the late 1880s, became involved with Socialism and Toynbee Hall in these years, and was a Liberal by the time he wrote his autobiography in 1930. Instead of a life of Church or Party, he pursued more solitary scholarship. Fred Kitchen's self-education was chronologically atypical. Having shut himself "out of the world of books" at fourteen, fearing the other farm lads' jeers, he joined a Workers' Education Association late in life and began to write.[50]

Working-class women also found it harder to fit their lives and the search for knowledge into the mold of political narratives. Expected to help at home, many young women had less leisure time than single young men did. Most women also had fewer opportunities to use their literacy skills to get better jobs. Girls might train to become pupil teachers if their parents could afford to sacrifice their wages or labor at home, but few women could hope for the paid positions in trade unions or the Labour Party that Snell, Tillet, and Griffiths had, or for access to the clubs and mutual improvement societies where men exchanged ideas and practiced speaking publicly.

For Hannah Mitchell there was no pivotal period of study, but rather a "lifelong struggle for education." She characterized herself as determined and ruthless in her desire for education—a desire that many men could take for granted because they would not have shared her guilt at taking time from her family to read and engage in political activity. If few women included chapters titled "Intellectual Awakening" in their autobiographies, perhaps it is because they had little time to read (a common complaint among Women's Cooperative Guild members) and few opportunities to turn the search for knowledge into sustained political careers.[51]

Margaret Bondfield revised this gendering of political opportunity (in part, by remaining single). Having worked in dressmakers' shops since the age of fourteen, she would become Britain's first woman Cabinet Member. For Bondfield, and for Clara Grant, a Board school teacher and settlement worker, the move from smaller cities to London in the 1890s opened up an uncharted world of independence and intellectual opportunity. Bondfield later saw her move to London in 1894 as the turning point in her life. She joined progressive clubs, made new friends, created a new life. Soon she was active in trade-union work, which led to long-term engagement in labor politics. Having left teachers' training college still "thirsting" for more knowledge, Grant found London to be a "veritable Temple of Learning" with open doors.[52] For Bondfield and Grant, place—specifically London—was vital to their intellectual journeys.

The autobiographies of Mitchell, Bondfield, and male labor politicians fit into gendered and generational patterns of educational and political opportunity and into a shared tradition of self-education that stretched back to the Chartists of the 1830s and to eighteenth-century radicals before them. For each generation, self-improvement was linked to larger social aims, and serious readers in the late nineteenth century still faced many of the obstacles that their predecessors had.[53] Working-class homes still provided little quiet or privacy, and gas lighting was still not universally available.[54] On the other hand, as David Vincent writes, after 1850 individuals' "access to the social mobility provided by formal education and the modern trade union and Labour Party bureaucracies transformed the significance" of the pursuit of knowledge.[55] As social context and opportunities changed, so did the meaning of the "search for knowledge." Working men and women had more access to study groups and to evening classes. But for many women and men, the gap between political desire and educational opportunity remained wide into the twentieth century, giving the pursuit of knowledge continued importance, as autobiographers' expressions of intellectual hunger and their detailed catalogues of reading conveyed.

Among the cohort of mostly middle-class women who joined the suffrage movement of the 1900s, some described a linkage of political awakening and self-education similar to that of politically active working-class women and men. Emmeline Pethick-Lawrence, Helena Swanwick, and Margaret Rhondda described restless teenage years when each felt dissatisfied with their dependence and lack of direction. Rhondda, awkward in her new role as a young lady during her first "Season," wrote that she was "miserable during those early, futile, unoccupied years."[56] For Pethick-Lawrence and Swanwick, restlessness in their teens coincided with a period of reading that helped to provide new perspective on themselves and their situations. "At a critical juncture," Pethick-Lawrence read a novel about life in London's East End that "made a profound impression." She saw it as one factor in her decision to leave home and take up social work at the West London Mission. Swanwick, resentful that her brothers' educations were given precedence over hers, discovered "feminist" books by John Stuart Mill and others that showed her that her "inarticulate revolt linked up with a world-movement."[57] She later won a scholarship to Girton College, married, and took up the constitutional suffrage cause in 1905, a year before Pethick-Lawrence joined the more militant Women's Social and Political Union. Rhondda's period of self-education followed college, marriage, and membership in the W.S.P.U. She had made a "temperamental" rather than an "intellectual" conversion to the women's suffrage movement. "Having made up my mind, however, I had to discover why I believed what I did. Through the following year I got and read every book and every pamphlet for and against suffrage." From this reading, "a dozen paths led out into other subjects, each of which bore on feminism in one way or another, and each of which needed exploring."[58] Both Rhondda and Swanwick, like Margaret Bondfield, began more systematic reading when called on to make political speeches.[59] Restless in the face of the dependence and limited educations that were the lot of most middle-class girls, Pethick-Lawrence, Swanwick, and Rhondda took up individual searches for knowledge that they retrospectively understood as crucial to their political beliefs and actions.

Memories of childhood reading served a number of purposes in the autobiographies of men and women born in Victorian and Edwardian Britain. They provided a language for explaining familial and private times, imaginative play and intellectual progress, and for conveying the emotions and beliefs associated with childhood and its end. In reconstructing these moments of reading, autobiographers were exploring and explaining the links between the childhoods they remembered and the adults they understood themselves to be.

Part Two

Constructing a
Literature of Childhood

"Real and Wholesome Pleasure": Critics Guard the Boundaries of Children's Literature

S candal hit London in the summer of 1885 when the journalist W. T. Stead published "The Maiden Tribute of Modern Babylon" in the *Pall Mall Gazette*. Stead's exposé of child prostitution provided readers with images of hardened working-class mothers, the villains of Stead's melodrama, and their helpless daughters whose purity had been sacrificed to dangerous, sexually voracious rakes. "My object," Stead explained, was to strengthen laws that stood "between infants and the brutal lust of dissolute men."[1] Demonstrations and controversy erupted in the wake of these revelations about the traffic in young girls in London's streets and brothels. Stead's series is also credited for spurring passage of the Criminal Law Amendment Act, which raised the age of consent for girls from thirteen to sixteen and made illegal "indecent" acts between consenting male adults. Stead himself was found guilty of abducting the young girl whose story was central to the "Maiden Tribute" and spent two months in Holloway Prison, only to emerge "a martyr to the cause of social justice and social purity."[2]

The year before Stead's "Maiden Tribute" appeared, Miss E. Barlee employed a similar narrative of lost innocence in her book, *Pantomime Waifs*, that warned of the dangers of employing children as entertainers. The laboring children she described were threatened by urban pleasure-seekers of another kind. These dancers and actors were sacrificed, morally and physically, for the entertainment of populations "both high and low." While upper-class children and their parents returned to their "happy homes" after attending a performance, the little entertainers encountered horrible temptations that made a "Shipwreck of their Innocence and Purity" as they made their ways home to fireless grates. Among the worst of these temptations was that terrible "poison" of female virtue, "lower-class literature." Left to their own devices, these children were "allowed to throw away the golden possibilities of their childhood[s]," falling from "desecrated Girlhood into the still darker abyss of a lost Womanhood." While Stead looked to the law, Barlee looked to philanthropy to save working children who were "immolated on the alter of Public Amusement."[3] Speaking the language of moral outrage, she called upper-class women to contribute time and money to London's missions and refuges. *Pantomime Waifs* and the "Maiden Tribute" raised uncomfortable questions about the sexual, class, and gender boundaries of childhood.

Barlee's identification of literature as a crucible of children's morals tapped into upper-class fears about the degeneration of popular culture that were being expressed through—and defined by—evaluations of the British public's reading habits. Literary critics' and reformers' desires to draw boundaries between uplifting and degrading literature were particularly strong with regard to children's literature.[4] Although not new in the late nineteenth century, concern about what children read took on greater importance in the context of heightened concerns about the future of the British "race," the composition of its political sphere, and the cultural influence of the popular commercial press.[5] A widely shared understanding of reading as consumption—you become what you read—lent urgency to the question of whether children were imbibing wholesome or poisonous fare.[6]

Historians have often read children's literature as texts that reinforced the dominant cultural ideologies of their period.[7] Children's stories written before midcentury, with their overt religious and moral didacticism, and late nineteenth-century boys' adventure tales, with their celebrations of the British empire, lend themselves to such interpretations.[8] While accepting this definition of earlier children's literature, a number of literary historians have viewed the late Victorian and Edwardian years as a "golden age" of writing for children, a time when the genre gained imaginative freedom and offered pleasurable stories and natural child characters.[9] More recently, scholars have begun to reconnect historical and literary evaluations of children's literature. Claudia Nelson writes that "when children's fiction began its golden age in the mid-nineteenth century, entertainment may have formed its limbs and outward flourishes, but didacticism remained its backbone."[10] Nelson argues that children's writers practiced a subtle emotional didacticism that centered on teaching boys a manliness based on "selflessness, emotional warmth, and purity," qualities more commonly associated with womanliness. By century's end, when many scientists, educators, and writers were anxious to distinguish more sharply manly and womanly attributes, this androgynous ideal was undermined by a more aggressive, physical ideal of boyhood.[11] Nelson and others have shown how children's literature, even at its most subversive, was still inseparable from the culture in which it was produced.[12] It not only participated in that culture, but gave more subtle and powerful expression to Britain's racial, class, and gender-bound ideologies.

We can view from several angles the integral role children's literature played in the formation of late nineteenth-century British culture. Critics and writers struggled with the tensions between the ideal of a universally shared, innocent childhood that they were trying to create and the class- and gender-divided childhoods they actually saw and that many depicted. The child prostitutes of Stead's "Maiden Tribute" rarely surfaced in reviews of the children's stories intended for middle-class budgets and nurseries, but the specter of cultural degeneration they represented shaped reviewers' discussions of the nature of childhood. Stead reminded middle-class readers that children were not universally protected or innocent. His work highlighted existing images of working-class girls as vulnerable to the streets' corrupting influences and as child laborers whose very bodies and purity had become commodities.[13] The girls' vulnerability and corruption could be blamed on their parents and on street culture, and thus be distinguished from their middle-class counterparts' protected innocence. But the disturbing association between childhood and sexuality could not be completely erased; nor could the reminder that working-class children were obliged to enter the adult world as laborers, gaining a degree of economic independence frightening to middle-class observers.[14]

The ideal of middle-class childhood itself was not completely stable. Reviewers and writers of children's literature had to work to reconcile the desire to see childhood as an innocent, insular world with the equally strong need to inculcate child readers with responsibility and morality as insurance against their corruption and to prepare them for adulthood. Portrayals of delightful, pleasing children and uplifting, reforming messages often coexisted uneasily within a single story.

This idealized image of childhood was presented in children's literature as much for the pleasure of adults as it was for children. A few critics complained about this trend. E. M. Field argued that too many stories were not "*for* children, but stories *about* children. . . ." Canon Alfred Ainger agreed that too many contemporary children's authors wrote "with one eye on the *child* and the other on the *grown-up person*. . . ."[15] Most critics, though, glossed over this crucial element of the commercial success of nineteenth-century literature for children. They joined other adults who wrote, published, bought, and read children's literature in constructing a modern vision of childhood as the opposite of adulthood that is only now being dismantled.[16]

Authors themselves had to negotiate cultural rules about gender, work, and morality. Because women were considered children's natural caretakers, they were also seen to be naturally suited to write for children. Some women parlayed this belief into successful writing careers, but it could also become a trap for women who sought to write for both child and adult audiences. Once labeled children's writers, women often found themselves excluded from consideration as serious writers for adults. With more access to an increasingly professionalized literary market, a number of men successfully moved between children's and adult fiction. Like women, though, they had to present themselves as concerned for the moral welfare of their child readers.[17]

Written by educators, Church leaders, authors, and cultural critics, and published in the major periodicals of the day, reviews of children's literature captured the tensions being played out in children's literature. These centered on the content and impact of popular culture and popular education, relations between rich and poor, between men and women, and most immediately, on the definitions of "appropriate" children's literature and of childhood itself. Writers and critics struggled over when and how to differentiate boys and girls, echoing contemporary battles over the separation of men's and women's spheres. Child labor legislation and the beginning of state-sponsored elementary education in 1870 had raised the possibility of extending the structure of middle-class childhood to working-class children and sharpened controversies over how far this extension should go. This chapter will map the cultural and political terrain of critics' reviews of children's literature, tracing how critics and authors worked to reconcile the tensions inherent in this redefinition of childhood and contributed to refashioning adults' relationship to children.

Nineteenth-century literary critics served as cultural interpreters during a century when the very concept of an English culture was being formed.[18] Their task of instructing and consolidating a middle-class readership was made increasingly difficult by the need to reinvent a public sphere that had been fractured by class struggle, commercialization, and the fragmentation of reading audiences.[19] In reviewing children's literature, critics presented themselves to their middle-class adult readers as guides and coconspirators, promising to act as custodians of British culture and childhood.

Critics began with the premise that properly judging children's books depended on the ability to recognize that children were uniquely impressionable and different from adults in vital, basic ways. In 1860, an anonymous critic asserted in the *London Quarterly Review* that the parent must consider the selection of children's books as one of "his most important functions," for children's "innocence and happiness are at stake."[20] Edward Salmon, an essayist who frequently wrote about children's literature, suggested in 1887 that the period of childhood was "not only impressionable, but charged with the gravest potentialities." Salmon, though, shifted the task of selecting books to mothers, the "responsible parties in this matter."[21]

The second major premise—that children were not like adults—was given this interpretation by the author of the 1860 *London Quarterly Review* article: children, he insisted, "are beings in whom certain intellectual powers are far more active, and certain moral attributes are in a condition of greater purity . . . than in later life."[22] The Socialist editor Robert Blatchford wrote in 1903 that children lived in their own world "of Makebelieve." In his view, they had no notion of time or distance, nor could they "draw a precise line between the real and the imaginary."[23] Some reviewers maintained that childhood's great distance from adulthood made children's minds virtually unfathomable, though they remained confident in their ability to diagnose the impact books had on children's characters.[24]

This linkage of childhood with purity, imagination, and impressionability shaped critical evaluations of children's literature. "Appropriate" literature, it was commonly agreed, mirrored child "nature." Narrative, plot, language, even illustrations, should be simple and accessible, with the kind of purity or transparency that adults saw in children themselves.[25] Reversing earlier generations' rejection of folk and fairy tales as insufficiently didactic, critics now considered them especially well-suited for children because they connoted traditional purity and simplicity.[26] "Naturalness" was also important, meaning that children should be depicted as they really were. This naturalness should also extend to the story itself. Criticizing overt didacticism as tiresome and old-fashioned, Salmon and E. M. Field argued that lessons were best conveyed through the plot and the characters themselves. Field praised stories that provided "real and wholesome pleasure," and Salmon called for a blend of the real and the ideal.[27]

Discarding earlier utilitarian and evangelical insistence on factual accuracy, critics and authors revived the Romantic linkage of children with imagination and defended fiction as vital food for children's minds.[28] This association of childhood and imagination served as an umbrella for two different, but reconcilable, visions of children and their books. Some viewed imaginative literature as a refuge from the adult world that was all the more necessary because of childhood's fragile and fleeting nature.[29] In 1853, Charles Dickens had declared fairy tales were more important than ever in the current "utilitarian age . . . [for] a nation without fancy, without some romance, never did, never can, never will, hold a great place under the sun." John Ruskin argued in 1868 that children needed fortification "against the glacial cold of selfish science," and the artist Walter Crane declared in 1879 that, in a "sober and matter-of-fact age," children's books afforded "perhaps the only outlet for unrestricted flights of fancy."[30]

Imaginative literature served not only as a refuge from a utilitarian world, but also to prepare children to enter that world armed with countervailing ideals. Critic and journalist J. Newby Hetherington declared that while fairy tales could teach little about worldly success, they could "develop the whole nature, and so make life beautiful, useful and happy."[31] Hetherington, writing in 1897, an anonymous critic writing in 1860, and author E. Nesbit, writing in 1913, all argued that imagination could teach children empathy by helping them to see from other perspectives.[32]

At least a few critics believed that children's purity shielded them from any inappropriate messages a book might contain. E. M. Field argued that a child could be let loose in a library without risk of moral taint because "to the pure all is pure."[33] Andrew Lang argued that children did not even comprehend the parts of novels that adults feared would corrupt them. "In the Egyptian wizard's little pool of ink, only the pure can see the visions, and in Shakespeare's magic mirror, children see only what is pure."[34] Most critics, though, maintained that adults must shelter children, and worried about the quality of children's books, believing that fine literature could teach children to appreciate great literature later in life, while "trashy" books could irreversibly demoralize them.[35] Margaret McMillan, a Socialist and child development theorist, urged that "the finest literature" should be children's only literature, serving as a "touchstone" for judging books later in life. Primarily concerned with poor children's mental and physical development, McMillan refused to divorce children's reading from their physical environment. She argued that two conditions for providing children with "deeper sympathies, finer intuitions," and better culture were "Time and Space—long days and wide horizons."[36] Few other writers dwelt on the conditions necessary for reading, probably taking for granted the comforts of middle-class childhood.

This concern for giving children the finest literary fare was heightened by a belief that the expanding book trade was introducing a dangerous mediocrity. Canon Alfred Ainger argued in 1895 that "after the gaudy hot-pressed, profusely illustrated, smartly bound children's books of today, a new one every month, when each is just tasted and then thrown away," it would be hard to reintroduce children to older, more wholesome stories. For "even brown bread and butter is apt to be insipid after a surfeit of chocolate-creams and hard-bake."[37] But, lest parents worry needlessly, Edward Salmon and other critics promised to guide them in buying those children's books that had become an indispensable part of the Christmas holiday.

The problem of shielding lower-class children from "trash" was more acute. Even Field's faith in the protection children's purity afforded was shaken when she considered that some might have only the "garbage of police reports and the lowest possible fiction to read."[38] Miss E. Barlee feared that mass education had worsened cheap literature's threat by creating new generations of unregulated readers.[39] Edward Salmon warned that to compulsorily educate working-class children, "whilst allowing them to digest" unwholesome fiction, was to court their moral and material ruin. While Barlee called for government regulation of publishers and production of cheap religious literature, Salmon argued that clergymen and visitors to the poor must induce parents to monitor the fiction their children devoured. "Only the most jealous regard to a boy's or girl's mental food will give him or her moral armour capable of resisting the insidious encroachment of depravity."[40]

For the most part, reviewers concentrated on books that, judging from their prices, were destined for middle-class nursery shelves, discussing working-class children's reading practices briefly, if at all. After all, working-class children were beyond middle-class control, except when in school, whereas middle-class children could be reached through their parents, who presumably shared critics' preoccupations. Edward Salmon described boys' books as the "mental food for the future chiefs of a great race" and books for girls as the mental food "for the future wives and mothers of that race." Thus it was imperative that middle-class parents select children's reading carefully and that working-class parents be guided in helping their children to select books. The future of the British race hung in the balance.[41]

The delicacy of the task of defining appropriate children's literature is illustrated by critics' responses to two writers' stories. Mrs. Molesworth had a long, critically acclaimed career as a children's author. Oscar Wilde wrote two fairy-tale collections, *The Happy Prince* and *A House of Pomegranates;* reviewers loved the first and hated the second. The very different critical evaluations of Molesworth and Wilde were responses as much to their very different presentations of themselves and their work as to the contents of their writings.

Mary Louisa Molesworth, together with *Little Folks Magazine,* which serialized much of her fiction, promised the balance between refuge from the adult world and the moral instruction of Britain's future "chiefs" and their wives that critics considered essential. Publishing over 100 books between 1875 and 1911, Mrs. Molesworth (1839–1921) became a popular author and a respected analyst of the field.[42] Journalist and novelist Alexander Shand placed Molesworth among the best children's writers of the late nineteenth century. Edward Salmon declared Molesworth the "best storyteller for children England has yet known" and praised *Little Folks* as one of the best children's magazines available.[43] Molesworth and her critics, during her lifetime and into the 1960s, agreed that she portrayed children naturally and appropriately. Salmon considered that Mrs. Molesworth's "great charm" was her realism, "realism, that is, in the purest and highest sense."[44] Molesworth explained to *Little Folks* readers that her stories were grounded in "real fact."

Her characters were modeled on her own children, and even her fairy-tale characters were "taken from nature."[45] Unfortunately, the *Little Folks* readers who voted her their favorite author did not explain their criteria or whether she had represented them accurately.

In her critical essays, Molesworth joined her contemporaries in defining childhood as a separate, purer state of existence: in "child-world," the "innocent beings [are] in some sense nearer heaven than are the grown men and women, sight-dimmed in the denser regions of earthly struggle and toil."[46] Writing for children required the ability to see and feel as children did. But it was also important to remain "in full possession of your matured judgement, your wider and deeper views." Only from an adult perspective could one write appropriately for children. She herself had only attempted it as a mother.[47] Just as authors guided children through new reading experiences, Molesworth's fictional mothers guided children through moral turmoil and recognized their childish innocence in ways that fathers (whom she usually portrayed as less sensitive to children) could not. Sharing an obligation to protect children's innocence, writers and mothers should become allies, urged Molesworth. Writers should provide wholesome stories and preserve the ideal of motherhood, for children's "belief in 'mother' is the very breath and sunshine of their lives. . . ." Mothers must live up to this ideal and choose books protective of their children's innocence.[48]

From its inception, *Little Folks* had depicted children as adorable and pure, their innocent beauty often serving to redeem the wayward adults around them. Mrs. Molesworth was one of the authors who, in the 1880s, incorporated curiosity and mischievousness into this depiction of childish innocence. The children of Mrs. Molesworth's "The Palace in the Garden" are curious and high-spirited. We watch through the children's innocent eyes as their curiosity leads their gruff, undemonstrative grandfather to reconcile with his sister, from whom he had wrongly estranged himself, and to become kinder to his grandchildren.[49] In stories like this one, childish innocence, coupled with physical beauty of the blue-eyed, blonde variety, is the vehicle for adult redemption.

A second kind of story is also based on the ideals of childish innocence and honesty. But the children of these tales of moral development have character flaws that are tempered by the harm their faults cause. In Molesworth's "Sheila's Mystery," the title character's jealousy and secretiveness alienate her from her family. She must go through a long, painful reformation process before a happy reunion can take place. In this kind of story, tension builds from installment to installment until the child's rehabilitation seems the only possible happy ending. Providing insight into the misery Sheila's traits cause her, Molesworth encourages readers to conclude along with Sheila that she can only gain happiness and approval by telling the truth, becoming more trusting, modest, and giving.[50]

Little Folks stories often incorporated subtle lessons in gender roles with celebrations of English "character." In the opening scene of "A Madcap," by Molesworth's contemporary L. T. Meade, six children and their mother have learned that their father is dead and that their home belongs to their half-Spanish cousin, Inez. When they meet her, the children remark that Inez is "not a bit English, not like us," and they fear that she will not look after the poor as they have. These cousins serve as foils for Inez's character. Sallow, passionate, and proud, Inez admires the oldest boy, David, who is selfless and strong. Violet, the youngest, has "rosy lips" and a loving "baby heart." When Dorothy, who is cultured and self-controlled, finds Inez "sobbing without restraint," she is kind and sympathetic, as her mother had urged her to be. Gradually, Inez reforms, learning self-restraint and finding happiness in her new family.[51] This story presents children as most appealing when they are trusting, unselfish, and controlled. The baby is lovable and loving, the brother strong, the sister cultured and self-restrained—desirable traits that are all tied to Englishness, gender, and class.

Just as fictional children had to fit into strict parameters of appropriate behavior, stories to be read by children had to pass critical scrutiny. Reviewers praised Oscar Wilde's *The Happy Prince,* a starkly beautiful collection of fairy tales published in 1888. Wilde created this collection of fairy stories in the mid-1880s, the years when he became a father and began to explore his homosexuality. Like much of his work, these stories contained tensions between the ideas of art as a vehicle for social reform and of art for art's sake.[52] Wilde described the title story as an "attempt to treat a tragic modern problem in a form that aims at delicacy and imaginative treatment. . . ."[53] The story opens with a description of a statue of the Happy Prince: he was "gilded all over with thin leaves of fine gold, for eyes he had two bright sapphires, and a large red ruby glowed on his sword-hilt."[54] He is visited by a little swallow who, because of a misconceived love for a reed, has stayed behind after his companions have flown to warmer climes. The prince tells the swallow that because he is a statue high above the city, he can "see all the ugliness and all the misery of my city" that he could not see while he was alive.[55] He persuades the swallow to pluck the red ruby from his sword-hilt and take it to a poor seamstress and her sick child. Next he convinces the swallow to pluck the sapphire from one eye and deliver it to a young writer, with "lips as red as pomegranates" and "large and dreamy eyes," who has fainted from hunger in his cold garret. A little match-girl who will be beaten by her father if she returns home without money receives the sapphire from the other eye.[56] Taking pity on the now blind statue, the swallow gives up his plans to fly south and stays behind to tell the prince marvelous tales of his travels. Reminding the swallow that "more marvelous than anything is the suffering of men and women," the prince sends the bird out again and again with leaves of gold to give to the city's poor. Finally, the swallow drops dead from the cold at the feet of the now barren statue, and the prince's lead heart breaks. The mayor and town councillors notice how shabby the statue has become and send it off to be melted down at the foundry. But the prince's broken lead heart will not melt, so it is thrown upon the dustheap next to the swallow's body.

In a letter to William Gladstone, Wilde described the collection of stories as being "really meant for children." Elsewhere, he described them as "meant partly for children, and partly for those who have kept the childlike faculties of wonder and joy. . . ."[57] Presented as a children's book, this first volume was well received by critics. "The gift of writing fairy tales is rare, and Mr. Oscar Wilde shows that he possesses it in a rare degree," wrote *The Athenaeum*'s reviewer. The tales contained "a piquant touch of contemporary satire." But it was "so delicately introduced that . . . a child would delight in the tales without being worried or troubled by their application, while children of larger growth will enjoy them and profit by them."[58] Walter Pater wrote to Wilde from Oxford to praise the book's "delicate touches and pure English."[59]

This stamp of approval was not extended to Wilde's second volume of fairy tales, *A House of Pomegranates* (1891), although these tales were also as much about compassion and empathy as they were celebrations of beauty. Wilde had published *The Picture of Dorian Gray* in magazine form in 1890; the book came out in April 1891. Richard Ellmann, Wilde's biographer, points out that *Dorian Gray* was not only about aestheticism, controversial enough, but also covertly presented homosexuality. Ellmann writes that the effect of *Dorian Gray* was "prodigious." No novel had commanded so much attention for years "or awakened sentiments so contradictory in its readers." His fans loved it; others condemned the novel as immoral.[60] *A House of Pomegranates* was published eight months later. When Wilde announced that his latest fairy tales were not necessarily for children, but were rather an expressions of aestheticism, critics attacked the book.[61] As Claudia Nelson argues, redefined as adult literature, the stories' homoeroticism "leaped into the foreground." Depictions of beauty deemed innocent in a children's book were now condemned as perversion.[62] Until very recently, Wilde's tales were virtually erased from histories of children's literature, no doubt because of the scandal attached to his name after his trial and imprisonment in 1895 for indecency and sodomy under the Criminal Law Amendment Act, which Stead's "Maiden Tribute" had helped to push through Parliament.

The very different responses accorded the tales of Oscar Wilde and Mrs. Molesworth demonstrate the extent to which personal reputation and statements of intent determined the reading of an author's work and marked the boundaries of acceptable children's literature. While Oscar Wilde invited ambiguous readings of himself and his fairy tales, Molesworth presented herself—in the complementary roles of critic, mother, and writer—as guardian of children's purity. Edward Salmon praised Molesworth's ability to write stories that both adults and children could enjoy. More importantly, she was an "almost infallible guide to the eccentricities of child nature."[63] Even before his trial, Wilde had challenged middle-class standards of masculinity with his aestheticism and self-presentation as a "dandy." The two authors' different reputations were shaped by the sexual taboos and gender boundaries that Wilde threatened and by the domestic ideology that defined women as natural guardians of children's morality.[64]

Wilde had tinkered with the purity critics considered intrinsic to good children's literature. W. T. Stead's "The Maiden Tribute of Modern Babylon," with its narrative of child prostitutes' sexual vulnerability, had reminded Britain of the divisions between working- and middle-class childhoods. By the 1890s, a new subject had caught Stead's attention. Noting that mass education had "practically created a new reading public," he introduced a series of penny booklets in 1896 intended to lower class barriers between child readers by providing quality literature at a low price.[65] One ad described these *Books for the Bairns,* issued monthly between pink paper covers, as "so cheap the labouring man can buy them for his children." They were "so good the Empress of Russia subscribe[d] for them," and Queen Victoria specially commended them. Introducing his seventh collection of tales, Stead expressed confidence that "good" would come from popularizing these "delightful romances of childhood" that had previously "been the Perquisite of the Rich. By the Books for the Bairns I hope to make them the Privilege of the Poor."[66] Stead meant to produce a series that would narrow the class divisions between children that his "Maiden Tribute" had exposed and simultaneously teach Christian morality. The prefaces to his early volumes provided readers with cues for finding the Christian lessons in the tales he presented. Either his didacticism was relatively subtle or children skipped his prefaces altogether, because at least three fans, Dora Russell, Leah Manning, and Phyllis Bentley, remembered the collections of Bible stories, fables, and fairy tales in *Books for the Bairns* as welcome departures from their usual "moralizing" Victorian children's books. Manning remembered the little pink paperbacks as "a bottomless well of enchantment. . . ." Bentley remembered spending her "Saturday penny . . . on those splendid *Books for the Bairns*" in the 1900s. Encouraged by her family to buy them, the six-year-old's "only difficulty" had been which to choose from the "shelfful of these darling penny paperbacks" on the porch of the local news agent.[67]

The year after Stead launched his *Books for the Bairns,* Oscar Wilde, having just finished his prison term, wrote a letter to the *Daily Chronicle* about three children who had been at Reading Prison with him because they had been convicted of snaring rabbits and could not pay their fine. This time he relied on his own experience, rather than allegory and beautiful images, to evoke his readers' empathy. He had glimpsed the children standing in the central hall, the smallest too tiny for his prison clothes. "I need not say how utterly distressed I was to see these children at Reading, for I knew the treatment in store for them. The cruelty that is practised by day and night on children in English prisons is incredible, except to those that have witnessed it. . . ." People no longer understood what cruelty was: "[It] is simply stupidity. It is the entire want of imagination." Prison officials had good intentions, but did not understand "the peculiar psychology of a child's nature." Unlike adults, children could not grasp that their punishment was inflicted by society, so they experienced prison as "limitless" terror. A child could not comprehend whether he is in prison on remand or after conviction. "To him the horrible thing is to be there at all. In the eyes of humanity it should be a horrible thing for him to be there at all."[68] Having traded forums, Wilde using the press and Stead fairy tales, the two men again threatened to explode the vision of a universally safe, carefree childhood that authors like Molesworth offered in her fictional world of middle-class nurseries. Stead, by trying to bridge the cultural gap between working- and middle-class children with high quality, cheap literature, and Wilde, by pointing out the continuing vulnerability of poor children, reminded Britain that the tensions and contradictions contained in the notion of a universally shared childhood were far from being resolved.

Chapter Four

Creating a Magazine World

Critics could write about children's literature all they wanted. In the end, authors, editors, and publishers had to please their audiences. The history of the successful, long-running children's magazine *Little Folks* (1871–1930) provides a window onto the relationship between producers and consumers of children's literature. Launched in 1871 by the publishing company Cassell as part of its expanding line of children's literature, *Little Folks* could not rely on the captive audiences that church-affiliated magazines could. With each edition came the renewed challenge of enticing readers back for the next issue and another opportunity for reader participation. The success of this commercial magazine grew out of the convergence of a publishing boom with a reconfiguration of children as readers and as objects of adult concern and pleasure.

Little Folks was created in an era when publishers were increasingly differentiating young readers by age and sex. A slew of new magazines targeted older youths, boys in particular. Aimed at a slightly younger audience than magazines like *Boys' Own Paper* and *Girls' Own Paper*, *Little Folks* cast itself as being for both sexes. Collectively, these magazines conveyed the message that gender was acquired in stages and helped to redefine childhood and to create the category "adolescent."[1]

In a decade when much of its competition was from religious presses, *Little Folks* distinguished itself by offering a balance between amusement and instruction.[2] Its opening page proclaimed that the magazine sought to amuse children "and at the same time teach them to think and do a little for themselves."[3] Presenting the act of reading *Little Folks* as fitting into multiple aspects of readers' lives, the editor carried this dual theme of pleasure and improvement through the first few volumes, promising in 1872 to provide "pretty stories to make you smile; wonderful facts to make you feel surprised," and of course, Sunday reading, "for as much as I long to make you clever, dear children, I would much rather help to make you good, as then you are sure to be loving and loved. . . ."[4] *Little Folks* had traded in the dire warnings of sin and death prevalent in earlier children's literature for appeals to children's better natures. Over the next six decades, the magazine periodically updated its image and message, taking part in larger social transformations in children's literature and childhood.

All of *Little Folks's* editors, male and female alike, assumed one male voice, altering its tone to keep pace with shifting notions of childhood and its relationship to adulthood. With each monthly pledge to entertain and instruct his readers, the editor was also defining the magazine's purpose, creating an image of its audience, and setting the boundaries of reader participation.[5] *Little Folks's* editors adopted an avuncular tone and established for themselves a central role in the magazine by speaking directly to the readers, opening and closing each half-yearly volume with words of encouragement, advice, and sales pitches. These messages contributed to the seamless quality of the magazine, giving the impression that there was only one, unaging editor and that the magazine, while forever improving, always remained familiar.[6]

Little Folks had at least three distinct audiences within its readership. The actual audience can be partially reconstructed through fund-raising lists, contest results, and correspondence. The editor also addressed an intended audience that embodied the contradictions in childhood's construction as classless and genderless. The editor depicted the readership as universal, yet differentiated boys from girls and assumed readers' familiarity with middle-class domestic settings. In portraying little foreign "heathens" or poor English children to arouse the horror or charitable feelings of his readers, the editor presumably had in mind an audience of white, middle-class, mostly English readers who would recognize those darker or poorer children as different from themselves. Adults, the magazine's third audience, were most directly addressed in the advertisements at the back of each month's issue. The emphasis on instruction and depictions of innocent, cherubic babies must also have been intended to appeal to parents who bought—and possibly read—the magazine.

The editor stressed from the outset that the magazine was for children and that they would be welcome to contribute material to it. As for the inaugural issue, "we can but trust that it will be welcome to the great family of English little folks."[7] This intimate, familial relationship involved reciprocity. Asking readers to "try to spread amongst others the instruction and pleasure" the magazine had afforded them, the editor promised that, in return, he did all he could to please them.[8] In 1874, the editor promised a "New and Improved Series" that would be larger, with more reading and pictures, "all this without increasing the price!" Since the magazine was "such a welcome visitor to so many homes in England and abroad," he had decided to give readers "more of everything that is good . . . and I want you all to assist me by showing the next number of *Little Folks* to your schoolmates and neighbours. . . ."[9] In a Christmas greeting "to his Friends" two decades later, in 1895, the editor promised "a better time than ever." And since they wouldn't want to keep all the pleasure to themselves, "the best and kindliest thing" they could do would be to persuade other children that had not seen *Little Folks* to ask their parents or uncles and aunts for the next number. The editor was both acknowledging that few children could buy their own magazines and urging readers to participate in defining children as recipients of gifts from adult relatives.[10]

Keeping Up with the Competition

From the 1880s on, shifts in *Little Folks*'s contents accompanied the periodic reformatting intended to renew its appeal. No longer able to presume a captive audience as the publishing industry grew more competitive and specialized, established magazines began to use more gimmicks; even religious magazines began to emphasize the pleasures they offered. *Little Folks* weathered these changes by adopting a lighter editorial tone and featuring new story genres, but without eliminating didacticism altogether. In the 1880s, *Little Folks* touted its Sunday pages as "cheery" and full of stories and anecdotes and informed readers that serials had been "specially written" for them.[11] By the 1890s, the magazine was promising surprise "gifts," including a "Little Folks Autograph Book" and a "Little Folks Diary and Notebook," illustrated by Walter Crane. *Little Folks* had also gathered a stable of regularly contributing authors and illustrators, referred to as "old friends." This new reliance on name recognition is a measure of the increasing profitability of children's literature and of the role of the magazine in boosting the fame of regular contributors. A number of these authors and illustrators became famous precisely because of their identification with successful magazines.[12]

In 1895 a new editor, Sam H. Hamer, created a more vivid persona and a fantasy world for readers. Like all good fairy tales, this one began with "once upon a time there was a good, kind Editor, and he edited a most beautiful magazine called *Little Folks,* and he used to talk to his little friends, and tell them of all the good things he had in store for them." He was visited one day by "six little people" who showed that they understood that reading choices were sex-specific. One boy requested a serial "full of adventures and fighting," and a girl asked for a nice story that both girls and boys could read. These and other wishes for serials, pictures, and animal as well as fairy stories were all granted by the editor. The boy was offered "Race for Death," the girl was given "A Pair of Primroses." Finally, "bidding the Editor goodbye, they all trooped off . . . and they all lived happily ever afterwards."[13] No longer a disembodied voice, the editor was a kindly man sitting in his office, talking with his readers.

Readers were asked to help in this reimagining of the editor by drawing his picture. The resulting collage, mostly of bearded men, but including three women, was accompanied by a photograph of a man sitting behind a desk with a *Little Folks* magazine covering his face.[14] In 1897, the "shy, modest, good, kind Editor" poked his head out of his shell to announce that there would be new illustrated covers each month, a "Little Folks Entertainment Album," and more surprises. Thanking his readers for their gifts to hospitals serving poor children and urging them to do even better in the coming year, he broke off with, "Dear me, I am getting quite solemn and serious! This will never do. I must get back into that shell of mine." While still cajoling children into charitable work, the editor now kept his tone light and playful.[15] Against the backdrop of increasing competition among children's magazines and the cultural reconstruction of childhood, *Little Folks*'s editor had evolved from a fairly remote avuncular voice, who rewarded well-learned lessons with pleasant stories, into a teasing accessible figure who did magic tricks and believed in fantasy. The kind but distant patriarch had become a middle-class "weekend dad" who played with his children in his leisure hours.[16]

Shaping Reader Participation

Part of *Little Folks*'s success lay in its creation of a magazine world that gave producers and consumers a shared set of references and expectations. The ever-evolving opportunities for reader participation may also have fostered the magazine's longevity. By the 1880s, the loyal reader could expect that each month's magazine would contain serial stories, pictures, games, poems, correspondence columns, contests, and charitable funds. In the early stages, participation largely consisted of letters written for prize contests. Children were typically instructed to write about the Bible or natural history or to create stories from a series of pictures. The magazine generally printed letters that conformed to *Little Folks*'s messages about character and charity.[17]

Now and again, the editor stepped in to shape the tone of these essay contests. He commended letters from clever readers who "have *thought* as well as *read*," hoping that they would inspire others to keep trying until they, too, could get one printed and so win a prize book.[18] In 1875, the editor offered a new incentive: the writer of the best essay for each month would be rewarded with the usual book and a new bronze medal constituting them as officers in the new "Little Folks Legion of Honour," "an honourable distinction which I hope many will endeavor to deserve." An opportunity not to be missed: children could join the Little Folks army and wear a symbol of their intellectual prowess.[19]

The next venture in reader participation was also carefully structured. Responding to requests by "many of my readers," the editor offered a new "Question and Answer Page" in 1878 that would print short questions of general interest, "but no notice whatever [could] be taken of merely trivial questions."[20] Some of these questions appear to have been "plants," enabling the editor to explain contest rules and advertise future attractions. But now and then, readers took the page off on their own tangent, as happened when a reader asked if there was any evidence of "good being achieved" with old postage stamps. This set off a flurry of replies. Another reader reported having read "that the Chinese sell their babies for one hundred old stamps, as they value them so much for decorating their houses." The same reader had also heard that ladies had secured children places in orphanages by sending stamps to Japan. Other readers asked where stamps could be sent and offered to contribute to stamp-collecting efforts. Finally, the editor intervened, declaring that there was no good evidence that stamps could be used to send children to school or to save heathens.[21]

The "Little Folks Post Office" replaced the "Question and Answer Page" in 1888, during one of the magazine's periodic overhauls. The editor invited children to write of their pastimes, holidays, dolls, and pets. Children who had traveled to, or lived in, foreign lands were invited to describe the strange people who lived there. The editor also asked for suggestions, "from your own experience," as to how children could "best help those who need aid and sympathy."[22] The letters chosen for publication closely followed the editor's guidelines. One thirteen-year-old correspondent described the bazaar she had held to raise money for a mission church. It had done a brisk trade, earning over five pounds, and she hoped to inspire children to follow her example, "for besides the good the money would do, there is a great deal of enjoyment and fun."[23]

Letters printed over the next eighteen years settled into discernable patterns. At first, children invariably wrote about pets, wildlife, or travel, as the editor had instructed. After a few years, it became standard to list favorite parts of the magazine—usually serials. Later, the litany expanded to include the number of years readers had taken *Little Folks*.[24] It is impossible to know how well these letters reflected readers' interests or whether correspondents tried to conform to the editor's and parents' expectations. Nor are these correspondents necessarily representative of the entire readership, since some kinds of letters must have been selected for printing over others. Nonetheless, these letters provide some of the best evidence we have about the composition of *Little Folks*'s audience.

Girls outnumbered boys in every category of participation, and they tended to read *Little Folks* for more years. Both sexes read the magazine between the ages of 6 and 16, but while girls continued to write and participated in contests in large numbers through age 14, boys' participation dropped off after age 11. This difference in participation makes sense in that juvenile boys were targeted as a separate reading market by the 1870s, while older girls were mostly left to choose between nursery literature and, if their parents permitted or did not notice, adult literature. Most of the mail came from within Great Britain, but many letters also came from Europe and the British colonies.[25] Correspondents' postal addresses and descriptions of their travels, nannies, and nurseries indicate a middle- and upper-class readership. In a memoir sprinkled with references to her family's ties to the British aristocracy, Angela Forbes describes winning a *Little Folks* competition when she was eight.[26] The magazine appears to have been especially popular in clergymen's families, or at least those children were prolific letter writers and fund-raisers.

Besides providing glimpses of *Little Folks*'s audience, "Little Folks Post Office" also provides clues about how the magazine was bought and read. Adult relatives bought children subscriptions as gifts, sometimes using the magazine to reward good behavior. Grandparents who sent the magazine to children living abroad were perhaps using it to maintain familial and national ties.[27] Some parents read the magazine with their children. One girl passed on her mother's description of the "Good Kind Editor"; another child wrote that even her father read the magazine; and a number of children asked that their letters be printed as a surprise for their parents.[28]

While adults participated in selecting and reading *Little Folks*, siblings had to work out how to share it. One eight-year-old boy explained that he, with his brothers and sister, had taken the magazine for two years and had each volume bound.[29] A second letter described how siblings of different ages read the magazine, together and separately: one seven-year-old girl read the short stories to a younger sister. "It is very amusing to see how earnest they are over it, and we all have chats" about the stories, and "do the puzzles, and write the answers in a book until the following number comes, and we see if they are correct."[30] These families' multiple uses of *Little Folks* illustrate the bonds forged between siblings in middle-class domestic circles.[31] The magazine was passed from sibling to sibling and from generation to generation. Children often began letters with the information that they had taken *Little Folks* "many years" or "as long as I can remember." By the 1890s, children were writing that their own parents had read the magazine as children and had passed their bound volumes on to a second generation of subscribers.[32]

While trying to retain the allegiance of readers ranging in age from four to sixteen, and "from every quarter of the globe," the editor differentiated readers by sex, giving papers on carpentry to boys and sewing lessons to girls and making it clear who was to read which serials.[33] Girls' stories were set within the domestic sphere, while boys' stories roamed further afield into exotic places and schools. In 1898, "Self-willed Family," about a family of sisters, was presented as girls' fare, while boys were given "Running Away to School." But some readers resisted being categorized by gender. One letter writer explained that she took *Little Folks* and her brother took *Chums,* but that both liked the former. Another girl wrote that Henty, the boys' adventure writer, was her favorite author, but she was also grateful to have a story for girls in "Self-willed Family." A twelve-year-old boy expressed approval for both "Running Away to School" and the domestic serial with which it was paired.[34] In a "dialogue" with some visiting "little folks" in 1897, the editor patiently explained to the girls who claimed the domestic serial for themselves, and to the boys who claimed the adventure serial, that the stories were really for both sexes equally. In this instance, the editor managed to affirm children's "natural" inclinations and to acknowledge the readers' practice of reading across gender lines.[35]

When the "Good Kind Editor" appeared in 1895, his call for both praise and criticism was apparently met by a flood of letters. Now the "Little Folks Post Office" often ended with a note indicating that hundreds more letters had been received than could be printed. The letter writing formula expanded to include the plea that this letter be printed, since the previous few had not been.[36] In keeping with the editor's new tone, children were given more latitude to shape the "Post Office." First one child wrote to ask for a foreign pen pal or a partner in trading postcards, then others followed suit, until finally, in 1898, the editor appended a "Stamp and Correspondence Column" to the "Post Office." By 1904, the "Column" had its own page and a steady stream of correspondents.[37]

Some readers built on the editor's make-believe world. In 1896, students at a Bavarian Young Ladies' College wrote a series of letters about the "Little Folks" club they had formed and the twelve-year-old president invited "King Eddie Tor" to join.[38] Other readers used *Little Folks* as inspiration for their own magazines. A ten-year-old wrote that she used *Little Folks*'s stories for her own magazine, which she distributed to friends.[39] They were in good company; Virginia Woolf and other future writers began by producing family magazines. Margaret Rhondda, founder of *Time and Tide,* edited her own magazine as a child in the 1890s. A student of marketing, she announced in her editorial page that the upcoming Christmas edition for 1899 would be "twice the usual size, besides having—perhaps—sketches and pictures in it."[40]

Magazine Philanthropy

Many of *Little Folks*'s stories were intended to arouse readers' sympathy toward less fortunate, often motherless, children. In one common variation on this theme, middle-class children, usually coached by their mothers, learned unselfishness by helping poor children. In these stories, poor children served as vehicles for improving middle-class children's characters. Elsewhere, *Little Folks's* readers were presented with complicated messages about class and philanthropy. They were instructed to pity children who lived in the turmoil and dirt of London's streets, yet these children were also shown playing and laughing in recognizably childlike ways. Child labor was depicted as firmly part of a dangerous past or as amenable to charity. In one series, "Little Ones of the Streets," a "Gentleman" hears the stories of appealing, hard-working young flower sellers, match sellers, and crossing sweeps. In each case, the gentleman provides assistance, whether buying the flower seller's stock or steering the crossing sweep to a new job.[41] Like W. T. Stead's "The Maiden Tribute of Modern Babylon," these depictions of child labor obscure the structural reasons for, and consequences of, child labor.[42] When suffering is involved, charity is at hand. *Little Folks* invited readers to contrast their presumably cozy, safe lives with those of London street arabs. At the same time, by blunting the consequences of poverty, the magazine presented childhood as a universally shared period of innocence and play that both adult and child readers could enjoy. These stories reinforced and framed *Little Folks's* charitable appeals during a period when the British middle class was increasingly uneasy about the social gulf dividing them from the poor.[43]

Little Folks invited readers to do more than read about philanthropy. It organized a series of long-running charities that added another dimension to the *Little Folks* world.[44] While the magazine structured each charity drive, participants added their own nuances and determined its success or failure. In 1875, the editor initiated a "Special Prize Competition" that would be repeated annually for more than thirty years. The editor explained that he wanted to employ readers' fingers and heads "to the benefit of other poorer children, whose ways do not lie in pleasant places." He offered prizes "to our girls and boys," asking them to "help us in a work that in itself will, I am sure, be a great pleasure and delight to many." The girls who sent the neatest dolls clothes would be "rewarded by a handsome guinea book, the second best by a half guinea book, the third by a five shilling book." The boys who sent the best model boats would win equivalent prizes. After being judged, the dolls would be sent to children's hospitals "as offerings to the young inmates from their more fortunate little brothers and sisters." The editor was sure that "many heavy eyes" would "brighten at the sight of even the humblest of these kindly gifts."[45] For the next five years, competitors were invited to make quilts for children's cots, illustrated texts, dolls' costumes, toys, scrapbooks, or color in painting books sold by Cassell. The addition of age divisions in 1882 (those thirteen and under could compete as Juniors, fourteen- to seventeen-year-olds could compete as Seniors) and their further refinement in 1886 suggest that the magazine was using competition results to gauge its readership's composition, and to secure the greatest possible number of participants.[46]

Girls participated in these contests in larger numbers, in more categories, and for more years than boys did.[47] There were always a few fourteen- or sixteen-year-old male winners, but boys' participation dropped off after age twelve, while girls tended to compete until age sixteen. These variations by age and sex can be linked to the composition of the magazine's readership and to the gendered nature of philanthropy. Goods for bazaars and for distribution to the poor were produced in the private sphere inhabited by women, girls, and young boys.

Appealing indirectly to parents by pointing out that the contests provided occupation for little hands and produced "a spirit of healthy emulation," the editor spoke directly to readers, urging those who had not won to remember that theirs was "a labour of love to help those less fortunate little ones who have not, with you, kind parents and relations to care lovingly for your welfare." Wishing that readers could see the pleasure their donations brought to the sick children, the editor invited them to "watch" patients like "poor little Lizzie" who had undergone "a severe operation and much suffering. All through the long weary weeks of pain and weakness her dolls have been her great solace and amusement."[48] As further encouragement, a "Little Folks Exhibition and Bazaar" was held in 1876 at the Crystal Palace to display and celebrate "Little Folks'" contributions. Reporting on the festivities, the editor described the "throngs" of visitors, the presentation of prizes, and the singing of 400 orphans.[49]

By 1890, "Contest Adjudicators" were critiquing children's endeavors, leaving the editor free to praise readers' "hearty and generous response." Commenting first on the toys and scrap albums, so that boys would not have to "wade through" accounts of knitting and stitching, the adjudicators used most of their column to lecture girls on neatness and tasteful choice of colors. They expressed surprise one year that the maker of an engine was actually a girl with a penknife. "But have you got all your fingers sound?"[50] In time, the magazine's lighter tone reached even these stern lectures, now presented as dialogues between Miss Judy Cator, Mrs. J. Udge, and the Good Kind Editor.

In 1880, five years after the first prize competition, the editor announced a new "Cot Fund." This charity drive opened with Viscountess Enfield's description of her visit to the East London Hospital children's wards. She begged the "dear children" to help keep the wards open, reminding them of their good fortune and philanthropic duty: "those amongst you who are sick and are lovingly nursed by tender mothers will be even more anxious to help the poor little ones who live in miserable homes, where they cannot be well nursed or cared for." Picking up this accent on the presumed contrast between the lives of readers and patients, the editor followed with Browning's "The Cry of the Children," explaining that the poem had been written on behalf of children who had labored in coal pits. This danger had been ended, but children still lived "in sickness, misery, and want in the dark courts and alleys of our great cities . . . [with] no gentle mother by their side to soothe and comfort them. . . ." Visiting London's East End, he had found "amid the mud and dirt . . . a group of half-clothed children, with cold, pinched faces, and with scarcely a sign of childhood's grace."[51] Having shown readers pathetic images of motherless and unchildlike children, the editor asked them to raise 1,000 pounds to endow a hospital cot. By December, the money had been collected, and the editor asked readers to try for a second cot. Explaining that "all classes, from the highest to the humblest" had assisted, the editor praised readers' self-sacrifice and hard work. A few letters "selected at random" told the stories behind the subscriptions. One girl had taken her new doll from house to house to collect money, in imitation of a Yorkshire custom practiced when a baby was born. One seven-year-old sent a "birthday shilling," and a father wrote that it had taken "very little to persuade" his children to send their Christmas coppers to the fund.[52]

As the "Cot Fund" drew to a close in 1882, with a final tally of 1,755 pounds, *Little Folks* offered another opportunity for philanthropic participation, this time tapping into Victorian interest in animal welfare and enabling the magazine to bypass contentious debates over pauperization involved in philanthropy to poor children.[53] The editor introduced the "Little Folks Humane Society" by calling on readers to "make the world better and happier" by protecting "weak and defenceless" animals. The fight to overcome the "Giants" of ignorance, cruelty, and thoughtlessness would lead to greater mercy and deeper reverence for God. Evoking religious and masculine themes, the editor suggested that boys were apt to think that kindness was "derogatory to manliness, and they would be almost ashamed to be seen abstaining from stoning frogs . . . [or] to show a tender-heartedness that might lay them open to the charge of being womanish and wanting in spirit." To the contrary, the bravest hearts had the most tenderness in them. He called on readers to "band themselves into an army to fight manfully for the weak and defenceless as the chivalrous knights used to do in old times." This stress on manliness, echoing muscular Christian themes, suggests that boys were considered more elusive as readers than girls and more in need of conversion to the cause. Girls were brought back in for the final sales pitch: "as all of you will like to grow up to be brave, noble, thoughtful men and women . . . , it is my desire to lead your minds in this direction" by forming the "Little Folks Humane Society."[54]

The rewards for participation were plentiful: readers who returned the attached membership forms received "Certificates of Membership," had their names published in the magazine and inscribed in the "Little Folks Humane Society Register." Those who convinced 50 more to join were made officers and received a medal and a book. Apparently, the magazine had successfully presented this as an appropriately masculine cause: the first list of 750 names, ranging in age from 6 to 16, was fairly evenly divided between boys and girls. By the publication of the sixth list, the names of new members filled 8 pages, reaching a total of 8,180, with Princesses Louise, Victoria, and Maud topping the list. The final list, published in 1884, tallied over 50,000 members, and the "Little Folks Humane Society Form of Promise" was published periodically for twenty more years.[55]

Pulling the animal protection theme into other parts of *Little Folks,* the editor offered prizes for the best poem about a dog's fidelity and for essays on kindness to animals.[56] The Christmas Annual for 1883 featured an address by the well-known philanthropist Lord Shaftesbury. Reminding readers that animals had rights "quite as clear and imperative as those of servants in relation to their masters" and of subjects in relation to their sovereign, Shaftesbury presented kindness to animals as training for the philanthropy that cemented the political and social structures. Sometimes, readers took the initiative. When Jumbo the Elephant was to be sold by the London Zoological Gardens to P. T. Barnum, the circus master, "Little Folks Humane Society" members inundated the editor with pleas to rescue Jumbo. Urging readers to follow the example of members who had given a "Humane Society Entertainment," the editor explained that similar events could benefit the cause of "Humanity to Animals" and provide officers a chance to wear their medals.[57]

By 1896, the magazine was repackaging its philanthropy. The "Good Kind Editor" had added essay categories and new prizes to the "Special Prize Competition," shifting the competition's focus from philanthropy to *Little Folks* itself. Girls could now win Little Folks brooches, and boys could win Little Folks knives for writing the best essay about "How I Would Edit 'Little Folks.'" In 1897, ten books by Mrs. Molesworth were promised to readers who could predict the secret to be revealed in the author's current serial, "The Secret of Greyling Towers." Competitors in other categories could win "suitable" and more expensive prizes. A doll costume could bring a doll worth seven pounds; needlework could secure a little needlewoman a workbox.[58] By 1900, the now semiannual competitions put greater emphasis on prizes, the new essay categories turned attention to *Little Folks*'s world, while accounts of suffering hospital patients were moved into the background. The magazine also offered more competitions that were detached from charity and skill. Offering watches and bikes as prizes, these contests served purely as enticement for readers, making them recipients rather than makers of gifts.

But seriousness had not been banished altogether. Beginning in 1901, a monthly "Ward Page" was devoted to raising money for Little Folks' cots at a Children's Hospital in Bethnal Green. Author Bella Sidney Woolf led the effort, leaving the editor free to cheer on his readers. By 1904, the goal of 2,000 pounds for 6 cots had been reached, and Woolf called on readers to try for another 1,000 pounds, using pathos and example as incentives. She described the "melancholy face" of one "little martyr" and wrote that her "heart ached" at the cot of a little boy who had lost a leg.[59] Accounts of fund-raising efforts, mostly by girls, followed these images: the girls of St. Nicholas School had raised 13 pounds with a play and bazaar; another girl had raised 4 pounds selling her own magazine. A reprinted newspaper article told of a schoolgirls' fund-raising "Entertainment" of songs, recitation, and dances. In a column devoted to fund-raising notices, one reader offered prizes for the best items donated to a bazaar; another advertised toffee and peppermints for sale. Just as the "Little Folks Humane Society" had defined appropriately masculine concern for animals, the "Ward Fund" helped to train young girls for womanly charity, providing the incentives of recognition in a magazine and participation in a community of "Little Folks."

Little Folks marked the ward's opening with a celebration. The "Good Kind Editor" was spotted on the platform with Princess Louise. Miss Woolf took the opportunity to remind readers of their duty to help people with as much "craving for happiness and pleasant things as we have, yet doomed to a life of hard, hard work, few pleasures—and those not always the right ones—much suffering and want." Presenting the poor as a group apart, their poverty as natural, and their actions as sometimes imprudent, Woolf reinforced *Little Folks*'s message that readers ought to engage in philanthropy that was safely mediated by the magazine.

While *Little Folks* invited readers to aid poor children and animals, it was also making readers themselves into the recipients of magazine subscriptions from parents and prizes from the magazine. Images presented in *Little Folks,* and confirmed in readers' letters, showed these watches, books, and magazines being consumed in domestic settings. In targeting the home as the site of consumption, the magazine both depended on a particular vision of family life and helped to transform that domestic setting. Entering the private sphere, it helped to differentiate its members by age and gender.[60] Editors invited children to consume as children, and as boys and girls. Adults were invited to consume the magazine as parents and to take pleasure in its depictions of innocent childhood.

Commodifying Children

The visual images of children contained in the illustrations and advertisements that filled *Little Folks*'s pages invited admiration of their physical beauty. Making the most of improvements in printing technology that allowed for better quality, more detail, and color, the magazine's editors heralded colored frontispieces and foldouts as special attractions and featured rosy-faced children in full-page pictures and border decorations.[61] A color picture of "Grandpa's Little Darling" was accompanied by a poem that invited readers to share the man's pleasure as he holds the girl's face in his hands: "Warm lips like ripe-red cherries, [a]nd a face so sweet and fair."[62] John Ruskin was one adult who admitted to taking pleasure in such images, praising British artists' rediscovery of children, "all dazzling and pure. . . ."[63] Such sensual images could be enjoyed as long as they were explicitly associated with childhood innocence.

Advertisements, grouped together in the magazine's final pages, were clearly aimed at adults. In the early years, the products advertised ranged from insect powders to cough lozenges, cambric frilling to baking powder. A few products promised to meet children's grooming needs, but most were intended to purify or soothe the bodies of adults or to ease household labor. By the early 1880s, advertisers were more likely to address potential customers in their roles as parents. Now, alongside ads for laxatives, pens, and soaps, appeared those for infant foods used in the royal nursery, children's laxatives featuring a picture of a baby, and "whispers" to mothers, urging them to ensure that their daughters would not lose their teeth. In 1884, there were creams for making children's skin smooth and Eno's Fruit Salts offered a "Nursery Card" with information in case of accident or common childhood illnesses. By 1894, Nestlé's food had become the "only" substitute for mother's milk, and alongside ads for corsets and teas were those for Mellins foods, which featured pictures of plump, partly nude children and testimonials from mothers, including the empress of Germany.[64] By the late 1890s, at least half the ads promised to benefit children: Hovis offered wholesome delicacies for little folks; Quaker Oats promised to make fretful children good-natured by building their bodies with "pure" food.[65] By century's end, sentimentalized images of rosy, plump children permeated advertisements, illustrations, and stories. These images and texts played on ideas of children as both appealing and delicate and portrayed women as mothers nurturing their children with books and wholesome foods. They anchored women to their homes and their roles as consumers on behalf of their families, at a time when women were demanding the right to join the public sphere as voters and entering the public world of shopping, where the pleasures of consumption threatened to outweigh the responsibilities of providing for one's family.[66]

    Little Folks responded to and shaped the changing literary market with its fiction, articles, correspondence, and competitions. This imagined community of readers sometimes took on a life of its own, but the editor always kept contributors within the bounds the magazine had established, while responding to their demands in commercially savvy ways. *Little Folks*'s magazine world mirrored the vision of childhood as a separate space being articulated by middle-class adults, but it also conveyed the message that children must take part in a larger world divided by class and gender. The tensions between designating children as givers and receivers of gifts, between making childhood insular and preparing children for adulthood, came to the forefront as the market in children's literature grew more competitive and childhood was reconfigured.

Chapter Five

"Another Ladder Altogether": Writing for Children

According to Mrs. Molesworth, the successful children's author, writing for children required the "peculiar gift" of being able to "see" and "feel" as children did. Andrew Lang and Edith Nesbit, who wrote for and about children between the 1880s and 1900s, shared this belief that children's authors had special insight into childhood.[1] Lang, through his "Colour Fairy Books," and Nesbit, through *The Wouldbegoods, Five Children and It,* and other popular children's novels, presented childhood as a separate and uniquely imaginative stage of life. Both also gave a central role to reading in their portrayals of children's imaginative play and participated in reworking the genre of children's literature.

Molesworth argued that writing for children was "not so much a question of taking up one's stand on the lower rungs of the literary ladder, as of standing on another ladder altogether—one which has its own steps, its higher and lower positions of excellence."[2] Nesbit's biographer, Julia Briggs, has suggested that the fluidity of children's literature in the late Victorian and Edwardian years was the source of its strength and lure. Some subjects like sexuality were out of bounds, "but the lack of fully developed rules and patterns left children's fiction as one of the freest and most versatile forms of the nineteenth century."[3] Children's writers could incorporate Romantic and supernatural themes no longer considered suitable to serious adult literature in an age when realistic fiction was ascendant.[4] This freedom, besides its commercial potential, may have attracted Lang and Nesbit to children's literature. It provided a forum for presenting their understandings of childhood and children's reading and for their political, intellectual, and spiritual preoccupations.[5] Lang's "Colour Fairy Books" were expressions of his anthropological theory of cultural evolution; Nesbit's Fabian socialism found subtle expression in her later children's books.

The relative freedom of children's literature was also due to its marginality. As popular as it was, children's literature was not accorded the status of adult literature. Nesbit, like Frances Hodgson Burnett and other women writers, had difficulty convincing publishers to take her seriously as a writer for adults once she gained a reputation as a children's author. Men, with greater access to an increasingly professionalized literary industry, and less associated with childrearing in the popular imagination, ran less risk of being labeled as children's authors. Lang, like J. M. Barrie, Oscar Wilde, and other men who experimented in children's literature, was not identified primarily as a children's writer in his lifetime. This chapter is as much about how gender shaped Lang's and Nesbit's professional opportunities as about how both constructed children as imaginative beings and as readers.[6]

Andrew Lang (1844–1912)

Andrew Lang was a "literary landmark" in late nineteenth-century London.[7] Passing easily from scholarly work to journalism to fiction and poetry, he contributed to the developing field of anthropology, took a central role in the late Victorian literary battle between Romanticism and realism, and is now remembered primarily as the editor of the popular "Colour Fairy Book" series. These seemingly disparate activities were united by his theory of literature's historical role in society and by his memory of its formative role in his own childhood.

The oldest of seven children, Lang was born in 1844, in Selkirk, Scotland. He grew up in a middle-class home, cared for by a Scottish nurse who introduced him to local folk and fairy tales. He went from grammar school to Edinburgh Academy and then on to the University of St. Andrews in 1861. Finishing his undergraduate work at Oxford, Lang then spent seven more years there as a Fellow of Merton College. His academic career ended in 1874 when he married and began to establish his writing career in London. Lang's wife, Leonora Alleyne (1851–1933) came from a family of Barbados planters. Growing up in England, she educated herself in several languages and became Lang's assistant and collaborator.[8]

The Langs arrived in London in 1875, a time when aspiring journalists could find many forums for their work in a growing numbers of periodicals. A prolific writer, Andrew Lang sold his book reviews and articles to a variety of magazines, including *Punch* and the *Fortnightly Review,* and he became "perhaps the most influential critic" of the late nineteenth century. Journalism allowed him to write about a variety of subjects—from anthropology and literary criticism to sports—but he also continued to produce scholarly work, including widely used translations of classical literature.[9]

At a time when the social sciences were coming under the influence of natural science methods and evolutionary theory, Lang broke new ground in anthropology and popularized the subject by writing about it in mainstream magazines. He wrote about anthropology for lay readers in part because he could not count on an audience within academia. His rival, Max Müller, an Oxford professor, kept anthropology tied to his own discipline of philology, forcing evolutionary anthropologists, including Edward Tylor, James Frazer, and Lang, to find other forums for their work. During this unique phase of its development (1860s–1890s), anthropology was conducted outside university walls. While it was, argues Henrika Kuklick, "anthropological ideas were elaborately linked to social practices in a fashion without parallel since."[10] Müller himself contributed to the blurring of lines between academic and popular discussions of anthropology by carrying out his theoretical feud with Lang in nonacademic journals.[11]

Lang and Müller disagreed about why similar myths and folklore existed in geographically and culturally distinct civilizations. Müller used a theory of language diffusion to explain why the same myths and folklore appeared in "primitive" and "civilized" societies. He maintained that certain linguistic symbols, originating in "Aryan" cultures, had migrated outward and been misinterpreted by other cultures.[12] Lang argued for an alternative theory of cultural evolution. He maintained that myths, folklore, and fairy tales grew out of early societies' need to explain their world and preserve their cultures. Handed down and refined over centuries, these stories could still be found in "backward" and peasant cultures. Viewing these contemporary stories as holdovers from early cultures, Lang was among the first to use literature to reconstruct past civilizations in the way that other anthropologists used fossils. He believed that the explanation for similarities between different cultures' myths and stories lay in early humanity's "universal" need to explain their natural and supernatural surroundings. He accepted that some stories might have been transmitted from one culture to another through migration, intermarriage, and war. But his basic argument was that certain universal experiences, translated into epics, myths, legends, and fairy tales, had evolved along similar lines in separate cultures.[13]

Lang saw folktales as records of "the ladder-like ascent of all men, regardless of their race or language."[14] Students of this lore could "look back and see the long trodden way" behind them, "the winding tracks through marsh and forest . . . the caves, the camps, the villages, the towns where the race has tarried."[15] Joining the Folk-Lore Society after its founding in 1878, he became part of a team of anthropological folklorists who championed cultural evolutionism against Müller's diffusionist school. The society sought to establish a science that would reconstruct prehistoric peoples' worldviews from contemporary folklore. Lang presided over the society's first International Folklore Congress, held in London in 1891.[16]

Lang's interest in identifying universal stories was tied to his exploration of literature's role in society. Placing himself at the center of a contemporary literary battle, he sided with his friend Robert Louis Stevenson and other late nineteenth-century Romantics against realists like Henry James. He argued that fiction should provide entertainment and escape from the world and criticized realists for their didacticism and depictions of squalor and dreariness. Realists, in turn, attacked Romanticism as a reactionary threat to literature's artistic advancement.[17]

As a prolific, popular critic and a respected reader for Longmans publishing house, Lang was in a position to publicize his views and to promote favorite authors like Robert Louis Stevenson and H. Rider Haggard.[18] His literary theory and championship of romance grew out of his experience with contemporary society and his anthropological studies. He was critical of the effects of urbanization and industrialization and pessimistic about Britain's evolution into a democracy.[19] Lang's dislike of England's urban present fed his desire for escapist fiction and his admiration for writers like William Morris, who found a better society in England's past.[20] His preference for fiction that allowed mental escape from the present was reinforced by his theory of cultural evolution. He believed that literature, in both oral and written forms, had preserved important cultural statements that civilization built on and altered as it matured. Lang believed that society had now reached a point when anthropology and the other social sciences had inherited the burden of cultural preservation, freeing literature to be used for escape and pleasure. This did not mean that literature could abdicate all responsibility. It should allow imaginative freedom within a "morally acceptable framework." Fairy tales and adventures provided precisely that: clearly defined good and evil and the ultimate triumph of goodness.[21]

Tracing romance's origins to early humanity's prescientific imagination, Lang believed that these roots in "universal elements of the imagination" provided the basis for its modern popular appeal. Literary critic Joseph Weintraub argues that Lang saw romance as the only medium that could "reunite the artist with a public that had already ceased to listen." He sought to recapture a mythic midcentury tradition of "a novelist in perfect accord with a national audience."[22] His championship of romance, and his self-declared alliance with those who read fiction "for the purpose of forgetting their woes" grew out of pessimism, nostalgia, and anthropological study. This critical stance, argues Weintraub, often put Lang in "the position of spokesman for the amusing, but ephemeral literature of the marketplace." Lang's tastes may have been middlebrow as Weintraub and Eleanor Langstaff, and Henry James before them, have argued. But Weintraub and

Langstaff also demonstrate that Lang's literary criticism was consistent with his theory of literature's diminished role in modern society and his insistence on his own subjectivity as a critic.[23]

Lang gained his greatest fame and profit as editor of the "Colour Fairy Books." Publishers were initially skeptical about launching this series into a children's book market dominated by the "realistic" fiction of Mrs. Molesworth, who also wrote the kind of modern, allegorical fairy tales Lang detested.[24] But *The Blue Fairy Book,* published in 1889, was immediately popular. It was followed by eleven more "Fairy Books," alternating with "Story Books," "Animal Stories," and "Rhymes," that sold well on the Christmas market. The "Colour Fairy Books" were frequently reprinted, and Longmans issued smaller volumes as prize books and schoolbooks until the London Blitz in World War II.[25] As editor, Lang combined profit, scholarship, and the pleasure of presenting the kinds of stories he had liked as a child.

The "Colour Fairy Book" series included *Aladdin* and *Gulliver's Travels,* translations of stories popularized by Charles Perrault and the Grimm brothers, old chapbook favorites, as well as less familiar tales from around the world. Lang's role was to find sources, edit, and write prefaces to the books. A team of women, consisting of Leonora Lang, the Langs' relatives, and other scholarly women, translated the folktales from their original languages. Andrew Lang was paid 100 pounds in 1889 and 200 pounds in 1899, while the women received between 3 and 15 pounds in 1889 and 10 to 40 pounds a decade later, depending on the number of tales they translated.[26] Leonora Lang ensured that the stories' vocabulary and sentence structures were accessible to child readers. Her percentage of the profits rose in later years, when she took over most of the translating and began to write and compile the nonfairy books that Andrew Lang edited, although her work was never fully acknowledged. Lang once explained that he selected the stories and traced their origins, while Mrs. Lang translated and adapted them for children: "[M]y part has been that of Adam, according to Mark Twain, in the Garden of Eden. Eve worked, Adam superintended."[27]

Lang brought to the fairy tales a scholarly stamp of authority that ensured the initial attention of publishers and the public.[28] Using the prefaces to transmit his message that fairy tales were anthropologically and culturally important, as well as pleasurable and morally sound, he announced that the stories had been gathered on scientific principles. The literary equivalent of fossils, they showed links between past and present civilizations and between geographically separate cultures. "As old as anything that men have invented," these stories were first narrated by "naked savage women" to their children in a time before science.[29] Long after the rich and educated had forgotten these stories, "the country people" had continued to hand them down from generation to generation. Then learned men "collected and printed the country people's stories, and these we have translated to amuse children."[30]

Lang stressed the fairy tales' universality: stories in many different languages contained "the same adventures and something like the same plots." Giving flesh to this idea of fairy tales as bridges across cultures and time, he explained that "all people in the world tell nursery tales to their children. The Japanese tell them, the Chinese, the Red Indians by their camp fires, the Eskimo . . . the kaffirs of South Africa," and the peoples of Europe.[31] These storytelling peoples differed in "colour, language, religion, and almost everything else." But they all loved "nursery tales" that embodied the shared moral truth that "courage, youth, beauty, kindness, have many trials, but they always win the battle; while witches, giants, unfriendly cruel people, are on the losing hand."[32]

Lang used the prefaces to convince adults of the tales' cultural importance, making it clear that he expected that adults would select the books and might participate in their reading. He made room for adult readers, and for his own roles as editor and scholar, by suggesting that adults who retained the "heart of a little child" could continue to enter the "enchanted realm." These stories could be read "both scientifically and in a literary way, without losing the heart of childhood."[33] Lang believed that children had a special affinity for fairy tales because their original tellers "were much like children in their minds long ago."[34] Like other post-Darwinian scholars, Lang was fascinated by the idea that children's minds were like those of mankind's earliest ancestors and of contemporary "primitive" peoples. He argued that contemporary children shared early mankind's "unblunted edge of belief, and his fresh appetite for marvels." Lang saw a shared imaginative quality and simplicity in his child audience, the peasants who had preserved the fairy tales, and the early peoples who had first told them.[35]

Lang described the writers he admired as having a special relationship to childhood. Hans Christian Andersen was "akin in imagination to the primeval fancy, so near the secret heart of childhood."[36] Robert Louis Stevenson had a "genius" that "*all* children possess," but that died out "in the generality of mortals."[37] Likening schoolboys to a savage tribe in his essay "The Boy," he argued that boys' imaginative powers were lost upon entering school, where they conformed to school rituals and codes and immersed themselves in sports. Lang regretted this loss of imagination, but considered the "savage" life better—apart from the bullying—than the alternatives he presented: the "awful infancy" of the scholarly young John Stuart Mill or the premature aestheticism of some older schoolboys (this dig may have been aimed at such proponents of aestheticism as *Yellow Book* magazine and Oscar Wilde).[38] He was silent about how the imaginations of middle-class girls and working-class children were shaped by their different schooling experiences.

Bringing together his favorite themes, Lang opened his memoir, *Adventures Among Books,* by stressing the importance of books in his own childhood, which he presented as a time of innocence and imagination, and ended it with a discussion of folklore's relationship to anthropology. Recreating his encounters with books and stories in vivid detail, he described learning to read at age four by picking out the words of a poem he had memorized, listening to *Robinson Crusoe* and Scottish folktales, and doing his Sunday reading out of an old illustrated Bible. An evening spent reading Shakespeare's "A Midsummer Night's Dream" to himself gave him "an enchanted glimpse of eternity in Paradise; nothing resembling it remains with me, out of all the years." At age six, he discovered "another paradise, a circulating library with brown, greasy, ill-printed, odd volumes" of Shakespeare and the *Arabian Nights.*[39]

Like other children of his generation, Lang quickly moved from didactic children's stories to adult novels by the Brontës, Dickens, Walter Scott, and Thackeray. He described his discovery of these novels as a turning point in his childhood. He had been "rather an industrious little boy" who read a history of Rome for pleasure. But when Dickens's *Pickwick Papers* was brought into the house, " I felt a 'call,' and underwent a process which may be described as the opposite of 'conversion'. . . . From that hour it was all over, for five or six years, with anything like industry and lesson-books." A temporary ban on reading adult novels was soon lifted. Lang felt that such restrictions were pointless, arguing that children did not even comprehend the parts of novels that adults feared would corrupt them.[40] Implying here that children's innocence protected them in their reading of adult novels, he denied elsewhere that fairy tales were harmful to children, because they had enough common sense to recognize "make-believe."[41] In this autobiographical piece, Lang developed his argument that adventures and fairy tales tapped children's natural imaginative powers and credited his own contact with fairy tales for leading him to anthropology.

Lang's reputation as a scholar and popularity as a journalist contributed to the "Fairy Books'" success and protected him from being labeled as a children's author. He could inhabit the world of publishers and academics in a way that women of his time, his wife for example, could not.[42] But his subsequent reputation was shaped by changing tastes in literature and by the fleeting nature of journalistic reputations. While he had chosen the losing side in the battle between Romantic and realistic fiction, Lang's anthropological work continued to be influential, but within an increasingly narrow circle. The field was moving from the public domain into academia, as evidenced by St. Andrews University's series of "Andrew Lang" lectures held from 1927 to 1937. He might well have been irritated that he is now primarily associated with the "Colour Fairy Books," having worked hard to make it clear that he had not written these tales "out of his own head," although he had "written almost everything else."[43] Although he guessed that people did not read his scholarly prefaces, he might have been more upset to learn that they were deleted from some editions published after his death and that versions issued in the 1940s excluded all non-Aryan tales.[44] The continued reprinting of these "Fairy Books" indicate de facto acceptance of Lang's linkage of childhood and fantasy, but his anthropological messages of universality and evolution have been erased.

E. Nesbit (1858–1924)

Edith Nesbit (known professionally as E. Nesbit), the author of a series of popular stories for children published between 1899 and 1910, has been dubbed by her biographer, Julia Briggs, "the first modern writer for children." Alison Lurie argues that Nesbit's innovations make it possible to think about children's literature "before and after E. Nesbit." Others see her work as tied to nineteenth-century conventions and less important than that of J. M. Barrie or George MacDonald, and there are similar disagreements over her status as a feminist.[45] These conflicting evaluations of her writing and politics correspond with her biographers' presentation of her life as complex and full of "inconsistencies."

Nesbit's marriage to Hubert Bland was a mixture of bourgeois propriety and bohemian unconventionality. A Fabian socialist, Nesbit passionately condemned industrial capitalism in her writing, yet combined her socialism with a rigid sense of class and, like some other Fabians, with imperialist and racist attitudes.[46] Nesbit yearned to be a poet, but often instead did "hackwork" to support her family.[47] She finally had her greatest success with children's stories that were an amalgam of her politics, her sense of class and gender, and a distinctive portrayal of childhood imagination and reading.

Born in 1858 to Sarah and John Nesbit, in South London, Edith Nesbit was preceded by four siblings. John Nesbit ran a small agricultural college he had inherited from his father. When he died in 1862, he left his wife a "well-to-do" widow with five children. But years of traveling through Europe in search of relief for the consumption suffered by Edith's older sister Mary depleted much of the family's savings. In 1875, Mrs. Nesbit and her youngest daughter moved to Islington, where they could obtain cheap housing. By 1877, Edith Nesbit was selling her poetry to magazines. That year, she met Hubert Bland, who was employed as a bank clerk.[48] Although they did not marry until 1880, two months before the birth of their son Paul, Edith told her family and friends that they had married the year before. She did not learn until later that Hubert's reluctance to marry was partly due to his "understanding" with Maggie Doran, his mother's paid companion, who would bear him a son and remain his lover for ten more years.

In addition to the emotional stresses, the early years of their marriage were also financially difficult. Hubert Bland would eventually earn a good living as an essayist and reviewer. But just before they married, he had invested in a brush manufacturing venture that failed, and when he developed smallpox after Paul's birth, it was left to Nesbit to support the family. Her methods of earning money reflected the limited range of options available to a respectable middle-class married woman in the 1880s. She peddled her stories and poetry around to various magazines and sold greeting cards, decorated with flowers and verse, to printers' shops. In the meantime, their second child, Iris, was born in 1881, and Fabian was born in 1885.[49]

Nesbit and Bland were increasingly politically active during these years. They joined the Social Democratic Federation when it was founded in 1883; the next year they were among the Fabian Society's founding members. As Fabians, the Blands' political and social lives meshed. They became known for their social "evenings," and Nesbit dressed and carried herself as a "New Woman." She adopted "aesthetic" loose gowns, cut her hair short, and took up smoking. Nesbit also formed friendships with such feminists as Olive Schreiner and developed a radical critique of marriage. But her belief in women's mental inferiority put her at odds with other Fabian women who sought equality for women as voters and workers.[50]

Hubert Bland expressed shock at Schreiner's defense of free love, a response that belied his actions. In addition to his relationship with Maggie Doran, he kept up a long affair with Alice Hoatson, whom Nesbit had met while trying to sell stories to Hoatson's employers at *Sylvia's Home Journal.* Hoatson became a family friend and came to live with the Blands. When she became pregnant with Rosamund, born in 1886, Nesbit offered to pass the child off as her own, probably because this seemed the only way to save the reputations of all concerned. She did the same with John, born in 1899, the year before her own son, Fabian, died during an adenoid operation. But Nesbit also seems to have decided that she would no longer play martyr to Bland's philandering. Biographers have speculated that she began to have affairs of her own.[51] Hoatson's presence freed Nesbit in other ways as well. Playing the role of live-in aunt, Hoatson took over much of the domestic work, giving Nesbit time to write. Letters to a friend capture Nesbit's life of juggling domestic tasks and paid work before Hoatson's arrival:

> Today I have washed my hair and . . . have done two sheets 'sides into middle'—written some paragraphs for a newspaper—cooked the dinner, nursed

Iris for a whole hour—in the vain hope of getting her to sleep. . . . I have also painted some cards [and] we have just finished a story about a dream. . . .

She resented the lack of "time to do any *good work.* . . ."[52]

Throughout the 1880s and 1890s, Nesbit wrote prolifically, producing poetry, novels, plays, book reviews, and children's literature, sometimes in collaboration with either Bland or Hoatson.[53] Her work appeared in a wide range of magazines and newspapers, including *Longman's Magazine, Temple Bar,* the *Star,* and, during a "Decadent" phase, in the *Yellow Book* magazine that Andrew Lang despised. Trying to sell such diverse writings put Nesbit in contact with almost 30 publishers during a period when authors were just beginning to secure royalties and overseas copyright protection and when publishers were sometimes underhanded about paying authors their share of profits. She appears to have been careful about negotiating and collecting the often small sums she was paid.[54] The next phase of her writing career put her in a stronger position to negotiate with publishers. She also acquired a literary agent, a member of a profession that emerged with publishing's increasing specialization.[55]

Beginning with the Bastable stories, the first of which, *The Story of the Treasure Seekers,* was published in the *Illustrated London News*'s 1897 Christmas supplement, Nesbit began writing popular children's stories.[56] Each of her children's books appeared first as serials in periodicals. Her second Bastable story, *The Wouldbegoods,* ran in *Pall Mall Magazine,* and the *Illustrated London News* (July 1900–July 1901), earning her 350 pounds. After its publication in book form, she earned 1,100 pounds in royalties in the first year, the most she would earn from any book.

Nesbit attributed her success in writing children's stories to an ability to remember her own childhood and to the belief that she was still, in part, a child. In a letter to her publisher at Macmillan in 1912, she wrote, "you know, really, I am a person who has never quite grown up (That is why I am able to write for children!)."[57] In "My School Days," an autobiographical series that ran in *Girls' Own Paper* in 1896 and 1897, she claimed a universality to her experience of childhood: "I was a child as other children, that my memories are their memories." Remembering that she had prayed "fervently, tearfully" that she would never forget what she "thought and felt and suffered then," Nesbit recalled that her fears of the dark and of her father's ghost were intensified by her inability to communicate them to her mother and older sisters. Elsewhere, she wrote of an unbridgeable "gulf" between children and adults. This image works against her claim that she could portray real children based on her own childhood memories, but reinforces the sense of childhood isolation she communicates in "My School Days."[58]

School and home became sites of clashing childhood experiences. Home and her mother—portrayed as cozy and angelic—provided refuge from the boredom, rules, and loneliness of boarding school. The best times occurred when adults were absent, as in the summer, when her mother let her youngest daughter "run wild," playing pirates and explorers with her brothers.[59] Remembering this as a "golden," enchanted time, the adult Nesbit reconstructed her childhood around these opposing themes of fear and play, school and home, childhood and adulthood.

The Treasure Seekers, the story that launched her success, was one of several manuscripts that Nesbit had in the works in 1898. She must have recognized its potential, because she continued to demand 50 pounds for the book and a high royalty of 16.5 percent after she was turned down by several publishers, writing to her agent, Morris Colles, "I am very much in love with this book, and I think it should be a great success."[60] T. Fisher Unwin's reader urged that they prepare *The Treasure Seekers* for the Christmas market, describing the book as amusing and "quite modern in tone," but reminiscent of the "excellence and good taste" of Mrs. Ewing's *Aunt Judy,* "the most rational child's magazine ever published." The Bastable stories have been considered innovatively realistic because Nesbit portrayed the children as sometimes bored and quarrelsome, eager for adventures and imaginative play, and as ultimately powerless in a world controlled by adults. Unlike didactic stories of the time, the children do not grow morally or redeem adults with their innocence. Yet she made it clear which character traits were admirable in English children, and her stories provided implicit, occasionally explicit, commentary on contemporary British society. T. Fisher Unwin's reader described *The Treasure Seekers* as a "very charming picture of *English* Family life—the best characteristics, the best in the English temperament, and manner of educating children is here." It was "just the sort of thing to appeal to the British mind."[61]

By telling the story from the perspective of Oswald, the second eldest Bastable child, Nesbit allowed readers to see the world through his eyes and be amused by the way he unthinkingly gives away his identity by shifting from third to first person narration or by praising his own insight and courage. Her innovative use of a boy narrator's voice was also commercially savvy, given that girls would read about boys, but boys were less likely to read a story told by a girl. When the stories were first published as magazine serials, she and her editors were unsure whether they were intended for children or adults.[62] They were finally published as children's books, but their initial appearance in adult and family magazines ensured the dual readership crucial to commercial success. Her stories tended to work against the trend toward differentiating reading materials by age and sex.

Most of Nesbit's characters are solidly middle-class, and although the families in *The Treasure Seekers* and *Railway Children* have lost their money, everyone they encounter recognizes their status. She played a bit more with notions about gender.[63] Oswald and the other boys are especially conscious of what boys and girls should be like, and the children often conform to gendered roles. But adventuresome girls are also paired with timid brothers, and gender differences are balanced by a common code of decency and honor that epitomized Nesbit's portrayal of English middle-class childhood that T. Fisher Unwin's reader admired. Adults are conveniently absent from the stories, for adventures only happen when children are alone, as Oswald notes in *The Wouldbegoods*.[64] The few adults who can sympathize with, if not join in, the children's adventures are writers.

Nesbit's first children's fantasy, *Five Children and It* (1902), appeared initially in *The Strand*, which paid its writers well and had a wide circulation and a reputation for publishing well-known authors, including Arthur Conan Doyle, Rudyard Kipling, and H. G. Wells. This was to be Nesbit's longest, most profitable association with a magazine. She earned at least 30 pounds per episode, as much again for American rights, and then resold the book twice over—in Britain and America—giving her a potential income of 500 pounds a year.[65]

Nesbit established her trademark mix of fantasy and "gritty reality" by having the magic in *Five Children and It* take place in contemporary England.[66] Modeled after the Bastables, the children encounter magical beings who grant wishes and take them traveling across space and time. The Psammead, the first magical being they meet, is a sharp-tongued, furry, fat, sand fairy, thousands of years old.[67] The wishes that the Psammead grants by puffing himself up like a balloon inevitably land them in trouble. When they wish to be rich "beyond the dreams of avarice," the Psammead brings them mounds of gold guineas, but no shopkeeper will accept the guineas, and they are headed for jail on charges of thievery when, at sunset, the guineas disappear. As her biographer Julia Briggs writes, the source of Nesbit's mixture of magic and everyday life was her awareness of children's "lack of any real power other than the power of imagination."[68]

By the early 1900s, Nesbit had become less active in the Fabian Society, but had begun to put more of her politics into her children's stories, integrating critiques of industrial, urban Britain with her stories' magic. In *The Amulet* (1906), the children use half of the amulet to travel through time and space in search of the other half, so that they may attain their "heart's desire" of being reunited with their parents and baby brother. When the children bring the queen of ancient Babylon to modern London, she is disgusted by the condition of the poor. "How badly you keep your slaves," she comments. When the Psammead grants her wishes, she temporarily provides the poor with all they can eat and destroys the Stock Exchange. In another chapter, the children find a little orphan girl sobbing in St. James's Park because she is to be sent to the workhouse. They must travel back to the year when England was invaded by Julius Caesar to find someone who will care for the girl.[69]

Traveling into the future, the children find a utopian, smoke-free London, full of green parks and trees. Even the pigeons in the garden outside the British Museum are "bright and clean." People with strikingly calm expressions sit on the park benches, and babies play in the grass. "Men as well as women seemed to be in charge of the babies and were playing with them." In this future London, everyone must work, care for the environment, and have time to play, as well as a home and adequate food. The children contrast this, with amazement, to life in their own London. The boy who explains all this to them is named after H. G. Wells, the "great reformer" who lived in the dark ages, and "saw that what you ought to do is to find out what you want and then try to get it. Up to then, people had always tried to tinker up what they'd got."[70] Begun in 1903, *The Amulet* was completed in 1905. Nesbit's tribute to her fellow author and Fabian H. G. Wells acknowledged her debt to his *A Modern Utopia,* published earlier in 1905. Both contrasted contemporary London with a more beautiful future city where personal fulfillment and civic and social justice are intertwined. Like William Morris, with whom she also shared political and social circles, Nesbit used the past to critique the bleakness of industrial England.[71] Rejecting the emphasis on personal moral growth typical of most contemporary children's stories, Nesbit presented an alternative didacticism with her images of societies, past and future, that were more compassionate than the present one.

Nesbit used time and space travel to critique British society, but also to assert Britain's racial superiority. When the queen of ancient Babylon visits the present, she appears gaudy and indecent in London's streets, and one of her priests proves less honorable than the children as he competes with them for the amulet. Another time, when the amulet takes the children to Egypt of 8,000 years before, they encounter fair-skinned, peaceful villagers who are attacked by "cruel, dark, big-nosed" invaders.[72] This mix of racism and progressive politics is most overt when the children encounter people of other societies. There is less room for either in Nesbit's Bastable stories, because the children remain within middle-class English settings.

Nesbit presented books as integral to her own childhood and to those of her fictional children. In "My School Days," she described books as sources of pleasure. She "devoured" them to escape from boredom. During adolescence, her stash of books, kept in the hollow of the roof, represented privacy and escape from chores.[73] Her fictional children's adventures are shaped by their imaginations, which, in turn, are shaped by the books they have read.[74] In *The Wouldbegoods,* the Bastable children recreate Kipling's *The Jungle Book* in their uncle's garden. Later, in an attempt to stay out of trouble, they form the Wouldbegoods Society. Here Nesbit pokes fun at the pious, improving books that inspired the Wouldbegoods. She also suggests a gendered response to such books: two girls initiate the society, while Oswald and his brother are determined not to stand for any pious "rot out of *Ministering Children.*"[75] Nesbit's magical stories are similarly informed by books. After the children wish for the house to be a castle, Robert recognizes their besiegers' speech and dress from "historical romances for the young." Later, Cyril has just finished reading *The Last of the Mohicans* when his wish for Red Indians to appear in England is granted.[76] Both Oswald Bastable and the narrator of the magical stories play with the acts of writing and reading. Oswald experiments with different literary styles, trying to find the appropriate one. The narrator of *Five Children and It* explains in parentheses that "I" must say that the sun set in the west "because it is usual in books to say so." Another parenthetical instruction, to "please pronounce 'humph' exactly as it is spelt," anticipates that the book might be read aloud.[77] Nesbit wrote about books in a way that assumed that she and readers shared common cultural references, that readers would recognize and laugh at the pious books and could imagine the children playing scenes from Kipling's *The Jungle Book.*[78] Books and their corollaries, imagination and magic, enlarged the scope of her fictional children's world in exciting, sometimes dangerous, sometimes disappointing ways.

T. Fisher Unwin's reader correctly predicted that both children and adults would appreciate Nesbit's stories. Children wrote to tell her and Oswald Bastable that they liked her books.[79] As a child, Noel Coward would save his money to buy old numbers of *The Strand* from a secondhand bookstore so that he could read her serials. Once, when he discovered that a few numbers were missing, he stole a coral necklace and pawned it to buy the whole book. As an adult, Coward reread her books each year. He wrote in 1956 that "the stories, which I know backwards, rivet me as much as they did when I was a little boy. . . ."[80] Writing to Nesbit between 1903 and 1905, Rudyard Kipling described his family's pleasure in her books and complained that he had had "no peace" since his children had discovered that the "Psammead tales lived in the *Strand.*" Each installment had to be read and reread, and his children rejected as unsatisfactory the explanation that the magazine was only published monthly.[81] Andrew Lang praised her children's stories and wrote that "I hope that before *you* die, the public will know the worth of your work as I do."[82] H. G. Wells liked her writing for children better than her writing for adults and told Nesbit's biographer, Doris Moore, years later that he considered the former underrated. In a letter to Nesbit, he predicted that her destiny was plain: "You go on every Xmas never missing a Xmas, with a book like this; and you will become a British Institution in six years. . . . Every self respecting family will buy you automatically and you will be rich beyond the dreams of avarice. . . ."[83]

Wells's predictions did come true in that her children's books continued to sell well, but they did not end her financial worries. Even at the height of her success, she was often short of cash. Her relations with her literary agents would fall apart when she began to feel that they were not selling her work quickly enough. Anxious about family medical bills, she wrote to her agent in 1898 that she realized "that you would get me better prices if I could afford to *wait*. But I can't. Needs must when the devil drives!"[84]

After three decades of almost constant writing, Nesbit's pace slowed after 1911.[85] Hubert Bland's death in 1914 left her emotionally devastated and substantially reduced the family income. After her second marriage, in 1917, to "Skipper" Thomas Tucker, she continued to write for children and adults, to receive royalties from reprints of her children's books, and to seek ways to eke more money out of her work. She wrote several letters to Macmillan between 1917 and 1920, urging them to reprint her work. But in 1921, she confided to a fellow writer that "publishers tell me that children don't want my sort of books anymore."[86] Nesbit's writing for children began and ended in attempts to support her family. She could produce each chapter quickly for serialization in magazines, often in a house full of guests and children. Production in this forum meant that both adults and children would read them and gave her incentive to add the element of suspense that kept Kipling's children on the lookout for the next installment. She had never wanted to be known solely as a children's writer, but it was her children's stories that people continued to buy.

Women authors in Victorian and Edwardian England had less access to the public world of publishers, editors, and academia than their male colleagues. Needing to earn enough to support her family, Nesbit and other women writers felt compelled to produce children's literature, but were consequently taken less seriously as writers for adults. Lang, in contrast, moved easily between fairy tales, journalism, and academic writing. Only in the twentieth century has Lang's journalism been forgotten, while his "Fairy Books" are remembered. Apart from their different experiences in the professional world of publishing, Lang and Nesbit shared a middle-class background and similar visions of childhood. While Nesbit seemed more conscious of children's powerlessness in an adult world than did Lang, both depicted childhood as a state separate from adulthood and connected childhood, reading, and imagination in their work. Both authors also evoked childhood memories as key to their ability to write for children. In linking childhood and imagination, Lang and Nesbit also gave voice to political and spiritual yearnings less easily contained in adult literature. Lang viewed children as uniquely able to share the imaginative vision of ancient peoples. Both Lang and Nesbit located a better society in Britain's past, but while Lang was pessimistic about Britain's urbanized, democratic future, Nesbit gave her fictional children special access to magic and imagination that allowed them to see a utopian, egalitarian future. Lang and Nesbit helped to popularize a conception of childhood as a moment of special vision. They turned to children's literature at a time when it offered a space to write about fantasy and imagination that was being closed off in adult fiction. The fact that their children's stories were read by adults points to childhood's importance in the wider middle-class British culture. Ultimately, their children's stories were about the adults who wrote and read into them their own childhoods, as well as their investment in children's reading and imaginative play as links to the past and to a potentially better future.

Part Three

The Politics of Literacy
in London's Board Schools

Chapter Six

An "Efficient and Suitable" Elementary Education

The year 1870 was a turning point in the history of British education. With the Elementary Education Act, the British government for the first time provided Board schools for working-class children. This legislation was supposed to provide school accommodations for "all the children resident in such districts for whose elementary education efficient and suitable provision is not otherwise made." Districts lacking adequate educational facilities were required to form school Boards. Although children of the lower middle class would also benefit from the new school system, it was intended to fill "gaps" left by voluntary schools in the education of children ranging from "street arabs" to "respectable" working class. Elementary Board schooling was also to be self-contained, ending by or before a student's thirteenth birthday, and "not preparatory to a grammar school or any other education."[1]

Over the following decades, the government would gradually expand the scope of its activities and the definition of its role as a provider of education. But it was by no means a foregone conclusion in 1870 that this Education Act would be followed by a series of acts making schooling compulsory and free and introducing related labor and health provisions. Concentrating on Board schooling in London, the nation's largest city, these final chapters examine how individual educational initiatives were formed out of conflicting agendas that, in turn, were shaped by battles over religion, class, gender roles, parental rights, industrial growth, and the role of government.[2]

Certain tensions were inherent to the development of mass education. By educating the majority of British children, educators and politicians courted the danger of disrupting hierarchies of class and gender.[3] Reformers, conservative and liberal, felt they were walking a fine line between giving working-class children the skills necessary to become citizens and enter the workforce and giving them analytic tools that could be used against the existing social system. This chapter necessarily focuses on middle-class adults' attempts to define working-class children's education. The voices of working-class parents and children emerge only sporadically, filtered through official school Board accounts of disputes in which they were involved.[4]

History of the 1870 Education Act

To make sense of the history of education after 1870, it is important to look back first at the concerns that fueled educational initiatives earlier in the century. The French Revolution, English radicalism, and industrialization had left upper-class opinion divided as to whether the ability to read was a dangerous tool in the hands of the masses or an instrument that could be used to shape their morals, and thus their actions. Gradually, the Evangelical vision of education as a vehicle for inculcating morality and combating worker unrest won the day. Religious organizations dominated education provision before 1870, with the Anglicans—supported by the landed classes and the state—outstripping the Nonconformists. Rationalist, utilitarian, and Owenite schools did not last long, but their secular curriculums were later adopted by church schools.[5]

A few historians remind us that education was not always imposed upon the working classes from above. Thomas Laqueur argues that working-class people could and did appropriate Sunday schools for their own ends. In his reexamination of the private adventure and dame schools that historians have written off as ineffective, Philip Gardner argues that these schools served well the working class communities that created and financed them. The teachers accommodated families' seasonal economic cycles and gave children the kind of education their parents sought for them.[6] When the government began to supplement funding of educational provision for the poor in the 1830s, schools were increasingly divided between those given by government grants and those that were not. By the 1860s, a clear distinction had been made between government-aided church schools and unfunded private adventure and dame schools.

Late nineteenth-century religious and political battles, as well as economic and class concerns, formed the more immediate context for the 1870 Education Act and subsequent educational legislation. Anglicans and Nonconformists had taken opposing positions regarding the question of government intervention into schooling for the poor. Fearing secular competition, the Anglican and Roman Catholic churches formed a rare alliance in defending voluntary schools against the new state-run Board schools. Nonconformists, lacking the means to compete with the Anglicans in maintaining a national network of schools, generally favored the introduction of public, secular elementary Board schools. Religion spilled over into politics. Liberals usually sided with Nonconformists, pushing, sometimes halfheartedly, for expanding government's role in educating the poor. Conservatives could be counted on to protect Anglican interests and to argue against any expansion of Board school education they viewed as encroaching on voluntary schooling. These divisions are of course too neat, because politics crossed religious and ideological lines. But this broad characterization holds true for most participants in educational battles.

Added to these political and religious divisions were middle- and upper-class fears about maintaining social order. Extension of the franchise in 1867 had raised anew the specter of political power in the hands of the uneducated masses. As in the 1790s and 1830s, one response was to educate the "masses" in their civic duties and thus bring them into a unified political culture. While the franchise was not the only factor shaping the 1870 Education Act, it certainly influenced the repeated insistence on teaching children about their civic duties and future stations in life. Fueled by journalists' depictions of "outcast London," fears of physical and moral degeneration, embodied in working-class children, also became important catalysts behind the extension of elementary education.[7]

By the 1880s, the organized working class had hammered out its own position on elementary education. Labour joined the most radical Liberals in demanding free, compulsory education. Ultimately going beyond the Liberals to demand secondary education for all, Labour unsuccessfully challenged the gulf between working- and middle-class education.[8] In the early 1900s, calls for universal secondary education were defeated by the counterproposal for expanding the scholarship pool. Rather than build a broad stairway between elementary and secondary schools, the working-class children deemed most intelligent would be given a "ladder," and the majority would continue to receive a limited education.[9] In reality, family poverty and their limited Board school educations prevented many students from taking advantage of scholarships to secondary schools. The battle over whether Board schools should open doors to lifelong learning and, possibly, to social advancement or reflect and reinforce existing class and gender divisions would be revisited time and again in the decades after 1870.

The School Board for London

Run by elected Boards from 1870 to 1903 and overseen by the Education Department, a centralized bureaucracy, Board schools represented a new departure in the education of working-class children and in their relationship to the state. Curricular decisions, inspection, fee collection, and measurement of attendance rates dovetailed into social concerns about how to train

British children in class- and gender-appropriate ways. School Boards collectively forced a rethinking of the scope of government and took central roles in reworking the circumstances and meaning of working-class childhood, with the School Board for London (SBL) usually leading the way.[10]

Funded by local rates and government grants, school Boards were empowered to pay administrators, attendance officers, and teachers; build and equip schools; set and remit student fees. Boards also controlled teacher appointments and set curriculums, within the limits of Education Code requirements. Powerful as they were, the Boards were not autonomous. The Education Department could and did override Board decisions that conflicted with departmental philosophy.

All ratepayers could vote in school Board elections, including single and widowed women with property and those working-class men enfranchised in 1867. School Boards were elected every three years by cumulative vote, meaning that voters could cast as many ballots as there were seats on the Board and cast all their votes for one person. This last provision helped minority factions gain seats. Because there was no property qualification for Board members, seats were open to both married and single women. The SBL attracted well-known Liberal, feminist, and radical reformers, as well as Anglican clergy and Conservatives who were determined to limit the Board's activities. By the 1880s, battle lines had been drawn between two parties on the Board. The Progressives generally represented Liberal, radical, and Nonconformist positions and educational development; the Moderates represented Anglican and Conservative positions and were the voice of economic conservatism.[11] SBL records contain the often dissonant voices of Board members, inspectors, government officials, teachers, and other lobbying groups, all competing to define the Board's objectives.

Ostensibly concerned only with overseeing curriculums and student behavior within schools and through school lessons, the SBL was repeatedly forced to acknowledge the voices of parents, reformers, politicians, journalists, and philanthropists and to deal with events taking place outside school walls. In these moments, SBL debates became sounding boards for a number of questions that were being asked in new ways: questions about parental rights and duties; about the protection and care of children; and about public and private agencies' respective roles in defining and addressing the causes and consequences of poverty.

Getting Children into School

Located in Britain's largest city, the SBL was faced with the difficult task of providing schools for a large, concentrated population of poor children. London's slum conditions were considered so dire that London alone was exempted from having to prove the need for supplementing voluntary schools with Board schools. But providing schools was not enough. Getting children into Board schools and keeping them there proved an ongoing and time-consuming challenge. In December 1871, the SBL publicized its attendance requirements for children ages 5 to 13 with 2,000 posters and 50,000 hand-bills: "The School Board therefore gives Notice that Parents of children who are absent from School without sufficient reason are liable to a penalty, and that steps will be taken to carry out the law."[12]

The Board's determination to compel children to attend school brought its officials into conflict with parents, magistrates, and church groups. As the Board's most visible arm, visitors (attendance officers) sent into London neighborhoods to find truants attracted much of this resentment.[13] Particu-larly vociferous were church schools partisans who viewed Board schools as encroaching on church schools. Board Member Reverend Riggs protested that the Education Code, "invidious and oppressive" class legislation, in-vested visitors with the authority to judge which houses contained children whose educations were being neglected. Charles Reed, the Board's second chairman and a Liberal, viewed the visitors' work more positively. They had succeeded in "drawing the children to school, but only to have to return day after day to these lazar houses of modern life." Now the streets of London were no longer "infested by large numbers" whom nobody cared for until they committed a crime, for the visitors knew all their names and "their training in the arts of crime [was] successfully hindered." The Board heard working-class parents' stories of poverty and intimidation only indirectly through courtroom reports, and they were drowned out by inspectors' alle-gations of parental incompetence and recalcitrance.[14]

Child labor laws, difficult to enforce and littered with loopholes, plagued the SBL from the outset, limiting its ability to compel attendance.[15] Un-sympathetic magistrates often blocked the SBL's efforts to fine the parents of truants. Magistrates hearing truancy cases gave priority to parents' economic circumstances in reaching their decisions. One father, a "labourer in regular work," was fined for keeping his two children from school. The Board su-perintendent asked for imprisonment, considering it less injurious than a distress warrant authorizing seizure of the man's possessions. The magistrate gave a distress warrant instead, explaining that he used imprisonment only when a man was a drunkard and the family better off without him for a time. An indication of how one judge understood family dynamics, this case also offers a glimpse of the demarcation line between public and domestic authority. The father was the one prosecuted, but it was the mother who pre-sented the family's case, explaining that she had intended to send her son to school, but not her daughter, perhaps because she realized that the girl's ab-sence would be more easily overlooked.[16]

In the above case, the magistrate upheld the Board's right to discipline parents for their children's nonattendance, but magistrates were inclined to side with parents, bringing a protest from SBL Chairman Reed in 1882 that magistrates indulged parents' desire to turn their children into income. A case brought against the employer of a twelve-year-old girl named Duggan became a symbol of this battle between magistrates and the Board. Mrs. Duggan came to court to explain that the family needed her daughter to work for their neighbor because the father's 18 shillings a week was insufficient to support a number of small children. Considering this argument reasonable, the magistrate dismissed the summons. The SBL appealed, believing an "Important Question of principle" to be involved, but the Superior Court upheld the first decision on the grounds that a child had a "sacred duty" to help support her parents.[17] In 1886, another magistrate used slightly different economic reasoning to oppose school Board prosecutions. He refused to send defendants to prison unless he was sure that their inability to pay fines did not arise from the "prevalent want of employment and distress among the working classes."[18] This time, it was less a question of whether children's educational needs conflicted with their familial duties than of whether the state should bend its rules in the face of general economic distress. Board efforts at compulsion were also frustrated by magistrates who charged minimal fees and by the difficulty of pushing cases through overcrowded court dockets.[19]

At odds on most issues, school officials did share with parents and magistrates a different set of expectations about boys' and girls' attendance records. In 1871, the Board was hopeful that new Infant classes would free girls from child-minding, thus removing one of the chief obstacles to their regular attendance.[20] But visitors and inspectors were up against the accepted premise that girls' family responsibilities overrode their educational needs.[21] One inspector commented in 1878 that from what he had seen himself "of sickness and misery about the very doors," he could well believe that kindhearted visitors would not have the heart to insist on girls' regular attendance.[22]

In truancy cases, the goal of securing children's attendance was often pitted against familial economic needs. Battles over fee collection threw political tensions over working-class children's education into stark relief. School fees, averaging two pence a week in London in the 1880s, could cut deeply into the budgets of working-class families and impeded efforts to compel attendance. But contemporaries viewed fees as necessary insurance that the poor were contributing to their own educations.[23] The Board undertook fee collection with a combination of paternalism and free-marketeering: it would avoid creating hardship by "carefully adapt(ing)" fees to the conditions of each neighborhood, and by occasionally remitting fees when circumstances warranted.[24] Early on, the SBL Attendance Committee urged that the power to remit be used sparingly because untested allegations of inability to pay would be a "great evil, as tending to pauperize a class of the population who should rather be stimulated to a sense of their duty" and to a manly spirit of independence.[25]

To avert the danger of demoralizing the poor, the Board's Byelaw Committee decided each fee remission case on its merits. The committee factored family income, size, and health into its decisions about eligibility, only presenting for the full Board's approval cases that met certain unstated criteria. It typically described women deemed eligible as hardworking, poor, and widowed or deserted—absence of a man and demonstrated efforts at self-support were crucial; eligible men were described as out of work or ill, meaning that they were victims of circumstances beyond their control. This practice of reviewing each remission case soon became overwhelming. In 1878, Chairman Reed reported that even the lowest fees were beyond the means of many. In that year, 3,219 London schoolchildren's fees had been remitted, and 2,355 more remissions had been renewed.[26]

Throughout the 1870s, Board Members' calls for lowering or eliminating fees were alternately ignored or voted down by the majority of the SBL or blocked by Education Department officials who argued that lower fees would drive away respectable working-class children. But by 1889, a contingent of Progressive Members, arguing in terms of social justice and efficiency, was able to rally a majority to petition Parliament for free schools.[27] The Board's new position echoed the mood of some of its constituents. The Independent Labour Party had called for free education, and in October 1889, the Board received from the "Schoolboys of Kennington and Lambeth" a list of demands drawn up at a meeting on the Albert Embankment, including free education, "one free meal a day. No home lessons. No punishment (by caning)." The "boys and girls" would "keep away from school," and "parade the streets, and extend it to the whole of London," if their demands were not met.[28] The Board's response has either disappeared or was not forthcoming. But the state was moving toward a more activist approach to public education. By 1892 the abolition of fees, almost unimaginable in 1870, had been largely accomplished in London. It would take longer elsewhere.

The SBL had become entangled in London's social fabric. In bringing together London's poorest children and sending out a host of visitors to gather information about them, the SBL made it possible to assess the conditions of London's poor more systematically than ever before. The Board relied on public and private agencies for information about schoolchildren and their families, and itself became a conduit for such information.[29] It was an SBL inspector who helped direct the nation's attention to the problem of

London's housing shortage. In his annual report to the SBL for 1883, then in letters to *The Times,* Board Inspector T. Marchant Williams cited severe overcrowding as a major impediment to children's ability to learn.[30] Williams's findings were confirmed by a Royal Commission in 1885, but the SBL waited four years to define overcrowding as an educational issue that demanded its attention. In a memorial to the Committee of Council of Education in 1889, the SBL argued that education was hindered by overcrowding children into "unhealthy" homes. The resulting moral and physical atmosphere was not "conducive to making good citizens"; when children returned home from school "they unlearned everything they [had] acquired during the day."[31]

The SBL was slow to act on problems of fees and housing because such issues exceeded the limits of its jurisdiction as defined in 1870. In the early 1870s, Board Members had lobbied for creating Industrial Day Feeding Schools that would provide for children "deprived of education through the extreme poverty or neglect of their parents or guardians; or who are unable to attend school from lack of food."[32] After consulting with public and private agencies that dealt with this group of children, the committee assigned to investigate the proposal rejected it on the grounds that it would place a burden on the SBL that belonged on the poor rate and that it might pauperize and demoralize its intended beneficiaries. Such children should be compelled to attend school, and their parents should be compelled to obtain poor relief, but the SBL must not overstep its educational jurisdiction. Philanthropy should be relieved of burdens rightly within the "duties of public bodies," while the remaining, less easily classified cases could be dealt with "under the elastic rules which private benevolence can allow." By maintaining these distinctions, public and private agencies could work in harmony.[33]

The Charity Organisation Society (COS) was one private agency that the Board could work with because its concerns about the dangers of pauperization meshed with the views of the SBL's more conservative members. Fearful that if the SBL offered free services indiscriminately it would weaken parents' sense of familial responsibility, the COS, in 1872, offered to give the SBL information on parents who claimed to be unable to pay school fees. In 1875, SBL Member Francis Peek offered the COS a personal donation of 1,000 pounds a year on the condition that the COS deal with cases of distress referred by the SBL. In 1883, seeking greater efficiency in processing such cases, the SBL adopted a form that provided space for information on parents, children, the visitor involved, and for the COS report.[34] This arrangement reflected both the cooperation between state welfare and private charity of the period and middle-class ambivalence about aid to the poor.[35]

Board School Curriculum and Practice

Having brought children into schools, Board officials had to provide lessons in accordance with the Education Code and SBL instructions. Codes issued by the Education Department set forth the goals to be pursued by school Boards, teachers, and inspectors. Throughout the first decade of Board schooling, the system of payment by result, a legacy of the 1860s, shaped teachers' and educators' work. This free-market approach to educational assessment tied a portion of teachers' salaries to their students' performance on examination day.[36] Educators also enacted educational policy based on assumptions about class, gender, and age divisions, their concern for sexual differentiation increasing as children grew older. London Board school buildings were divided into at least three departments. Boys and girls below age seven were put together in Infant departments. The decision whether to put boys and girls ages seven to ten together in Junior departments was to be made on a case-by-case basis, since "so much depend(ed) upon the previous training of the children, and upon local circumstances." Senior boys and girls were put in separate departments.[37]

The Education Department's "New Code of Regulations and Instructions," issued in 1885, reminded school managers that they should make personal contact with parents and provide sympathetic encouragement to teachers. The code's final section addressed the managers' responsibility for scholars' mental, moral, and physical welfare and for seeing that "they are brought up in habits of punctuality, of good manners and language, and of cleanliness and neatness. . . ." Teachers should impress upon the children "the importance of cheerful obedience to duty, of consideration and respect for others, and of honour and truthfulness in word and act."[38] This mandate captured the essence of elementary schooling, as conceived of by education officials: children's morals, minds, and bodies were to be the objects of Board school education. The degree of emphasis given to each component varied over time, reflecting changes in pedagogical theories and in the social concerns of educators and politicians. The early overriding concern with children's morality gave way slightly to increasing concern for their physical and mental development by the mid-1880s. Personal opinion was another factor. Inspectors' reports, often rich sources of commentary, ranged from depictions of working-class children as rebellious and rough to pleas for sympathy for their hunger and ill health. Two children's advocates, Lord Shaftesbury and Margaret McMillan, would have agreed that there were moral, mental, and physical components to children's education. But while Shaftesbury, an Evangelical philanthropist, saw morality as the crucial factor, McMillan, a child theorist and Socialist, viewed the condition of children's bodies as the primary determinant of their well-being.[39]

School officials measured morality by outward behavioral signs or "habits," projecting maps of London's neighborhoods on the bodies and attitudes of Board school children.[40] Reporting in 1875, an inspector linked children's "character and habits" to the conditions of the districts they inhabited: in "flourishing localities," children were "clean, tidy, and tractable. . . . [i]n poor and densely populated parts," children's education had been "almost, if not entirely, neglected, from apathy, wilfulness, or inability on the part of their parents." Such children often attended school only under compulsion and were "characterized by their dirty and untidy habits. . . ." Correlating economic status and character, the Inspector attributed poorer children's faults to their parents and the streets:

> in the very lowest districts, the Teachers' work is rendered still more difficult by the presence of children who learn in the streets to swear, and lie, and pilfer, and in whom these habits seem to be fostered rather than checked by the example of their parents.[41]

Inspector Ricks reported in 1878 that children's "moral discipline" was unsatisfactory; yet he cautioned against the "repressive," harsh tone he saw in some schools. Despite his criticisms, Ricks concluded that "under great difficulties and depressing influences . . . immense strides [had] been made towards bringing the vast shoals of ignorant, neglected, and not infrequently mutinous children of this great metropolis" into habits of order, regularity, neatness, cleanliness, and truthfulness.[42]

Board officials expected teachers, and the very process of schooling, to counter the effects of children's parents and neighborhoods. Sometimes parents themselves were the presumed beneficiaries of teachers' influence. Inspector Noble commented in 1877 that parents' attempts to make themselves clean and tidy before meeting the teacher indicated that, like their children, they were feeling the schools' "wholesome influence."[43] Parents in the "lowest neighborhoods" were reportedly giving teachers less active opposition, in the forms of violent language and rough conduct. In 1881, Inspector Landon reported that Board schools were reclaiming the "social residuum": "[s]teadily and surely we are reaching down to the lower depths of ignorance and vice, and drawing their victims out to the light of knowledge and virtue."[44] While difficult to verify, these reports by middle-class school officials coupled anxiety about working-class children's potential unruliness with a strong belief in education's power to eradicate such threatening tendencies.

Inspector T. Marchant Williams's report for 1883 provided a different perspective on the neighborhoods that Board school children inhabited. Like the rest, he noted that children of the "lowest districts" had the most irregular attendance records. But he located the problem not solely in the moral atmosphere, but also in children's poverty-stricken conditions, reporting that 82 percent of the families of children attending one school occupied just one room. The "half-starved" children of Seven Dials and St. Lukes were "little astonished" by Bible stories of 40 days of fasting, because they resembled their own experiences. The benefits of teaching these hungry, ill-clothed, and ill-housed children, he argued, would be meager until housing was systematically improved.

In his more detailed letters to *The Times* in 1884, Williams challenged the popular belief that parental intemperance was the only cause of children's poor conditions, pointing out that in neighborhoods where Board schools were heavily attended, high rents consumed between one-third and one-fourth of tenants' wages. "Improvidence, want of employment, indolence, and intemperance are, doubtless, the main causes of poverty in this country, although, too, it very commonly happens that poverty and overcrowding . . . lead to intemperance."[45] Williams' concentration on social conditions distinguishes his reports from those of other inspectors. But since his job was to inspect schools, not build houses or feed children, Williams followed the rest in placing his hopes in schooling's influence, noting that teachers who treated children firmly and considerately made them loyal in "thought and act."[46] Collectively, these reports paint Board schools as havens from the outside world the children inhabited.

Moral discipline was to be reinforced by physical discipline, although the SBL could not find a method of enforcement free of controversy. In 1871, it cautiously upheld the use of corporal punishment, stressing that its frequent use was a sign of incompetence, but its occasional, exceptional use was necessary. Over the years, it managed to satisfy neither teachers, who wanted more control over administering corporal punishment, or radical and working-class groups that called for its abolition.[47] As historian Dina Copelman writes, the ongoing battles over corporal punishment illustrate "the physicality of state education: the struggles to control the bodies of children."[48]

The teaching of military drill, provided for in the Elementary Education Code, touched off another controversy. In 1875, the Society for the Encouragement of the Arts offered to provide a prize if the Board would hold annual drill inspections. Protest met the SBL's acceptance of this offer. The Workmen's Peace Association sent a deputation to the Board to state that it had led meetings for five years to "wean" men from a "love of military glory and warlike pursuits" and teach that arbitration was more humane, civilizing, and economical. By helping to undo this good work, the Board was "forwarding the realization of conscription." The Women's Peace and Arbitration Auxiliary sent a memorial calling military drill an injustice to the parents who did not want their sons' minds diverted from the "pursuit of honourable and honest labour. . . ." They explained that they believed "in the power of the well developed mind to resist evil, and not in the bodies of the children being scholastically rendered more capable machines for killing their fellow creatures." The "Ratepayers and Inhabitants Residing Within the Jurisdiction" of the London School Board and the Hackney Working Men's Club also registered their disapproval of military drill's introduction.[49] Benjamin Lucraft, one of the few Labour Members of the Board, called for an end to the drills. But his motion was superseded by an amendment pointing out that the drills promoted "ready obedience, orderly behavior and good temper," all benefits that outweighed any potential evils.[50]

Both parties to this debate believed that military drill could influence children's minds, and both used moralistic language to make their arguments. But while military drill's defenders saw it as a means of containing working-class disorder, its opponents linked Board school education with the pursuit of "honourable and useful labour."[51] Although suspended shortly after this uproar, it was soon reintroduced and given the official blessings of the SBL, the Church of England, and the crown. The Archbishop of Canterbury made Lambeth Palace grounds available for the annual drill inspection; in 1882, School Board Chair Edward Buxton acted as judge; and in 1883, the Prince of Wales awarded the winning school its prize.[52]

While the merits of military drill for boys were being debated, questions about physical exercise for girls and the youngest children in Infant classes were also raised. One inquiry found that most girls were given only desk drill, which was "rather a means of securing prompt discipline than a physical exercise." If teachers, however, were scientifically trained in physical development, they could do much to remedy children's often ill-developed conditions. In this instance, physical exercise was not meant solely to instill discipline, but also to repair children's bodies.[53] When the subcommittee appointed to deal with the "Question of Physical Education" filed its report in 1883, it recommended the "Swedish system" because it developed all parts of the body. The subcommittee also urged that Swedish drill be introduced into Boys' departments, taking care not to interfere with military drill.[54]

The growing interest in physical education brought together people with differing agendas. Some wished mainly to strengthen and repair children's bodies. Others tied bodily exercise to morality and discipline. By century's end, many linked the condition of the empire to the condition of children's bodies. In 1883, Lord Brabazon, speaking before the Board as chairman of the Metropolitan Public Garden, Boulevard and Playground Association, argued that physical exercise was an antidote to the "physical degeneration of large towns." It would improve children physically, mentally, and morally and diminish their predisposition to crime and drunkenness.[55] Speaking from another political perspective, opponents of military drill proposed calisthenics and gymnastics as constructive alternatives. In a similar vein, kindergarten proponents and child theorist Margaret McMillan argued that bodily strength and dexterity must precede mental growth.

While the SBL devoted attention to Board scholars' moral and physical well-being, they also worried about the academic portion of their educations and how it would prepare them for adulthood. In addition to reading, writing, and arithmetic, Board schools could offer other subjects, including British history, geography, and grammar. From the start, SBL curriculum provided for age-appropriate learning. During curriculum-planning sessions in 1871, the Board gave Infant departments special attention as the sites of children's initiation into Board schooling. Board members were convinced that a properly run Infant department could ensure educational progress: children were "not only withdrawn from evil and corrupting influences, and disciplined in habits of order, attention and cleanliness," but they also received "positive instruction" that facilitated their further education. Even the environment of the youngest students was given careful thought: their rooms were to be outfitted with reading sheets, alphabet boxes, and kindergarten toys, and the walls would be covered with diagrams and illustrations.[56] The SBL's original curriculum also called for object lessons in which familiar objects were used to stimulate children's minds and to introduce them to the physical world around them. These age-specific lessons were intended as preludes to science lessons and as a means of training children's powers of observation. Infants' lessons were to be of a "simple character," exercising their hands and eyes; Juniors' and Seniors' lessons were supposed to be "systematized," embracing a course of "elementary instruction in physical science."[57]

While the 1870 Education Act made no distinction between the educations of boys and girls, historians Dina Copelman, Anna Davin, and Carol Dyhouse have shown how the SBL's concern for gender-appropriate training resulted in increasing emphasis on the importance of needlework and domestic economy lessons for girls.[58] In his annual report for 1878, Chairman Reed affirmed the need for needlework lessons, contending that because it had been neglected in schools, few domestic servants could sew, and mothers were rarely capable of teaching their daughters.[59] The gendered division of work broke down in Infant departments where boys were taught needlework. But a survey of Infant mistresses conducted in 1885 showed that many thought needlework lessons were useless for boys and that young boys were less capable than girls of doing steady work, and therefore "more liable to Overpressure."[60] Probably begun as a way to keep little boys' fingers occupied while teachers gave girls their obligatory needlework lessons, this practice was now defined as unacceptable. Not only was needlework unrelated to boys' future work, they were constitutionally incapable of it.

Domestic economy, another vehicle for training future wives and mothers, was made a compulsory subject for girls in 1878. Eager to reinforce the importance of such training, the National Health Society offered in 1874 to establish annual prizes for girls' examinations in physiology. Despairing over poor examination results, the National Health Society withdrew the prize competition in 1884, but offered to try again in 1886 with a new examination on the Laws of Health and Domestic Economy, which brought its work into step with the current national efficiency campaign. The 1890 exam called for a knowledge of health applied to the domestic arena and the ability to work with limited economic resources. Girls were asked which joints of meat the "industrious classes" could purchase and prepare most profitably and to explain how the "inconvenience arising from the absence" of a bathroom could be lessened. The National Health Society, with the Board's cooperation, was bent on turning working-class girls into women who could efficiently and scientifically care for their families without much money and in poor housing conditions.[61] Dina Copelman writes that women Board teachers resisted this differentiation of girls' educations in the 1880s, on grounds of practicality (they and their students were hard pressed to fit needlework and domestic lessons into their full schedules) and fairness to the girls' academic training. But, by the 1900s, most women teachers supported domestic economy and a vision of education based on sexual difference.[62]

Class joined gender as a factor in the SBL's curricular decisions. In 1871, Board members argued that the condition and station in life of the children to be educated in Board schools should determine the instruction given. Lessons in social economy became one area of the curriculum where this mandate was carried out. In 1883, a committee of SBL members recommended extension of social economy lessons:

> because of the importance of instructing the children of the working classes upon such topics as the need of industry and thrift; the causes which regulate the rate of their own wages and the employers' profits, the inability of laws to create wealth, the basis of private property. . . .[63]

Standard I of the social economy syllabus would teach the functions of labor and capital in producing wealth and the ineffectiveness of each without the other. Under this heading went lessons on how thrift, honesty, and forethought influenced the wealth of the community and individual well-being. Standards II and III were also designed to give students a clear understanding of their roles in the economic machinery of industrial society and to see that machinery as natural and inevitable.

During the first two decades of Board schooling, educators worked to carry out their mandate to provide an "efficient and suitable" elementary education. Many sought to maintain class and gender boundaries and to re-shape working-class homes through military drill, physical exercise, and lessons in domestic and social economy. Others sought to expand Board schooling based on visions of a more democratic educational system. The overpressure crisis of 1884 would bring these agendas into collision, forcing the SBL and the nation to reexamine Board school practices and to decide who was responsible for its poorest students.

Chapter Seven 🙠

Overpressure in London's Board Schools, 1883–1884

In 1883, London's state-funded elementary Board schools were plunged into crisis: young working-class students were allegedly dying from the effects of educational overpressure. One doctor reported that nine-year-old George Leach had died of "overtaxed brainwork"; the mother of eleven-year-old Emily Frost recounted her attempts to pry her daughter's schoolbooks from her hands shortly before Emily died, apparently of "congestion of the brain." Under the headline, "Schooled to Death," *Lloyd's Weekly Newspaper* told the story of young Sophia Raybould, who had "talked and raved about her school work, uttering unceasingly, almost with her last breath, 'I can't do it; I can't do it.'"[1]

Argued over in the press, Parliament, and London School Board (SBL) meetings, the overpressure crisis became an opportunity to reexamine the purpose of elementary education, and what the state's role should be in caring for the children who received that education. Doctors, politicians, educators, working-class parents, and ratepayers (taxpayers) competed to define overpressure's causes. For reformers, overpressure was a sign of children's poverty and malnutrition; for some conservative politicians, it proved that working-class children were being "overeducated" and that the state was growing unwieldy. Some viewed it as an indictment of a too rigid educational system; others considered it the result of parents' moral failings and working-class degeneration.[2]

By 1883, Britain was thirteen years into its experiment with publicly funded elementary education. Facing greater economic competition from abroad and agitation for extending the franchise at home, British leaders were trying to decide whether to take elementary education in a more literary or a more practical direction. This was also a time of anxiety about the limits of human energy. Historian Anson Rabinbach, writing about the proliferation of studies of fatigue and "overwork" in Europe during the 1880s, argues that the resulting medical discourse on fatigue intersected with general social anxieties about modernity and social decline (Germany, France, and the United States all underwent crises of "educational exhaustion" in the 1880s).[3] Already linked to debates about the education of middle-class girls, this preoccupation with fatigue found its way into efforts to diagnose overpressure. Doctors argued that if a body's limited supply of energy was siphoned off for brainwork, other organs might suffer, and that, if forced to exert itself without sufficient energy, the brain itself would suffer.[4] In particular, the overpressure controversy sheds light on a "crisis of liberalism" that challenged existing boundaries among the state, the individual, and society.[5] The overpressure debate was messy and heated precisely because this was a moment when notions about the appropriateness of state intervention into children's lives—and about the possible benefits of such intervention—were being reimagined.

Chronology of Overpressure

In late 1883, four headmistresses were diagnosed as ill from overwork, and three student deaths from typhus and meningitis were linked to overstudying.[6] As more cases surfaced early in 1884, the medical and popular press began to cover stories like that of Sophia Raybould, the six-year-old who had raved about her schoolwork with her last breath. The *British Medical Journal (BMJ)* described her as a "little martyr" who, "weak and debilitated after scarlet fever," was "driven into school when she ought to have been resting at home, and was there plied with brain-work, which induced functional hypercemia, merging rapidly into congestion and meningitis, which killed even in its first stage."[7]

Throughout the spring and summer of 1884, newspapers carried dramatic headlines attributing children's deaths to overpressure in Board schools. By the end of 1884, 22 cases of alleged overpressure had been reported to the Education Department. A number of these children had been ill, possibly from typhus or scarlet fever, before their deaths.[8] Two members of the SBL, Mrs. Fenwick Miller and Miss Hastings, were among the first to offer an explanation for the crisis. Late in 1883, they argued that needlework lessons, on top of the rest of their classes, were too great a burden for girls and their teachers, and that overpressure was the consequence.[9] By early 1884, their concern was matched by a public outcry.

On February 4, 3,000 people had reportedly turned out in Bradford for a demonstration against overpressure in elementary schools.[10] On February 23, the *East London Observer* described an "immense gathering" of people at Burdett Hall, Limehouse, there to express opposition to overpressure in schools. Miss Hastings, who chaired the meeting, was received "with cheers" when she condemned the practice of overburdening young children with needlework. After hearing from several other SBL members, the assembled crowd voted unanimously that needlework requirements should be modified because they were excessive and caused overstrain.[11]

On March 26, Lord Shaftesbury presided over a large meeting at Exeter Hall, convened to protest overpressure in schools. Dr. Forbes-Winslow, who had made a career for himself as an expert medical witness, warned that overpressure led to disease among schoolchildren and demanded action by the government.[12] MP Stanley Leighton, supported by fellow SBL members Mr. Grove and Mrs. Surr, declared that a more cruel system for children than had been adopted under the present Education Code could not have been devised.[13]

These SBL Members and their allies had swiftly defined overpressure as the result of a burdensome Education Code. Just as quickly though, other groups seized on the overpressure crisis as a means of publicizing their more sweeping condemnations of elementary education. This loose coalition included champions of "voluntary" or church and other privately funded schools, those who believed that anything more than the most basic elementary education was unnecessary, and those who simply wanted to keep public rates (taxes) low.[14] Many in this coalition viewed overpressure as proof that some poor children were hereditarily unsuited for education and that the state was overstepping its educational mandate.

Throughout the overpressure controversy, deputations representing ratepayers' groups and factions in the SBL and Parliament raised cries of SBL extravagance.[15] *Lloyd's* linked the two issues by pairing condemnation of SBL "extravagance" with the story of Sophia Raybould, "a poor little girl, who was . . . schooled to death."[16] *The Times* reported in March 1884 that a large deputation, including several MPs, had visited Mr. Mundella, vice president of the Committee of Council for Education, to urge that the government rein in the SBL's power to build new schools. Edwin Hughes, an SBL member and chairman of the Metropolitan Association for Limiting the Expenditure of the London School Board, "insisted that the SBL was making provision for more school places" than necessary. Mr. Mundella corrected him: there was actually a deficiency of school places in London. Children "could not be treated as if they were something to be warehoused, and schools must be in the immediate neighborhood." To counter the cries of educational extravagance, Mundella noted that the SBL was responsible for only a fraction of the increase in London's expenditure from 1875 to 1882.[17] Apparently Mundella did not mollify the SBL's critics. Later that month, the press reported on a "stormy" meeting of ratepayers, convened to protest "School Board extravagance."[18]

Ambivalence of the Popular Press

The press watched closely and helped to shape the unfolding overpressure controversy. It was *Lloyd's* that paired condemnation of SBL "extravagance" with news of a child's death, allegedly due to overpressure. Along with the *East London Observer* and the *East London Leader, Lloyd's* covered the meetings held in the spring of 1884 to protest SBL expenditures and overpressure and published accounts of inquests into schoolchildren's deaths.[19] In other, more indirect ways, newspapers illustrated how complicated the conditions surrounding overpressure were. News stories and editorials reminded readers of ongoing conflicts between education authorities and parents over compulsory attendance. Under the headline, "Harsh School Board Regulations," the *East London Leader* told the stories of parents summoned before a sympathetic magistrate to answer for their children's truancy. In October 1884, the *Pall Mall Gazette (PMG)* boldly suggested that compulsory attendance could only be accomplished if education were made free.[20]

The curriculum prescribed by the Education Department also came under fire. In August 1884, the *East London Leader* reported that Lord Reay, presiding over a recent education conference (held during the International Health Exhibition), had denounced the Education Code. Given that the "great bulk" of the nation was not intended to read and write, and that inequality was "a law of nature," he declared that one educational standard could never meet the needs of all individuals and localities.[21] *The Times* reported that Earl de La Warn had warned his fellow Members of the House of Lords that children were overworked in Board schools, leaving them "mentally damaged and unfitted for the duties of after life." He argued that recent increases in Board schools' education standards had raised the question of how far that trend would be allowed to go.[22] During the fall of 1884, the *PMG* ran a series called "School-Board Idylls," by former teacher James Runciman. These vignettes depicted Board school teachers being ground down by government inspectors' excessive and capricious demands during their yearly examinations.[23]

While Lords Reay and de La Warn spoke pessimistically of some children's capacity for learning, and "School-Board Idylls" warned of the heavy toll that examination standards took on teachers and students, the *East London Observer* suggested that elementary education was opening up new opportunities to the children of its neighborhoods. The paper celebrated the festivities that marked the opening of new Board schools and annual school Prize Days. In November 1884, the paper published an article titled, "The Education Ladder," praising recent advances in providing education for "our youth": "genius, hitherto unrecognised or smothered by the ruthless and irresistible forces of circumstances" might now go on its way "until the goal of ambition is reached."[24]

These contradictory assessments of Board schooling accompanied a steady stream of reports about the larger social context in which Board schools operated and children lived. Newspapers depicted a world in which children were endangered by the adults around them. Eye-catching headlines, like "Boiling a Child to Death" and "Alleged Murder by a Baby Farmer," appeared frequently in London papers, usually followed by wrenching but sketchy stories of violence and neglect.[25] These stories of children victimized by violent, desperate adults competed with depictions of children as potential agents of crime and immorality. Early in 1883, the *East London Observer* warned that many of London's destitute children consorted with criminals, learning "cunning and tricks" from them.[26] Throughout 1883, the paper ran a string of articles about young girls caught frequenting brothels and charged with "not being under proper control." Court disputes in these cases centered on the moral characters of the girls' mothers, and on whether they had known what kind of establishments their daughters were entering. The descriptions of the girls involved are unusually detailed: Ellen O'Donnell was a "rather goodlooking" little girl of eleven, Charlotte Richley a "rather interesting looking little girl" of nine. W. T. Stead's "The Maiden Tribute of Modern Babylon," published in the *PMG* in 1885, would solidify this sexualized image of young girls connected to prostitution.[27]

The question of what to do with these endangered and dangerous children invariably became entangled with concerns that philanthropy would weaken parental responsibility. In July 1884, a meeting was held to establish a London Society for the Prevention of Cruelty to Children.[28] The speeches, recounted in the *East London Observer,* struck a common chord: the threat of degeneration loomed large in London's streets; it was embodied in poor children, and parents were to blame. J. A. Picton, an MP and former SBL member, described the marks of degeneration on one little girl, three or four years old, whom he had encountered in the streets of Liverpool. Her face was withered, "almost like that of an old worn out woman . . . her whole vitality almost exhausted by starvation." But she had been rescued and was now "a fine, healthy, promising girl." If degeneration could be reversed so dramatically, surely the urge to rescue children could win out over logic and the laws of political economy that warned against interference with "parental responsibility," he concluded.[29]

Other news stories undermined the emphasis on parental immorality and neglect. In late 1884 and early 1885, the *East London Leader* and *The Times* printed a number of stories on the "Depression of Trade." While the *East London Leader* blamed unions for the economic ills, it sympathetically reported on mass meetings of the unemployed, organized to demand public works projects.[30] These papers provided multiple readings of children's circumstances and schooling: they were both innocent victims of cruelty and neglect *and* potential sexual temptresses and criminals; their poverty was due to parental irresponsibility *or* to larger economic forces; Board schooling was wasteful *or* a positive benefit that society owed its children.

By late summer, the battle over who would define overpressure had taken a turn. Both Parliament and the press now closely followed a heated argument, largely conducted in letters to *The Times,* between Mr. Joshua Fitch, a chief inspector of schools, and Dr. James Crichton-Browne, a Chancellor's Visitor in Lunacy and coeditor of the journal *Brain.* Their debate over who was fit to judge whether Board-school education benefited or harmed its students became the one to which everyone else felt obliged to respond.[31]

In June 1884, several Members of Parliament addressed Mr. Mundella, vice president of the Committee of Council for Education, asking whether he had received a report by Dr. Crichton-Browne about overpressure in London's Board schools. If so, why had he not produced it? Mundella responded that it was not an official document and that its findings were questionable. Rushing to his own defense in a letter to *The Times,* Crichton-Browne reconstructed the origins of his report. Having publicized his opinion early in 1884 that homework was harmful to young children, he had been invited by Mundella to visit London's Board schools with an inspector and to report to Mundella his observations "as to the effects of the present system of education on the health of the children." Crichton-Browne had been "reluctant" to undertake the duty, given his heavy schedule, but "yielding" to Mundella's "persuasion," had consented. Devoting "every interval of leisure" he could secure, he had visited Board schools in Lambeth with Mr. Fitch, then submitted the results of his inquiry to Mundella in May.[32]

His report contained "strong evidence" that overpressure existed in elementary schools and was "injuriously affecting the health of the children," threatening "a rich harvest of degeneration." Crichton-Browne felt entitled to feel "a little aggrieved" that while refusing to publish his report, Mundella had disparagingly referred to it as "'highly controversial'" and as "being a sort of farrago of 'medicine, lunacy, ethics, and social and vital statistics.'" In fact, Crichton-Browne maintained, his report was "judicial rather than controversial in style" and founded on inquiries "conducted by scientific methods."[33]

Crichton-Browne's letter to *The Times* fueled interest in his report. The *School Guardian* and *The Times* called upon Mundella to make the report public, the latter suggesting that it was "perhaps somewhat problematical" whether "anything practical" would result from publishing a report that advocated "the periodic weighing, measuring, and medical examination of every child in every elementary school in the kingdom." But, "taking into account the high reputation Dr. Crichton-Browne undoubtedly" possessed, it was regrettable that a communication addressed to a public department was still as "thoroughly unknown as if the present were a pre-Reformation age and an Index of prohibited books was in full force."[34] In late August, *The Times* reported that Her Majesty's inspectors of schools, "with scarcely an exception," had in their annual reports declared overpressure nonexistent or exaggerated. The newspaper advised the public to "study attentively" the evidence from various official reports, but to suspend judgment pending publication of Crichton-Browne's "much-talked-of essay," which would "doubtless throw considerable professional light upon an important social question."[35]

Meanwhile, Crichton-Browne continued to make his views known through other media. In what the *BMJ* called a "powerful and eloquent extempore speech" before a conference on school hygiene (held at the International Health Exhibition), Crichton-Browne maintained that the Education Code "led to an amount of pressure, both on the teachers and the scholars— the latter too often ill fed—in elementary schools, which was productive of the worst results." School inspector T. Marchant Williams, author of a recent series of letters to *The Times* about schoolchildren's poor living conditions, supported by SBL member Dr. Gladstone, "attempted to controvert" Crichton-Browne's conclusions, "insinuating most unfairly" that "his method of inquiry was not deserving of confidence." But Mr. Greenwood, president of the National Union of Elementary Teachers, "ably confirmed" Crichton-Browne's conclusions. Both the Metropolitan Board Teachers' Association and the National Union of Elementary Teachers would later formally support Crichton-Browne's position.[36]

Finally, in September, by resolution of the House of Commons, Dr. Crichton-Browne's report and Inspector Fitch's rebuttal were published together as a Parliamentary paper. In his report, Crichton-Browne charged that overpressure was a universal problem, particularly affecting the brightest and the most "backward" schoolchildren. The brightest students were hurt morally and mentally by being held back, while the backward were "stimulated to a rank, spongy brain growth, and to a straining effort that wrenches the whole system and may permanently damage health." He attributed overpressure to inspectors' failure to withdraw from examination children who were ill or of delicate health: "it is not in the power of an inspector to decide by a look or even by a few well-devised questions whether or not a child" was physically or mentally strong enough to be examined. He suggested that teachers, while better able to gauge students' abilities and health, were compelled by inspectors and the system of payment by result to "press" children in preparation for examination day. Medical men, Crichton-Browne asserted, were most able to judge the fitness of schoolchildren, for they "could at once recognise the physical defects (which are often distinctive enough, although imperceptible except to the medical eye) which accompany mental weakness." Periodic medical inspection, enabling doctors to "protect" children from being "unduly pushed forward," would eradicate "overpressure and all its attendant evils" from elementary schools.

"But more valuable and trustworthy than even a medical report" would be a register of children's height, weight, head, and chest girth. Currently, schoolchildren were only classified by age, "no allowance being made for health, or development, or racial differences." But no one could walk through schools in different districts of London "without being impressed by the wide interval in health and development that separates children in the best from those in the worst. The latter are puny, dwarfish, pale, and feeble, when compared with the former." To judge a teacher of these children by the same standards as another "whose lot is cast among larger limbed and larger headed children, with richer blood and more constitutional vigour," was to do the former injustice and incite to overpressure. Such "injustice would vanish at the appearance of the tape measure. . . ."[37]

In his memorandum responding to Crichton-Browne's report, Fitch made it clear that he was writing at the request of the Secretary of the Education Department and that he had not known Crichton-Browne was conducting an official inquiry when they visited schools together. He described Crichton-Browne's judgments as "hasty and inaccurate. . . ." The doctor asserted but did not prove that the intellectual work required of students was either excessive or led to sickness. Fitch hoped that, before lowering educational standards, Parliament and the English public would ask for "some better testimony than that which can be furnished" by someone whose knowledge of the subject was "very recent and superficial" and who had "publicly denounced the machinery of popular education in England as a 'grinding tyranny' before his investigations commenced."[38] Reminding readers that he was "an inspector of many years' standing," Fitch argued that Board schools were not the places of drudgery and ill health depicted by Crichton-Browne, but rather improved children's health. Furthermore, in Fitch's view, it was precisely the "poorest and most neglected" children whom the doctor wished to exempt from "mental exercises altogether" that benefited most from school life.

Fitch did not dispute Crichton-Browne's argument that children needed to be fed before they had their lessons. But he reminded readers that public elementary schools had a "very limited and special function": they were "established for the purposes of instruction, and not for the purpose of dispensing new milk." A school "cannot control *all* the conditions which affect a child's life. It cannot protect him from all the evils arising from poverty, sickness, or neglect at home." He also strongly warned against measures that could diminish parents' sense of responsibility for their children's welfare: "if once it becomes understood that the State, or any public authority, is willing to provide nourishment and medical attendance" for children in public schools, "the influence on a large number of parents in diminishing their sense of responsibility may become a serious public danger."[39]

After the reports' publication, the two men exchanged a series of letters in *The Times*. Crichton-Browne wrote first to defend his medical credentials, and also to question Fitch's memory of their encounter.[40] Fitch responded that Crichton-Browne's memory was "wholly at fault": he had not apprised Fitch that he was engaged in an official inquiry. Fitch also defended his right to critique Crichton-Browne's report, stating that it was not "in any sense a medical report." The doctor's "most elaborate arguments and his most positive assertions" related to educational matters which lay "strictly within the official cognizance of an Inspector. . . ."[41] Crichton-Browne's rebuttal took two lengthy, sarcastic letters to *The Times*. Rather than catalog all of Mr. Fitch's "intricate errors and dense misapprehensions," Crichton-Browne would select "a few statements which lie at the base of his argument and showing how hollow they are I shall hope to shake confidence in the whole structure." Fitch had falsely claimed that Crichton-Browne was unqualified to investigate overpressure in schools, having never practiced general medicine or visited an elementary school. In fact, Crichton-Browne had engaged in general practice and had a long-standing interest in "education in connexion with the development of the nervous system." Fitch had also wrongly asserted that Crichton-Browne was "absolutely dominated by a foregone conclusion" and "ignorant of what scientific evidence really meant." Though Crichton-Browne had begun with "a provisional hypothesis that overpressure did exist in elementary schools," he would "readily have abandoned that hypothesis on encountering proof to the contrary." In Crichton-Browne's opinion, any prejudice was on Fitch's side. "At our first interview he repudiated the possibility of overpressure under the new Code" and later ignored "the gradually accumulating evidence of overpressure which I brought before him."[42]

Defending his controversial argument that the Registrar-General's mortality statistics revealed an "increase of nervous diseases," Crichton-Browne cited "a most masterly paper" by Dr. Rabagliati (himself embroiled in an overpressure controversy in Bradford) on the educational system's effects on the physical condition of children. Contrasting child mortality from nervous diseases for 1868–1870, before the Education Act, and 1879–1881, a decade into Board schooling, Rabagliati had proven "incontestably" that the Education Act was a major cause of schoolchildren's increased mortality from nervous diseases. "With glowing optimism Mr. Fitch smile[d] away such grave considerations." Crichton-Browne also accused Fitch of avoiding the "great problem of how to reconcile education with starvation." The doctor warned that while children's brains were growing, "forced cerebral activity" without adequate nutrition could be dangerous. When "breakfastless and dinnerless children" were driven into schools where they were, "while pinched with hunger, taught a great variety of subjects," it was under such circumstances that congestion of the brain was most apt to be induced, which had a "most pernicious" effect on development.[43]

Hoping for the final word, Fitch responded that he had Mundella's "express authority" to say that he had not commissioned Dr. Crichton-Browne to prepare any report for the Education Department. So how had the doctor, "in the absence of instructions, interpret[ed] the commission with which he supposed himself charged?" Instead of undertaking a medical inquiry, "for which, indeed, I have never questioned his competency," Dr. Crichton-Browne had delivered to Parliament, "under the guise of a medical report . . . a vigorous and able polemical pamphlet, assailing the whole system under which in England children are taught, teachers are trained, schools are inspected, and the Parliamentary grant distributed." Fitch did not deny that "undue strain sometimes exists in connexion with school work," but had confined himself to inquiring whether Crichton-Browne's report proved its existence. Given the importance of the Education Act's "credit and continued usefulness," Fitch thought it his duty to show that Crichton-Browne had failed to prove that overpressure even existed, much less that it was caused by education requirements.[44]

The Press Takes Up the Battle

Press responses to the reports by Crichton-Browne and Fitch expressed ambivalence over how to apportion parental and state responsibility for children's physical needs, and echoed Crichton-Browne's slippage between hereditary and environmental explanations for children's ill health. *Lloyd's,* always critical of the SBL, condemned Crichton-Browne's report as "deficient, inadequate, and unstatesmanlike" because he had based generalizations about the whole education system on observations of schools in Walworth, "one of the poorest and most crowded [districts] in London." While urging that public education be made more flexible to provide for differences of ability, the paper cautioned against falling "from that high standard it is our object to attain and to preserve. English schools cannot afford to lag behind in the great race which is now quickening the pulses and the energies of European nations."[45] The *Daily News* sided with Fitch, the *Daily Telegraph* supported Crichton-Browne, and the *PMG* straddled the fence, declaring that Fitch "made as much too little of overpressure" as Crichton-

Browne "made too much." As for "the great problem of 'how to reconcile education with starvation,' Mr. Fitch thinks we should educate children and leave the question of feeding alone; Dr. Browne, that we should feed children before we educate them. The commonsense conclusion is that if one should be done, the other should not be left undone." The state undertook education; private enterprise ought to be equal to organizing the feeding.[46]

The *School Guardian,* an "Educational Newspaper and Review" published by the Church of England's National Society, covered the overpressure controversy extensively, presenting to their readers the opinions of MPs, doctors, and educators—one teacher wrote to defend Crichton-Browne, a school principal called overpressure a "fad."[47] The *School Guardian*'s own position was marked by skepticism. Its editors argued that the cry against overpressure had been "groundlessly swelled by parents who disliked compulsory education, and by reactionists glad to find some new pretext for denouncing the whole system of Elementary Education." But, after allowing for "panic-created exaggerations, interested clamour, and irrational prejudice," there was no question that overpressure did exist. They had assurances from teachers and from medical practitioners who had treated the poor and had read it for themselves, "as anyone may, in the faces of too many of the children who attend our Elementary Schools." The system of payment by result under the Revised Code was to blame: overpressure had come in with it and had increased with each extension of the syllabus. It had converted children into "so much raw material to be manipulated for grant-producing purposes. . . ." This system hurt all children, but especially "children who are physically weak, or naturally dull, or irregular in attendance through no fault of their own, or who come from homes unfavourable to intellectual progress." The solution to this terrible situation was to give teachers greater freedom to withhold children from examination and to keep inspectors from setting "unreasonable" standards.[48]

The *School Guardian*'s editorial position clashed with that of *The Times,* which presented itself as both impartial chronicler of the debate and judicious defender of state-funded education. The paper admitted that isolated cases of overpressure were inevitable in an education system that treated all children as intellectual and physical equals, but was reluctant to lower educational standards, and so blamed individual inspectors and teachers for not making allowances for children's different abilities.[49] In March, *The Times* noted that "the philanthropists," having unearthed "a few cases . . . in which school lessons appeared to be telling upon the health and even the life of the weaker scholars," had been keeping up "such a running fire" of almost daily questions about cases of "so-called 'overpressure'" in both Houses of Parliament that they were leading the general public to believe in its existence. The economists, "again, taking fright at the great leap" in the education rate, had been making common cause with "voluntary educationists." Defending the latest Education Code against the attacks of these parties, *The Times* argued that it alleviated the threat of overpressure by relaxing requirements for subjects including arithmetic, geography, and needlework, while leaving out "nothing which is really useful and essential." *The Times* concluded that this code was more reasonable and had greater "regard for children's varying capacities" than any previous Education Code.[50]

While the public awaited publication of Crichton-Browne's report, *The Times,* in August, decided that it was time to get to the bottom of this issue. The question was whether, in the attempt to reach educational goals, "the minds of children in elementary schools are overstrained so as to . . . make their school lives a burden to them?" Advocates of the cry of overpressure loudly affirmed this was the case, some claiming that until payment by result was abolished, it would be "impossible" to ensure "that the next generation shall not be a race of nervous, excitable, shortsighted men and women, as weak in body as feeble in mind." Yet inquiries in Birmingham, Leeds, and Bradford had failed to substantiate charges of overpressure, except in the cases of a few delicate and unhealthy children. *The Times* agreed with Crichton-Browne that periodic medical examination was needed. The paper also affirmed that it was "little short of inhuman to try to force" poorly fed children through the same course of lessons "as their more highly-favoured fellow scholars." This was not to suggest that the rates should be used to feed hungry children. But here was an opportunity for "the well-to-do in society." Without "at all demoralizing or pauperizing certain classes of the community," they could "render very great service, and at comparatively little cost to themselves, to the cause of national education." Penny dinner programs had already markedly improved students' health and ability to pass examinations.[51]

When Crichton-Browne's and Fitch's statements were made public in September, *The Times* weighed in on Fitch's side, declaring that Crichton-Browne had failed to establish a connection between educational overpressure and alleged increases in disease rates. It was as much a question of style as of substance: the doctor's report asserted "a foregone conclusion in almost every page," its reasoning was "deplorably loose and inconsequent," and its style was "so rhetorical, not to say florid, as to deprive its conclusions of much of their weight and authority." This judgment was strengthened by perusal of Mr. Fitch's "temperate and able memorandum." A comparison of the two "in tone, temper, sobriety of language, and cogency of reasoning" inevitably led to the conclusion that the Education Department may far more safely be trusted in the matter of overpressure than Dr. Crichton-Browne."[52] Far from speaking with one voice, the British press did seem to have reached a rough consensus: there was need for flexibility in classifying and examining schoolchildren, and school meals would be useful, if provided by private sources.

Approaching this crisis from yet another angle than "economists," voluntary educationists, or the lay press had, the *Lancet* and the *BMJ* joined the debate over who had the authority to measure schoolchildren's health, both claiming to speak for parents and children whose voices were silenced by skeptical educators.[53] The two medical journals located overpressure's causes in a mismatch between the education system and the physical condition of children attending Board schools. Furthermore, in a decade when the medical profession was beginning to successfully claim authority based on its special knowledge, the overpressure controversy became an arena for these medical journals to police professional boundaries, defending doctors' special expertise and scolding those who acted unprofessionally.[54]

The *BMJ* reported in February 1884 that the doctor who had attended Sophia Raybould's death certified that she had died from meningitis and convulsions, adding his opinion that the present system of cramming was injurious. Mundella's response had been unsatisfactory and "blindly partisan." Medical men "and even the lay public" would understand that Mr. Bradley, "an independent practitioner of high standing" who treated the child during her illness, was much more likely to know the cause of her death than a government official who had formed his opinion on "documentary evidence" and who probably had "meager clinical acquaintance with disease."[55]

While the *BMJ* asserted that doctors were more qualified than education officials to diagnose overpressure, it joined the *Lancet* in insisting upon professional objectivity. Actually, the two positions reinforced one another: a reputation for objectivity made it possible to insist on doctors' indispensability. In March 1884, the *Lancet* reported that a group of doctors had sent a letter to the Bradford School Board, protesting that children were being harmed by overpressure in schools. Their spokesman, Dr. Rabagliati, whom Crichton-Browne cited in his report as an expert on mortality statistics, argued that the Registrar General's returns showed that "since the Education Act came into force," deaths from water on the brain amongst school age children had increased by twenty percent, "and from inflammation of the brain by fifty percent. . . ." The *Lancet* warned medical men against "the tendency abroad" to attribute every schoolchild's death to overpressure and scolded Rabagliati for failing to mention that the death rate of school-age children had declined 21 percent during the first ten years of the Education Act. The journal also commented on the difficulty of interpreting statistics, given ongoing improvements in standards for their collection: "there can be no question as to the probability that many deaths are now certified as due to hydrocephalus and cephalitis which would ten years ago have been merely attributed to convulsions." Whatever the arguments against the Education

Acts might be, they could not be based upon the Registrar-General's returns, which could not yet provide "precise statistics" on children's deaths.[56]

Sharing the *Lancet*'s concern with promoting professionalism, the *BMJ* urged "medical men and others to put themselves into the positions of judges, rather than advocates," in deciding whether schoolchildren's deaths bore any relation to their schoolwork. A recent case reinforced the importance of this advice: Adolphus Davis, age 11, had been attended by Dr. James, who attributed the boy's death to overpressure. The boy, described as excitable, had complained of being kept late to study for an exam, and his teacher had testified that the work was too much for pupils. Dr. James had strong prima facie evidence for his opinion, but nothing more, according to the journal. Had he said he could not give an opinion without a postmortem examination, he would have been "quite within the bounds of sound professional practice."[57]

Responding to Crichton-Browne's report proved a delicate task. While believing that overpressure existed and that doctors were best suited to identify it, both journals were leery of validating unsubstantiated opinions. The *BMJ* defended Crichton-Browne's right, given his expertise in mental disease, to "speak authoritatively on the question of mental overpressure." But it pointed out that Crichton-Browne had "laid himself open to the piercing shafts of his acute critic," Fitch, by indulging in "a florid kind of language" that was "not quite suitable to a scientific inquiry into a matter of great national importance."[58]

The two medical journals joined Crichton-Browne and other doctors in warning that overpressure was not confined to children in Board schools.[59] Crichton-Browne argued in his report that while dull children were overpressed in Board schools, it was the clever children in public and high schools who were strained by their efforts to win prizes, scholarships, and certificates.[60] The *Lancet*, for its part, warned against winter parties for well-to-do children. The excitement such parties produced, together with the dangers of chill and improper food and drink, incurred "wear and tear and waste" dangerous in this period of development.[61] Crichton-Browne and other doctors argued that middle-class schoolgirls were at greatest risk from educational pressure. According to Crichton-Browne, many physicians "of authority on the diseases of women" called for "a reduction and careful regulation of brain labour" in adolescent girls because of "the mischief to the individual and to society" resulting from "disregard of hygienic laws in the case of girls at this epoch of life."[62] This reproductive concern was less overt in discussions of the preadolescent elementary school population.

Dr. Elizabeth Garrett Anderson, a former SBL member, put a different twist on this discussion of overpressure of Britain's young. In a letter to *The Times,* she suggested that childhood would "always be a time of peril, the physiological strain which attaches to the processes of growth and development being what it is. . . ." But she was skeptical about the dangers of overpressure to students who were carefully tended by teachers and parents, stressing that "[m]oderate exercise of the brain" promoted its health, growth, and development.[63] A writer for the *Lancet* made a similar point. While children's brains could be damaged by overwork, just like muscles in the body, they needed exercise if they were to develop properly. He advised that educators engage pupils' brains for short periods, with intervals of rest.[64] This vision of education's benefits was at odds with Crichton-Browne's warnings of overpressure among dull Board school students, clever middle-class students, and adolescent schoolgirls.

Having reached no consensus about how to educate children safely, the medical community was able to agree that all growing and developing children were prone to fatigue and that poor children were made more vulnerable by inadequate diets and other demands on their strength, including after-school labor.[65] In the end, both medical journals refused to condemn Board schooling altogether, suggesting instead that children's bodies be fortified against the strain of learning. In the spring of 1884, the *BMJ* advocated feeding Board school children, but worried that such aid might "degenerate into wholesale demoralisation of worthless or indolent parents."[66] By October, while Crichton-Browne and Fitch were still arguing, the *BMJ* was advocating a government-sponsored program of penny dinners for schoolchildren. Society no longer tolerated ignorance in children, and "the day seems to have come for us to see that they are fed as well," even if this expanded governmental role should, as some feared, "revolutionise" society. "More than once in history," its editors concluded, "has logic had to give way to humanity; and no doubt this experience will have to be repeated before the human race has wrought its full development."[67]

Slightly more cautious, the *Lancet* warned that "the etiology of any breakdown in a child's health" was quite complicated and that "the injurious pressure of education" could not yet be proved by statistics. Yet every week, doctors saw proof "that schools may make or mar" children's future. Leaders had warned against entering into democracy with an uneducated people. "We have done worse than that; we have dared to educate a vast multitude of underfed and only half-developed brains." Statesmen must ensure that public education would benefit the nation both physically and intellectually.[68] The proper course was not to teach children less, "but to feed the little brains at work up to the level of organic health and efficiency."[69] Like Crichton-Browne, the *Lancet* repeatedly called for medical supervision of schoolchildren. Urging that "there should be no straining in training," the journal suggested that medical officers observe children as they studied for "indications of brain worry."[70] The two medical journals had reshaped the overpressure debate, substituting a scientific vocabulary of energy and fatigue for that of hereditary inequality and racial degeneration. By defining overpressure as a question of energy supply, the journals claimed roles for the medical profession and the state in ensuring that children could safely learn in Board schools.

The SBL in the "Silly Season"

The SBL had been drawn into the overpressure controversy from the start. Board members led public meetings to protest overpressure, and SBL meetings were consumed by the issue for months on end. For two months after Crichton-Browne's report was published in September, SBL members, roughly divided between Progressives and Moderates, debated whether overpressure existed, what caused it, and whether the Board should launch its own investigation.[71] In October, Progressive SBL Members Helen Taylor and Edward Lyulph Stanley took the opportunity presented by anxiety about overpressure to move to remit fees in all cases where family income was below 16 shillings per week. They suggested that overpressure resulted from poor families having to pay school fees out of their limited food budgets. Mr. Gover opposed the motion, fearing it would "benefit the drunkard and extravagant classes. . . ." Sir E. H. Currie responded that it was "very easy for well-clothed, well-fed, and well-housed people to class others as 'drunkards,' and 'extravagant,' but the fact was the very poor, whose poverty was increasing" due to circumstances beyond their control, "had not sufficient means with which to indulge in drunkenness." It was time the Board took this matter into its own hands by removing the hardships parents faced in finding the pennies to send their children to school.[72]

The debate over overpressure's causes consumed the next week's SBL meeting as well. Mr. Bousefield moved for appointment of a special committee to inquire into Crichton-Brown's allegations. Remarking that Dr. Crichton-Browne's opinions were not those of the medical profession generally, Sir Currie protested against the Board's valuable time being occupied week after week by a motion that was "the result of a passing excitement in the 'silly season.'"[73] Crichton-Browne lost little time in forwarding to *The Times* several letters he and Currie had exchanged in the following three days, ending with his own letter, in which he pointed out that he had "excellent reason for believing" that his opinions on the subject were shared by a majority of his "professional brethren."[74]

On November 14, after formal business was finished, the SBL again took up the overpressure question. The ensuing debate, lasting four hours and ending in deadlock, echoed the range of opinions expressed at public meetings and in the press. Those who believed in overpressure's existence assigned it various causes. Some blamed the Education Code and payment by result. One Board member maintained that overpressure was "due to lack of food, and not to excess of education." Others doubted overpressure's existence, but had concluded that an investigation was necessary in order to alleviate public alarm fueled "by the enemies of education."[75] The deadlock was finally broken, and, two weeks later, the SBL's chairman announced that he had selected a special committee of Board members to inquire into the allegations of overpressure in Board schools.[76]

The committee's mandate was to determine the veracity of Crichton-Browne's allegations of overpressure in Board schools. Teachers and inspectors called to testify before the committee offered conflicting testimony. Several teachers affirmed that schoolchildren did appear overpressed, citing their "ill health" and "weariness." One inspector considered overpressure "more of a sentiment than a reality"; another stated that "the cry of overpressure" was in inverse ratio to teachers' professional abilities.[77]

Beyond determining overpressure's existence, the committee also explored the parameters of the SBL's responsibility for the children in its schools. Committee members repeatedly inquired about the conditions of students' homes and about parents' attitudes toward their children's schooling. They wanted to know whether parents were using overpressure as an excuse to keep their children from school and whether parents pressed their children to finish school quickly in order to begin earning money. A few witnesses confirmed that parents did push their children through school so that they could contribute to the family's income.[78] Witnesses also reported that many of their pupils were very poor. A headmistress testified that "[t]his winter there has been more poverty than I have ever seen there."[79] Several teachers noted that programs offering penny dinners to schoolchildren markedly improved their ability to study. Children were better for their penny dinners physically and, "I think, mentally," testified one headmaster. The superintendent of visitors agreed that there were advantages to providing children with dinners. Asked to speculate whether parents would use that penny in "drinking and in extravagance" if dinners were provided free, he thought this would be a problem and agreed with the committee chair that parental "vice" caused children's poverty.[80] Like SBL debates and newspaper stories, witnesses presented conflicting testimony about parents' responsibility for their poverty.

In July 1885, the committee concluded that their inquiry had not disclosed "the systematic and universal overpressure" of children in Board schools. On the contrary, it had shown that children gained "physical, moral and intellectual benefit from attending school." As for the small number of cases where overpressure did exist, the committee placed most of the blame for it on parents anxious to push their children through school and with the material conditions of poverty.[81] The committee pointed out the Board's "difficult task" of educating children who ranged between two social extremes. In one group were children whose fathers made between 30 and 60 shillings a week. These children lived in comfortable homes and were well fed. The second group consisted of children of London's lowest classes, who lived in "crowded, squalid, dirty, bare, and infectious homes." Because the latter came from a class unused to "intellectual work or study," they were "as a rule, hereditarily unequal to the sustained learning and mental exertion attainable by others." The gravest difficulty the Board encountered in dealing with these poorest children was their hunger. Many went without breakfast and were "dull, listless, and inattentive." The Board was making "great efforts" to "attract and force" these children into schools, but it was "not responsible for their conditions," which must be left to philanthropy and legislation.[82] The report echoed Fitch's memorandum. It found the educational system to be sound. The problems lay with conditions outside the schools and therefore were beyond the Board's jurisdiction.

Just before the Special Committee on the Question of Overpressure released its report, *The Times* warned of the delicacy and importance of this issue. No statistical proofs of elementary education's progress could make education popular or "check a disastrous reaction against its further development, if the belief were once to take root that its spread was sapping the physical strength of the people."[83] Two days later, *The Times* printed an abstract of the SBL *Report on Overpressure,* followed by commentary. The Special Committee seemed to have "done their work carefully and thoroughly." Stating that the committee's opinions were "very much what the general public are prepared to accept and credit," the paper supported its conclusion that schooling was actually beneficial to children's health. Any cases of overpressure that did exist were not necessarily a consequence of the school system, but rather had a variety of causes, "some of which the School Board has no power adequately to control."[84] The Special Committee had decided early in its proceedings not to call medical experts as witnesses. *The Times* found this decision unfortunate but understandable. Less forgiving, the *BMJ* considered the value of the report "very much diminished by this circumstance. . . ." But the journal noted that the report had some value because it admitted overpressure's existence and because it suggested practical remedies (penny dinners, physical exercise, kindergarten, and more flexible classification of children according to their abilities).[85] The *Lancet*'s repeated calls for medical inspection went unanswered.[86]

The SBL was trapped between two paradigms: it had anecdotal and scientific evidence that feeding children helped them to learn better, yet several constituencies loudly warned against demoralizing parents and extending state powers. In the end, as Fitch had predicted, the Board lacked the authority to extend its responsibility for children in Board schools. The overpressure scare did prompt changes, however. In the next few years, volunteer agencies were allowed to increase substantially the number of penny dinner programs in Board schools, as the committee report had suggested. In the next decade, schools were made free, and medical inspection was approved.

Thirty years later, several authors of books about child welfare and education identified overpressure as an important but failed trial run for the crisis over physically inadequate recruits for the Boer War and the subsequent report by the Interdepartmental Committee on Physical Deterioration in 1904, which led to the Provision of Meals Act of 1906 and the Medical Inspection Act of 1907.[87] Confident that they lived in an era of more enlightened understanding of the ameliorative role state intervention could play, these writers overlooked some vital parallels between 1884 and 1914. SBL reports for 1889 and 1898 and a Board of Education report for 1912 all noted the prevalence of hunger among elementary school children.[88] Each of these reports also ignored the obstacles and humiliations working-class mothers endured in negotiating for their children's free and penny dinners.[89]

Writing from a further remove in 1937, former SBL Member Thomas Gautrey refocused on the curricular aspects of the overpressure crisis, arguing that it had brought "the biggest education agitation in the Board's history."[90] A template for conflicting beliefs and agendas, overpressure shaped subsequent decisions about the very purpose of elementary education. Debates over whether elementary education should be more "bookish" or more practical, already under way in the early 1880s, ended in reforms that shifted the curriculum towards technical education for boys and domestic economy lessons for girls. The specter of small children falling ill over their schoolbooks, in combination with larger political and economic anxieties of the period, effected this shift toward a "less bookish" education.

Chapter Eight

"A Power of Reading":
"The Key to All Knowledge"

In 1902, Parliament passed legislation mandating state aid to secondary schools for the first time. The 1902 Education Act also forced the government to mark the boundaries between a terminal elementary education for working-class children and a secondary education for middle-class children and a minority of working-class scholarship students. In her study of how J. M. Barrie's *Peter and Wendy* was made into an elementary school reader, Jacqueline Rose has analyzed how the new Board of Education (replacing the Department of Education) adopted two different forms of language to distinguish between classes of children after 1902. Rose argues that by 1912 state policy rigorously distinguished between a "language of elementary experience and one of cultural style," the former belonging in elementary school, the latter in secondary schools. The "natural" elementary school language then being constructed for working-class children was to be "carefully distinguished from literary language by its reference to experience, to the 'sights and sounds, the thoughts and feelings of everyday life.'"[1]

According to the Board of Education, this new functional, "natural" language would be taught through visual images and concrete objects. Its literature, based on physical actions "and on facts which could be added to the child's stock of information," should be read for the story, not for the form. The "literary" language taught in secondary schools would place more emphasis on cadence and quality in children's speech and structure and style in their writing. This "literary" language should become the model "of the child's own mental processes which reflect, not everyday concrete experience, but 'remembrances,' 'unconscious associations,' and a 'widening experience of life.'"[2] J. M. Barrie's story presented a problem because it wove together elementary and literary languages. So when *Peter and Wendy* was accepted for use in 1915, the offending "classical" or literary parts were simply removed and the story was abridged to fit the language requirements for elementary schools. This kind of editing points to the solution the education authorities had settled upon: working-class children were to be given a functional, terminal elementary education and were not to participate in the broader literary culture.[3]

This demarcation between "natural" and "literary" languages did not grow inevitably out of earlier educational policies of the Education Department or the School Board for London (SBL). The policies of 1912 must be viewed in light of an earlier generation of educators' faith in reading's power to unlock the doors of knowledge and of curricular changes spawned by compromises that had sometimes unintended consequences.[4] From 1870 on (and even long before that), reading lessons were placed at the center of battles over whether elementary education should provide working-class children with basic skills, the concrete facts necessary to enter the working class, or provide them with critical skills and imaginative powers—tools that could potentially be turned against a political and economic system built upon class and gender divisions. Furthermore, the ways in which school officials understood the problems of Board scholars' uneven attendance and ill health subtly shaped their evaluations of working-class children's cognitive development and educational needs. The debate over reading lessons was not just academic, but rather was closely related to controversies over fee collection, school meals, and overpressure. These education controversies, in turn, took place against the backdrop of fears about Britain's eroding position in the world economy, the disruption of political stability with the enfranchisement of property-owning working-class men in 1867 and 1884, and the growing strength of feminist and labor movements.[5]

Reading in Board Schools

In its first year of existence, the SBL appointed a subcommittee of the School Management Committee to compile lists of recommended and unsatisfactory books. The books were assessed in terms of their "intrinsic value, their appropriateness to Board Schools, their actual popularity, and their cheapness"; inspectors' and schoolmasters' recommendations were considered as well. In 1872, the approved list of 17 titles included *Cassell's New Code Series* and *Laurie's Technical Series of Reading Books*.[6] Once teachers had selected books from the recommended list, these were distributed through a central store; and, finally, after much debate, the Board decided to allow them to be used free of charge within schools.[7]

Frequently updated as publishers began to respond to this new book market, the Board's book lists drew a united protest from publishers in 1882. They argued that by so limiting teachers' choices, the Board hurt the publishers' trade and, ultimately, the "true interests of education." But the Board refused to change its practice, arguing that the market was flooded by inferior books and that some teachers were apt to choose those that only helped children pass exams without training their minds. Besides, publishers had apparently been pushing their wares on teachers, "holding out to them inducements of a corrupt nature," all the more justification for the SBL's supervisory role.[8]

The poet and cultural critic Matthew Arnold was someone who, in his capacity as one of Her Majesty's Inspectors (1851–1886), shaped discussions of books and reading before and after 1870. Arnold left a complicated trail with his writings on education, delineating a position that incorporated the tensions within late nineteenth-century liberalism. His desire to "humanise" students was born of his fear of mob rule following the extension of the franchise in 1866. But his writing, influenced by contact with teachers and students, also contained an egalitarianism in that he presented universal access to good education and ideas as a right, a contention denied by most conservatives; and he advocated pursuit of knowledge as an end in itself, a possibility ignored by utilitarians. The conflict between Arnold's egalitarian respect for imagination and his desire to civilize the lower classes was played out in his own and other school officials' evaluations of children's reading.[9]

As an inspector of voluntary schools before 1870, Arnold lamented children's lack of good reading material. A student's reading books were too often either crammed with facts or with "feeble, incorrect, and colourless" literature, written by third-rate authors. As a result, "he has, except his Bible, no literature, no humanising instruction at all." But good, sound, refining books could be used to teach children to read well and to inspire "quick scholars with a real love for reading and literature." For Arnold, books mattered immensely; in them lay the potential for "refining" and "humanising" children.[10]

Arnold believed that children's unawakened and uninformed minds posed the greatest challenges to educators. The "past life and circumstances of our poorer classes" might partially explain this, but so too could the "composite character of our language," a "fatal" but conquerable obstacle to instruction, as perhaps, he implied, the former problem was not. Developing this theme, Arnold explained: "[t]he animation of mind, the multiplying of ideas, the promptness to connect, in the thoughts, one thing with another . . . are what are wanted." Friends of natural science looked to it as a remedy for working-class ignorance of the laws of health. But this "positive knowledge" would not carry a man far unless he had been "moralised." The best moralizing agents were literature, poetry, and religion: "so let not our teachers be led to imagine . . . that their literary cultivation is unimportant," he urged. For the fruitful use of natural science itself depended "on having

effected in the whole man, by means of letters, a rise in what political economists call the standard of life."[11] In passages like these, Arnold threaded together language, reading, ideas, and quality of life.

In his report for 1878, Arnold urged that young children who from "circumstances of their bringing-up have an especially narrow mental range"
not be given too many subjects to study. Their scanty vocabularies, "the signal feature of their mental condition," constituted their "real inferiority to
the children of the cultivated classes. The ignorance of what we are accus-
tomed to consider things universally known is on a par with this want of
words and of the ideas which go along with the words." Hitting his stride,
Arnold warned that most elementary education had "nothing of that formative character" that education demanded. Sewing, calculating, and
spelling, though useful, certainly did not fit the bill. Even "the power of
reading [was] not in itself formative." But good poetry had "the precious
power of acting by itself . . . not through the instrumentality of that somewhat terrible character, the scientific educator." The good of poetry could
not be "got" unless the words were understood, but "more and more I find
it learnt and known." That "signal mental defect" of schoolchildren, "their
almost incredible scantiness of vocabulary," was being remedied. "We en-
large their vocabulary, and with their vocabulary their circle of ideas."[12]
Arnold considered "a power of reading, well trained and well guarded . . .
perhaps the best among the gifts which it is the business of our elementary
schools to bestow."

Inspectors' reports filed in the first decades of Board schooling echoed
Arnold's concerns about children's reading and the stifling effects of payment
by result.[13] Nearly 20 years after Arnold's early discussion of the importance
of good literature, Inspector T. Marchant Williams complained that one
Board school used only a dry, dull, difficult series of books. Given an "ex-
clusive diet" of "uninviting" topics, how were children to acquire a taste for
reading? The littlest children "cordially dislike their books and are therefore
never tempted, as are the children of other divisions, to dip surreptitiously
into their 'readers.'" Bad books were like bad medicine.[14]

Even worse than dull books were those that warped children's minds.
When "obscene" words were found scribbled in a girls' department reading
book, the investigating inspector argued that the children's "wretched surroundings" increased the importance of "maintaining in full vigour" the
good influences of the school "and of banishing from it whatever is likely to
promote vice or curiosity about it."[15] In a similar vein, the author of *Pantomime Waifs* (1884) argued that "in these days [of] universal rudimentary
education," poor children were given a "mighty power, which, if not turned
to good account, becomes self-destructive." The gift of reading engendered
a thirst for knowledge "which if not slaked at healthy streams, will quench

itself in noxious pools, whose very inhalations breathe defilement." Cheap, sensational literature was a poison that threatened to undermine young girls' virtue, producing a race of "premature child-women" who threatened the country's moral strength.[16]

The antidote for this poison was good books that had the power to instill a love of reading. Books could also have a more practical purpose as rewards for good behavior and correct knowledge. In 1876, Board Member Francis Peek maneuvered around restrictions on religious instruction by arranging for the Religious Tract Society to distribute Bibles as prizes to Board scholars who demonstrated excellence in biblical knowledge. While these negotiations were going on, the Board was establishing lending libraries in schools. Borrowing privileges could be won with good conduct and punctual attendance. Reward books, long used in voluntary schools, were also handed out for good behavior.[17] Given the high cost of children's books, some working-class children coveted these prizes and access to libraries. More to the point, educators believed strongly in giving children good books and teaching them to read well.

Inspectors complained that reading, "the most important" elementary subject, received the least attention with regard to teaching methods. Teachers were trained to get children to pass exams, not to develop their powers of observation and reasoning. Teaching methods were "defective" or nonexistent, and lessons became a dull grind: books were distributed, the first boy read the first line, had his pronunciation corrected, then the second boy read, and so on, without the words ever being explained in a way calculated to arouse the children's interest.

Inspectors made similar reports five years later, in 1880. Where reading was poorly taught, the alphabet was drilled through constant repetition, a process occasionally enlivened by calling a child up to match the letters. Then books were placed in the "little ones'" hands; the teacher spelled the first word, gave its sound; the children repeated it half a dozen times; then the second word was given. This process continued until 12 pages had been learned in 6 months. "So mechanical is the reading in a few schools, that the children are taught to read *one line* each, without any reference whatever to the sense or meaning of the passage read."[18] This regimen had apparently changed little 40 years later. Dorothy Scannell remembered that reading in a London school during World War I "was not a real pleasure, for all reading was aloud and as we read paragraphs in turn we had to keep pace with the slowest reader. Many times I tried to dash on secretly, but I could never keep the place in the book with my finger" and was inevitably caught when called on by the teacher.[19]

As time went on, inspectors suspected that children were learning to read more accurately and fluently, but not more intelligently.[20] One inspector argued that reading was not worthy of the name until the written word coalesced with the thought in the child's head. It was not enough that children could recite set pieces on examination day, he wanted evidence that they understood what they read.[21] Clara Grant, who began teaching in 1888 and was still teaching in London elementary schools in the 1930s, had a different view of the results inspectors reported while payment by result was in operation. An inspector, she estimated, gave 12,000 tests a year. "Is it any wonder that he could assess only the mechanical reading and counting, not the child's intelligence, and that teachers prepared accordingly?"[22] Inspectors were also troubled by London children's pronunciation. Some inspectors discerned improvements as children began to drop their "h's" and "g's" less. But others continued to find their working-class students' "dialectical peculiarities" too prevalent and thought their teachers unqualified to correct them.[23] In this case, reading was a means of eradicating the sounds of class and regional differences.

Having been informed repeatedly that children were not being taught to read well, the SBL set out to remedy this problem. In 1876, the Board appealed to the government to reform English spelling, arguing that a more consistent system that "represented in the simplest form the exact sound of every word" would be more economical and efficient. The Board pointed out that similar reforms on the Continent had saved half the time required to teach children to read. Since education was now national work, and since children could not leave school to work until they had passed required standards of proficiency, the government should see spelling reform as essential to educational progress and the national economy.[24]

In 1877, the SBL began to examine the methods used to teach reading. The resulting committee report cataloged the available methods and recapitulated inspectors' criticisms of and aspirations for reading. The committee found that the alphabetic method, in which lessons proceeded from letters to syllables to words, was "false" and tedious because letters' names and sounds did not correspond. More to the committee's liking was the phonic method, because it began with letters' "true sounds" and was "genuinely synthetic." Although it would require reformed spelling, phonics had "the great merit of cultivating the habit of distinct articulation, and of imparting to the ear accuracy and delicacy in the discrimination of sounds." With the phonetic method, words were spelled as they were pronounced, and the "ripened intelligence of children" taught to read with this system would in turn enable them to read with ordinary spelling. The best way to teach the alphabet was to classify letters and associate them with objects they resembled, thus helping to "satisfy the active imagination of children and to powerfully assist the memory."[25]

The greatest obstacles to good reading were the logistics of teaching large classes, together with children's limited vocabularies and their pronunciation. The difficulty of learning to read was doubled because "the language which children of the poorer classes" spoke and the language they read were "two different tongues." Their vocabularies must be enlarged, and "words must be set before them in their living organic relations with the other words of a sentence," not as columns of disconnected words.

Poetry could be a means of cultivating their imaginations and improving their vocabularies and delivery. It was crucial to interest children in reading by making it a source of pleasure and an end in itself, not just a means of transmitting information. If young children had more time to read, they could learn to do it with pleasure, and to employ this new power to acquire knowledge and cultivate their higher faculties.[26] This report identified reading as the key that could unlock children's mental powers, bring them into a common English culture, and homogenize their speech. Underlying the methods the Board advocated was the principle that teaching could be geared to the development of children's minds. The first stage involved making concrete associations between letters and words and children's physical surroundings; later stages built logically from there.

In subsequent reports, attuned more than ever to the problems the committee had identified, inspectors complained that reading was poorly taught and that children were not learning to read naturally or intelligently. One unusually empathetic inspector argued that for a young street arab, "used to all the life and variety of the London streets," a regimen in which each line was read "forwards and then backwards" and each word was spelled half a dozen times, was "past bearing." He fled, his spirit quailing, and the teacher was relieved to see him go, since his presence threatened the school's examination results.[27]

The committee's follow-up report on reading methods, submitted in 1883, was enthusiastic, and the SBL asked the Education Department's support in getting inspectors to relax rigid examination policies that discouraged experimentation. But the department refused on the grounds that the shortness of most children's schooling made undesirable any instruction that did not enable them to pass the required examination in reading and spelling at age eight.[28] There was simply no room for experiments that impeded the speedy, efficient, education of Board scholars. The Board's vision of making reading pleasurable and a key to higher knowledge was pitted against the Education Department's goals of providing a solid, basic education as efficiently as possible.

In this context, questions about reading were reformulated. Now questions of how children should learn to read were increasingly replaced by questions of when they should learn and how reading skills related to other educational goals. In 1883, Inspector T. Marchant Williams noted with displeasure that in one Infant school, reading was done seven hours a week—

out of books consisting of sentences about fat vats, rats, and fat men—while kindergarten and object lessons combined received less than two hours. With so little time given to kindergarten, it could not serve its intended purpose of training the senses to observe and compare, cultivating intelligence and social instincts, and satisfying the love of discovery and creation.[29]

Williams's call for greater attention to kindergarten was not new. Back in the mid-1870s, inspectors and Board members had enthusiastically embraced kindergarten, urging that it be more widely practiced. One inspector called in 1876 for the kindergarten "spirit" to permeate the Infant department, because kindergarten recognized play as the business of a child's life. Guided by systematic use of toys (gifts) and occupations, play was the basis for the physical, intellectual, and moral education "peculiarly adapted" to developing the "Infant mind."[30] Underlying inspectors' comments, and central to kindergarten literature, was the premise that there was an "Infant mind" to be studied and guided through stages of development. By the 1880s, as the child study movement gained momentum and educators worried more about suiting the curriculum to children's abilities, kindergarten had come to symbolize a developmental model of childhood education that centered on the relationship between mind and body.[31]

Shortly after Williams submitted his report, the SBL sent a memorial to the Education Department, calling for relaxed examination standards for children five and younger. After years of reading inspectors' complaints about teachers' failure to fully implement kindergarten, the Board seemed finally to have decided that the system of payment by result was a major impediment to their doing so. Echoing Williams, the Board argued that children were subject to "severe training": five to nine hours a week of reading, and only a little time for kindergarten and physical exercise. Such long hours of enforced stillness were "detrimental" to children's physical and mental growth. Their "restless energy, instead of being repressed, should be directed into channels in which observation, imagination and dexterity . . . can be cultivated." The strongest critique, later deleted, focused on reading: "the natural desire of young children to play, to touch and to see is not met by the dull mechanical work involved in a parrot-like repetition. . . ." Children's first lessons should be in language, given through the mediums of pictures and lively lessons on "common natural objects of daily life," and varied by physical exercise, games, singing, and "occupations calculated to train the eye and hand."[32] Current fears about overpressure and interest in kindergarten united here to bump reading aside in favor of more active and physical learning for the littlest Board scholars.

This interest in kindergarten and worry about overtaxing children's minds coincided with educators' growing concern for making elementary education more practical. While the SBL's memorial suggested that reading be postponed until children were developmentally ready, advocates of a more technical, manually oriented education sought to remove reading from the center of the curriculum. When, in 1879, a coalition of Progressive SBL members had argued for establishing technical institutions, on the grounds that most children in Board schools were "destined for handicraft occupations," the rest of the Board had responded without enthusiasm.[33] But a decade later, a new Board would take a different approach. Thomas Gautrey, secretary of the Metropolitan Board Teachers' Association in the 1880s and an SBL member in the 1890s, looked back on the period 1885–1896 as a time when the SBL's main objective had been to make "instruction less literary and less ambitious." He explained that SBL Members had experienced a crisis of doubt in 1885, concerned over teacher dissatisfaction with the Education Code, uneven inspection standards, payment by result, and overpressure.[34] The time had come to reconsider Board schooling's purpose, specifically to revisit the question of whether to include technical education. So, in typical fashion and after much debate, the SBL in 1887 appointed a Subjects and Modes of Instruction Committee to consider whether the present curriculum could be altered to ensure that, upon leaving school, children would be fit to "perform the duties and work of life before them."[35]

The committee reported back in 1888, having taken testimony from expert witnesses. They began by defining the object of elementary education as the harmonious development of the bodily and mental faculties with which children are "endowed by nature." Education's moral benefits were clear: it imparted "fearless truth, bravery, honour, activity, manly skill, temperance, hardihood, welded into a great national character," and it taught order, obedience, cleanliness, and courtesy. The question of the relationship among the physical, mental, and moral aspects of education was more vexing. The physical side had been neglected. As for the mental side, too much time was spent on memory work, not enough on cultivating intelligence.[36]

Professor Thomas Huxley, a member of the original SBL, had dug to the root of the problem: elementary education was "too bookish, too little practical," the faculties important to life, those of accurate work and of "dealing with things instead of words," were not being educated.[37] Another witness concurred, arguing that nothing in the present curriculum ennobled labor; instead it gave boys an "undue bent toward clerkly and nonmanual pursuits." Yet this testimony had been preceded by the remark that the curriculum did little to awaken children's reasoning faculties and thus laid a poor foundation for secondary education. How could these two concerns be reconciled? How could elementary education cultivate children's intelligence and be made less bookish, more relevant to children's future in manual labor? The solution was to recognize that mental and manual training were inseparable. It was time to heed the calls of educators, scientists, industrialists, and statesmen for bringing manual work to the aid of intelligence. Eyes, hands, bodies, and minds trained in scientific principles were indispensable to "industrial excellence."[38]

Industry's need for trained workers at a time of growing international competition undoubtedly influenced this interest in technical education. But this was not the committee's sole concern. They argued that study of English history was necessary for intelligent understanding of political and social issues. For it was as much the Board's duty, "in our present social condition," to prepare boys to vote as to enter the workshop. The strands of this report, one leading toward intellectual cultivation, the other toward practical training, indicate that male Board scholars were being prepared both to participate in a national political culture and to take their places within the working class of an industrial economy. Girls' educational needs had vanished from this discussion, but were picked up in the Cross Commission report, also presented in 1888. This commission, appointed by the Conservative government to inquire into the working of the Elementary Education Acts, recommended that code requirements in mathematics be lowered for girls to give them more time for needlework.[39] While men pondered politics, women must be able to sew a seam.[40]

The SBL committee pointed out that implementing technical education would require balancing mental and manual work and meeting the separate needs of children of different classes. The solution to both problems lay with using kindergarten methods throughout elementary school, since they developed children's intellectual and manual powers, providing basic lessons in science—motion, form, proportion, and color—and in the manual exercises that formed the "rudiments of handicraft." The full SBL decided that kindergarten methods should be developed throughout the standards "so as to supply a graduated course of Manual Training in connection with Science Teaching and Object Lessons," but without actually "teaching the practice of any trade or industry." By linking manual training to academic subjects, and proposing not to teach any one trade, the SBL hoped to conciliate both the opponents of manual training and the "Artisan class."[41] Thomas Gautrey commented in 1937 that this "almost forgotten" revulsion "against a 'too literary' education" was one of the "most important events in London's education." It had changed "the whole spirit" of elementary education, and subsequent progress could be traced to "this landmark."[42]

The SBL was not alone in rejecting a "too literary" elementary education in 1888. Joshua Fitch, the inspector who had tangled with Dr. Crichton-Browne regarding overpressure, suggested that "[t]here was a prevalent and increasing conviction among teachers" that education was "too verbal and bookish" and that a useful corrective was to be found in exercises that trained the body and promoted manual dexterity. He did warn, though, that teachers should regard handwork as a supplement, rather than a substitute, for intellectual exertion.[43] The Cross Commission, in its 1888 report, called "[t]he question, whether it is desirable to give manual instruction in elementary schools," one of "gravest importance." Technical instruction could help prevent too many boys from becoming clerks and shopmen, give "those who were naturally fitted for work with their fingers" an outlet for their talents, and promote "the growth of really skilled artisans which our present system of elementary education tends, it is commonly said, to discourage." The commission also regretted that boys were "limited," after the age of seven, "to a merely literary education."[44]

Not everyone agreed that Board schooling was too bookish. One witness before the Cross Commission, Thomas Smyth, a plasterer "representative of the working class" and of the London Trades Council, objected that the working classes did not want vocational training in elementary schools. He called instead for a more general, secular, and free education. Clara Grant, who began her teaching career in 1888, later commented that the curriculum of that era did not consider children's needs, but was instead designed to make children useful to employers.[45]

Ambivalence about the proper balance between literary and vocational education is the common thread between the reports of the Cross Commission and the SBL Subjects and Modes of Instruction Committee. Both documents stressed the value of teaching reading in Board schools. The Cross Commission had heard from witnesses, including Mr. Fitch, that there was insufficient time to teach children to read intelligently the amount required by the code, "so that they get to hate their books." The commission concluded that "it is plain that there is room for much improvement in reading." Much was at stake, for "a child who has thoroughly acquired the art of reading with ease has within its reach the key to all knowledge, and it will rest with itself alone to determine the limits of its progress."[46] The SBL committee urged that reading lessons should encourage children "to read for their own pleasure, both at home and after their school days are over," and they should be "specially directed to awakening an intelligent interest in the subjects read of, rather than as auxiliary only" to spelling and grammar.[47] Eleven years later, the government's "Revised Instructions to Inspectors" made a similar point: "The chief requisites of a school reading book are that it should be attractive to scholars, and should establish in their minds pleasant associations with the act of reading." The main object was to ensure that children retained the "reading habit" after finishing elementary school.[48]

Why did the SBL take so much trouble with reading? And how is it that the SBL and national education authorities could both embrace technical education as an antidote to a "too bookish" elementary curriculum and continue to express optimism that reading could open children's minds to life-long learning? These evaluations of reading—pitting a belief in the power of reading to enhance intellectual development against a desire to make education practical—were made within the context of tensions among Arnold's vision of a common "Culture," conservative fears of overeducating the working class, and progressive efforts to widen educational opportunities. Educators had been shaken by overpressure, and many genuinely believed that kindergarten offered a model for matching elementary education to children's stages of development. Some Progressive SBL members were trying to be realistic about the fact that most children would be done with school by age 13. Their concern for making education more practical meshed with widely expressed fears about Britain's industrial competitiveness.

In 1888, the Cross Commission pointed out that the 1870 Education Act had not defined the meaning and limits of the word "elementary." Some thought this a good thing, because it had given educators room to experiment and make progress.[49] The Cross Commission felt otherwise, noting that the Education Department had continued extending elementary education until it included subjects properly taught in secondary schools. It was "absolutely necessary" that instruction paid for out of taxes be fixed by the legislature. Until this was done, the limits of primary and secondary education could not be defined.[50]

The 1902 Education Act accomplished what the Cross Commission had suggested, distinguishing a terminal elementary education from secondary education for middle-class children and a minority of working-class scholarship students. Jacqueline Rose's study of *Peter and Wendy*'s transformation into an elementary school reader demonstrates how policy-makers intended to reinforce the difference between elementary and secondary education by teaching a "concrete" language in the former and a more "literary" language in the latter.

Of course the match between government policy and individual practice was never perfect. Educators continued to embraced the ideal of reading as a key to wider knowledge. Edmund Holmes, a former school inspector, wrote in 1911 that the "power to read" was a "key which unlocks many doors," while the consequences of not learning to read were "far-reaching and disastrous."[51] Alluding to Matthew Arnold's writings in 1930, Board teacher Clara Grant described the "amazing poverty" of children's vocabularies in East End schools. She insisted that training in "the mother tongue" was "the open sesame to the treasure house of books, which might enrich life at every point," and she warned against an education system that sacrificed "the general culture of the child to the narrower demands of written examinations. . . ."[52]

Every 20 years or so after 1902, the British government commissioned studies of children's reading abilities when concerns about literacy rates surfaced. In 1921, the Newbolt report stressed that the ability to read English "intelligently" was the key to all other learning. Revelations about high illiteracy rates within the armed forces during World War II prompted surveys of reading standards and a controversy over teaching methods. Following the social upheaval of the 1960s, a Select Committee of the House of Commons was set up in 1970 to investigate allegations that "progressive" ideas had resulted in unacceptably low literacy rates.[53] In 1974, the Bullock report on literacy, entitled "A Language for Life," found that existing educational practice, inherited from the 1900s, had the effect of arresting working-class children's development at a concrete level, something no longer acceptable in the workforce of the 1970s. The Bullock report advocated breaking down educational differentiation and presenting children with a unified culture, during the time when Basil Bernstein and others were developing a theory of linguistic "deprivation" to explain poor children's educational difficulties.[54] Matthew Arnold and Clara Grant might well have recognized the Bullock report and Bernstein's theory as related to their concerns about the consequences of poor children's "scanty" vocabularies.

The Bullock report takes us back full circle to the 1870s and 1880s, when the groundwork for the education policies of the 1910s and 1970s was being laid in interlocking debates about how technical education, kindergarten, and reading fit into the curriculum. Somewhere along the way, the idealism of Arnold and other educators, and their desire to give children access to knowledge and a love of reading—perhaps inextricable from their class fears—were overridden by the need to educate Board school scholars as working-class children. Engaged in an ongoing battle to control popular literacy, Arnold and his successors failed to acknowledge (or see) the rich tradition of autodidacticism within working-class culture. As many working-class autobiographies would attest, some workers had long known how to find "good" books for themselves.[55]

Postscript, 1996

In the spring of 1996, during a week when British newspaper headlines declared "The End of the Welfare State," the reading abilities of London's schoolchildren were once again the subject of controversy.[56] The Office of Standards for Education (Ofsted) had issued a report critical of poor reading standards in three London district authorities: Tower Hamlets, Islington, and Southwark. About 80 percent of 7-year-olds and 40 percent of 11-year-olds in the 45 schools examined read below the levels established for their chronological ages. The report, blaming "trendy" teaching methods and poor leadership by head teachers, followed nearly a decade of battles over the Conservative government's 1988 Baker Plan to implement a national curriculum and national testing and to allow parents to vote for their schools to opt out of local control.

In this charged atmosphere, the three local Labour authorities were not about to accept Ofsted's report uncritically.[57] They accused Ofsted's Chris Woodhead of a "preplanned political agenda," noting that the redrafted report had dropped passages outlining serious inner city problems. Representatives of a teachers' union pointed out that, besides blaming trendy teaching, the report itself identified other contributing factors: many of the schools' students spoke English as a second language; "high levels of social disadvantage; poor management; poor initial training." Inspector Woodhead responded that if it was political to want to raise educational standards, "I plead guilty."[58]

One hundred twenty-five years after the first Board schools were opened, children in London's poorest areas are again at the center of controversy. Once again, British politicians and educators are arguing over whether poor teaching or poor social conditions are to blame for children's disappointing examination results. It is no coincidence that government officials and teachers are agonizing over children's literacy at a time when Britain is being shaped by a global economic restructuring, and rethinking the balance of state, local, and parental responsibility for children. The issue of the power of reading, a key means by which a society defines itself in class and gender terms, has arisen each time modern British society has undergone major economic and social transformations.

Notes

Introduction

1. Mary Langan and Bill Schwarz, eds., *Crisis in the British State, 1880–1930* (London: Hutchinson, 1985), chap. 1; Robert Colls and Philip Dodd, eds., *Englishness, Politics and Culture, 1880–1920* (London: Croom Helm, 1986), chap. 1.

2. For the history of the reception of Philippe Aries's groundbreaking study of childhood, see Richard T. Vann, "The Youth of *Centuries of Childhood*," *History and Theory*, vol. 21 (1982): 274–92.

3. Carolyn Steedman, *Strange Dislocations: Childhood and the Idea of Human Interiority, 1780–1930* (Cambridge: Harvard University Press, 1995); Hugh Cunningham, *The Children of the Poor* (Oxford: Blackwell, 1991); Deborah Gorham, "'The Maiden Tribute of Modern Babylon' Re-examined: Child Prostitution and the Idea of Childhood in Late Victorian England," *Victorian Studies* (1978): 353–79; James Kincaid, *Child-Loving: The Erotic Child and Victorian Culture* (New York: Routledge, 1992); Viviana Zelizer, *Pricing the Priceless Child* (New York: Basic Books, 1985). Literary depictions of childhood are analyzed in Peter Coveney, *The Image of Childhood* (1957; Harmondsworth: Penguin, 1967); and Robert Pattison, *The Child Figure in English Literature* (Athens: University of Georgia Press, 1978).

4. Cunningham, p. 4. See also George Behlmer, *Child Abuse and Moral Reform in England, 1870–1908* (Stanford: Stanford University Press, 1982); Deborah Dwork, *War Is Good for Babies and Other Young Children* (London: Tavistock, 1987); Pat Thane, "Childhood in History," in *Childhood, Welfare and Justice,* ed. Michael King (London: Batsford, 1981).

5. Anna Davin, *Growing Up Poor: Home, School and Street in London, 1870–1914* (London: Rivers Oram Press, 1996). See also David Nasaw, *Children of the City* (New York: Anchor Press, 1985); Thea Thompson, *Edwardian Childhoods* (London: Routledge, 1981); and James Walvin, *A Child's World: A Social History of English Childhood, 1800–1914* (Harmondsworth: Penguin, 1982).

6. Leonore Davidoff and Catherine Hall, *Family Fortunes: Men and Women of the English Middle Class 1750–1850* (Chicago: University of Chicago Press, 1987); John Gillis, *A World of Their Own Making: Myth, Ritual, and the Quest for Family Values* (New York: Basic Books, 1996); Jane Lewis, *The Politics of Motherhood* (London: Croom Helm, 1980); Ellen Ross, *Love and Toil: Motherhood in Outcast London, 1870–1918* (New York: Oxford University Press, 1993).

7. Dina Copelman, *London's Women Teachers: Gender, Class and Feminism, 1870–1930* (London: Routledge, 1996), pp. 100–2.

8. Routledge compiled a "Catalogue of Juvenile Books" in 1875; 2,000 schoolchildren were polled about their reading preferences in 1888; and the *Bookman,* a trade journal, included a special children's book section in its 1896 Christmas supplement.

9. Kirsten Drotner, *English Children and Their Magazines, 1751–1945* (New Haven: Yale University Press, 1988); Kimberley Reynolds, *Girls Only? Gender and Popular Children's Fiction in Britain, 1880–1910* (Philadelphia: Temple University Press, 1990); Janice Radway, *Reading the Romance* (Chapel Hill: University of North Carolina Press, 1984).

10. Gillian Avery, *Nineteenth Century Children: Heroes and Heroines in English Children's Stories, 1780–1900* (London: Hodder & Stoughton, 1965); Harvey Darton, *Children's Books in England,* rev. ed., Brian Alderson (Cambridge: Cambridge University Press, 1982); Drotner, *English Children and their Magazines;* Mary V. Jackson, *Engines of Instruction, Mischief and Magic* (Lincoln: University of Nebraska Press, 1989); Claudia Nelson, *Boys Will Be Girls: The Feminine Ethic and British Children's Fiction, 1857–1917* (New Brunswick: Rutgers University Press, 1991); Jacqueline Rose, *The Case of Peter Pan, or the Impossibility of Children's Fiction* (London: Macmillan, 1984).

11. Edward Salmon, "What the Working Classes Read," *The Nineteenth Century* xx (1886): 108–17; W. M. Gattie, "What English People Read," *Fortnightly Review* xlvi (1889): 307–21; J. Ackland, "Elementary Education and the Decay of Literature," *The Nineteenth Century* xxxv (1894): 412–23; J. G. Leigh, "What the Masses Read," *Economic Review* xiv (1904): 166–79; Florence Low, "The Reading of the Modern Girl," *The Nineteenth Century and After* lix (1906): 278–87.

12. Florence Bell, "What People Read," *Independent Review* 7 (1905): 426–40; Andrew Lang and 'X,' A Working Man, "The Reading Public," *Cornhill Magazine* (1901): 783–95. See also, Tony Davies, "Transports of Pleasure: Fiction and Its Audiences in the Later Nineteenth Century," in *Formations of Pleasure,* ed. Frederic Jameson (London: Routledge, 1983).

13. Those who link literacy and objectivity point out that the printed page frees the mind from memory work, allowing reflection on the ideas and words fixed on the page. See Walter Ong, *Orality and Literacy* (New York: Methuen, 1982); Jack Goody, ed., *Literacy in Traditional Societies* (Cambridge: Cambridge University Press, 1968).

14. Gerd Baumann, ed., *The Written Word: Literacy in Transition* (Oxford: Clarendon Press, 1986); Jeffrey Brooks, *When Russia Learned to Read: Literacy and Popular Literature, 1861–1917* (Princeton: Princeton University Press, 1985); Harvey Graff, *The Literacy Myth* (New York: Academic Press, 1979); Carl Kaestle et al, *Literacy in the United States: Readers and Reading Since 1880* (New Haven: Yale University Press, 1991); David Mitch, *The Rise of Popular Literacy in Victorian England* (Philadelphia: University of Pennsylvania Press, 1992); David Vincent, *Literacy and Popular Culture* (Cambridge: Cambridge University Press, 1989).

15. Children's publishing has reportedly been one of the most profitable divisions in publishing during the past decade: "Van Allsburg's Express: Children's Books Are Big Business," *New York Times,* 24 December 1989, p. 15; "Old Title Reaps New Dollars for Publishers in Children's Books," *New York Times,* 13 June 1994, sec. D, p. 7. These are but a few examples of recent coverage of childhood and education: "Little Big People," *New York Times Magazine,* 10 October 1993, pp. 28–34; "Study Confirms Worst Fears on U.S. Children," *New York Times,* 12 April 1994, sec. A, p. 11; "Can the Schools Stand and Deliver?" *New York Times,* 24 March 1996, p. 4.

Chapter One

1. My study of British working-class autobiography began with John Burnett, David Vincent, and David Myall, eds., *The Autobiography of the Working Class: An Annotated Critical Bibliography,* vol. 2 (New York: New York University Press, 1987). See also, Nan Hackett, *Nineteenth Century British Working-class Autobiographies: An Annotated Bibliography* (New York: AMS Press, 1985); Simon Dentith "Contemporary Working-class Autobiography: Politics of Form, Politics of Content," in *Modern Selves: Essays on Modern British and American Autobiography,* ed. Philip Dodd (London: Frank Cass, 1986).

2. The studies I found most helpful in analyzing the relationship between individual life stories and historical context include John Burnett, *Destiny Obscure: Autobiographies of Childhood, Education, and Family from the 1820s to 1920* (1982; Harmondsworth: Penguin, 1984); Regina Gagnier, *Subjectivities: A History of Self-Representation in Britain, 1832–1920* (New York: Oxford University Press, 1991); Deborah Nord, *The Apprenticeship of Beatrice Webb* (Amherst: University of Massachusetts Press, 1985); Personal Narratives Group, *Interpreting Women's Lives: Feminist Theory and Personal Narratives* (Bloomington: Indiana University Press, 1989); Raphael Samuel and Paul Thompson, *The Myths We Live By* (New York: Routledge, 1990); Carolyn Steedman, *The Radical Soldier's Tale* (London: Routledge, 1988); David Vincent, *Bread, Knowledge and Freedom: A Study in Working-class Autobiography* (London: Europa, 1981). I read Mary Jo Maynes' excellent study, *Taking the Hard Road: Life Course in French and German Workers' Autobiographies in the Era of Industrialization* (Chapel Hill: University of North Carolina Press, 1995), as I was completing revisions of this chapter.

3. Studies of autobiography have proliferated in conjunction with growing interest in the formation of personal identity. See James Goodwin's bibliographic essay in his *Autobiography: The Self Made Text* (New York: Twayne Publishers, 1993). Philippe Lejeune's work, including *On Autobiography,* ed. Paul John Eakin, trans. Katherine Leary (Minneapolis: University of Minnesota Press, 1989), has shaped discussion of autobiography since the 1970s. The debate over how to define autobiography is taken up in the following works: Shari Benstock, ed., *The Private Self: Theory and Practice of Women's Autobiographical Writings* (Chapel Hill: University of North Carolina Press, 1988); Paul John Eakin, *Fictions in Autobiography: Studies in the Art of Self-Invention* (Princeton: Princeton University Press, 1985); Avrom Fleishman, *Figures of Autobiography: The Language of Self-Writing in Victorian and Modern*

England (Berkeley: University of California Press, 1983); Candace Lang, "Autobiography in the Aftermath of Romanticism," *Diacritics,* vol. 12 (1982): 2–16; Roy Pascal, *Design and Truth in Autobiography* (Cambridge: Harvard University Press, 1960); Linda Peterson, *Victorian Autobiography* (New Haven: Yale University Press, 1986); Karl J. Weintraub, "Autobiography and Historical Consciousness," *Critical Inquiry* (June 1975): 821–48. Feminist explorations of how women have been constrained by, and reshaped, autobiographical traditions include Estelle Jelinek, ed., *Women's Autobiography: Essays in Criticism* (Bloomington: Indiana University Press, 1980); Julia Swindells, *Victorian Writing and Working Women* (Cambridge: Polity Press, 1985). The ways in which differences of race, class, gender, and sexuality shape the telling of individual life stories are analyzed in Susan Groag Bell and Marilyn Yalom, eds., *Revealing Lives: Autobiography, Biography and Gender* (Albany: State University of New York Press, 1990); Bella Brodzki and Celeste Schenk, eds., *Life/Lines: Theorizing Women's Autobiography* (Ithaca: Cornell University Press, 1988); Dodd, ed., *Modern Selves;* Gagnier, *Subjectivities;* Françoise Lionnet, *Autobiographical Voices: Race, Gender, Self-portraiture* (Ithaca: Cornell University Press, 1989); Personal Narratives Group, *Interpreting;* Julia Watson, "Towards an Anti-metaphysics of Autobiography," in *The Culture of Autobiography: Constructions of Self-Representation,* ed. Robert Folkenflik (Stanford: Stanford University Press, 1993).

4. Beatrice Webb, *My Apprenticeship* (London: Longmans, Green & Co., 1926), pp. 1–2, 60; J.R. Clynes, *Memoirs* (London: Hutchinson, 1937), pp. 14, 18. Benjamin Tillet also wrote that he was bearing witness for his class in *Memories and Reflections* (London: John Long, 1931), p. 22. Margaret Bondfield, *A Life's Work* (London: Hutchinson, 1949), pp. 9–10; Graham Greene, *A Sort of Life* (New York: Simon & Schuster, 1971), p. 12; Dora Russell, *The Tamarisk Tree* (London: Elek Books, 1975), pp. 9–10.

5. Asquith's nephew edited and abridged her two-volume autobiography after her death. Margot Asquith, *The Autobiography of Margot Asquith* (1962; London: Methuen, 1985), introduction. Thomas Okey, *A Basketful of Memories* (London: J.M. Dent & Sons, 1930), p. v; J. Millot Severn, *The Life Story and Experiences of a Phrenologist* (Brighton: J. M. Severn, 1929), p. ix.

6. For discussions of how memory works, see Eakin, p. 3; Goodwin, pp. 10–12; Richard Johnson et al., *Making Histories: Studies in History-writing and Politics* (London: Hutchinson, 1982), pp. 207, 223–34; Lejeune, p. 171.

7. Arthur Ransome, *The Autobiography of Arthur Ransome* (London: Jonathan Cape, 1976), p. 33; Annie Kenney, *Memories of a Militant* (London: Edward Arnold, 1924), p. 136; Eleanor Acland, *Goodbye for the Present, The Story of Two Childhoods* (London: Hodder & Stoughton, 1935), p. 212; Bondfield, pp. 9–10. Winifred Peck believed her contemporaries' memories of the past were more objective than those of younger generations because they were "undimmed" by psychological theory: Peck, *A Little Learning, or A Victorian Childhood* (London: Faber & Faber, 1952), p. 13.

8. Dodd, ed., *Modern Selves,* pp. 7–8; Gagnier, *Subjectivities,* introduction; Mary Jo Maynes, "Gender and Narrative Form in French and German Working-class Autobiographies," in *Interpreting Women's Lives,* pp. 106–7; Luisa Passerini, "Women's Personal Narratives: Myths, Experiences, and Emotions," in *Interpreting*

Women's Lives, pp. 189–97; Samuel and Thompson, eds., Introduction; Vincent, *Bread, Knowledge and Freedom,* chap. 2.

9. Roy Pascal, *Design and Truth in Autobiography* (Cambridge: Harvard University Press, 1960), chap. 8; Valerie Sanders, *The Private Lives of Victorian Women* (New York: St. Martin's Press, 1989), pp. 55–56.

10. Burnett, *Destiny Obscure,* pp. 15–16; Richard Coe, *When the Grass Was Taller* (New Haven: Yale University Press, 1984), pp. 1–9, 117, 190.

11. Helen Corke, *In Our Infancy, Part I* (Cambridge: Cambridge University Press, 1975), p. 11. Corke and Graham Greene are among the few who use psychoanalytic terms.

12. Leah Manning, *A Life for Education* (London: Victor Gollancz, 1970), p. 23; Ben Turner, *About Myself* (London: Cayme Press, 1930), p. 22. See also Wilfred Wellock, *Off the Beaten Track* (India: Bhargava Bhushan Press, 1963), p. 13.

13. Asquith, p. 16; Emmeline Pethick-Lawrence, *My Part in a Changing World* (London: Victor Gollancz, 1938), p. 32; Clara Grant, *Farthing Bundles* (London: Fern Street Settlement, 1930), p. 3. See also Peck, *A Little Learning,* p. 80; Phyllis Bentley, *O Dreams, O Destinations* (London: Victor Gollancz, 1962), p. 30; Lady Angela Forbes, *Memories and Base Details* (London: Hutchinson, 1921), pp. 55–56. For evaluations of the roles that rebellious self-images play in the life stories of Italian and British working-class women, see Luisa Passerini, "Women's Personal Narratives," in *Interpreting Women's Lives;* and Anna Davin, *Growing Up Poor: Home, School, and Street in London, 1870–1914* (London: Rivers Oram Press, 1996), pp. 80–81.

14. See Katherine Chorley, *Manchester Made Them* (London: Faber & Faber, 1950), p. 11.

15. Severn, chap. 1. For further discussion of British children's first memories, see Burnett, *Destiny Obscure,* pp. 24–25, and Coe, p. 190.

16. Greene, pp. 15–17; Turner, p. 42; George Baldry, *The Rabbit Skin Cap* (London: Collins, 1939), p. 47.

17. Greene, pp. 47–48; Manning, p. 23.

18. Acland, p. 201.

19. Russell, pp. 23–24.

20. Rose Kerrigan in Margaret Cohen, Marion and Hymie Fagan, *Childhood Memories, Recorded by Some Socialist Men and Women in Their Later Years* (London: n.p., n.d.), p. 75 (thanks to Anna Davin for sharing this collection with me); Rev. J. H. Howard, *Winding Lanes* (Caernarvon: The Calvinistic Methodist Printing Works, 1938), p. 31.

21. Frank Benson, quoted in Paul Thompson, *The Edwardians* (London: Weidenfeld & Nicolson, 1975), chap. 9; William Bowyer, *Brought Out in Evidence* (London: Faber & Faber, 1941), p. 61.

22. Angela Rodaway, *A London Childhood* (1960; London: Virago, 1985), pp. 21–23. See Davin's examination of the meaning and costs of respectability, pp. 69–77.

23. Corke, p. 78; Frederick Willis, *Peace and Dripping Toast* (London: Phoenix House, 1950), p. 48. See also Florence Atherton in Thea Thompson, *Edwardian Childhoods* (London: Routledge, 1981), chap. 4.

24. Peck, *A Little Learning,* p. 31.

25. Acland, pp. 89–91.

26. Robert Roberts, *A Ragged Schooling* (London: Fontana, 1982), p. 124; Dorothy Scannell, *Mother Knew Best* (London: Macmillan, 1974), chap. 10; Howard Spring, *Heaven Lies Above Us* (London: Constable, 1939), pp. 12–17. See also, Bondfield, pp. 22–23; and Peck, *A Little Learning,* p. 25. Ellen Ross discusses Scannell's and other working-class fathers in *Love and Toil: Motherhood in Outcast London, 1870–1918* (New York: Oxford University Press, 1993).

27. Philip Ballard, *Things I Cannot Forget* (London: University of London Press, 1937), p. 13.

28. Minnie Bowles in Cohen and Fagan, *Childhood Memories,* p. 7.

29. Philip Inman, *No Going Back* (London: Williams & Norgate, 1952), p. 14. Dorothy Scannell remembered that her mother "was always there when I needed her," p. 32. See Arthur Goffin, "A Grey Life," manuscript, Brunel University Library, n.d.

30. Emma Smith (pseud.), *A Cornish Waif's Story* (New York: E.P. Dutton, 1956); George Meek, *George Meek Bath Chair Man* (London: Constable, 1910).

31. Kathleen Woodward, *Jipping Street* (London: Virago, 1983), pp. 3–20. In her introduction to Woodward's autobiography, Carolyn Steedman argues that Woodward's ambivalent presentation of the mother-daughter relationship undercuts the myth of the working-class mother as martyred saint found in male working-class autobiography. See also Maynes, *Taking,* chap. 3.

32. Asquith, p. 18. See Jane Poynder, quoted in Thea Thompson, p. 216.

33. Webb, pp. 10–12.

34. Sonia Keppel, *Edwardian Daughter* (London: Hamish Hamilton, 1958), p. 18; Pethick-Lawrence, p. 24. See also Greene, pp. 25–26; Chorley, p. 177; and Agnes Hunt, *This Is My Life* (New York: Arno Press, 1980).

35. For analysis of "ancestor myths," see Samuel and Thompson, p. 8. Most common in upper-class autobiographies, genealogies were also used by working-class writers to establish family traditions of respectability or radicalism and by some lower middle-class writers to show that their families had known better times.

36. Corke, p. 18; John Fraser, *Sixty Years in Uniform* (London: Stanley Paul, 1939), p. 18; William Collison, *The Apostle of Free Labour* (London: Hurst & Blackett, 1913), p. 3. See also Lillian M. Faithfull, *In the House of My Pilgrimage* (London: Chatto & Windus), p. 24; and Willis, pp. 17–18.

37. Pethick-Lawrence, pp. 38–47. Maynes argues that working-class women were most likely to find "usable models" of militancy through relatives, in *Taking,* p. 161.

38. Margaret Rhondda, *This Was My World* (London: Macmillan, 1933), p. x, chaps. 12, 13.

39. Russell, pp. 14–15, 29.

40. Acland, pp. 211, 246; Beryl Lee Booker, *Yesterday's Child* (London: J. Long, 1937), pp. 20, 42; Chorley, pp. 21–22, 149.

41. Corke, p. 75; Rose Gibbs, *In Service, Rose Gibbs Remembers* (n.p.: Ellison's Editions, 1981), p. 5; Thomas Morgan, quoted in Thea Thompson, p. 27; Turner, p. 38. See also Davin, chap. 5.

42. Helena M. Swanwick, *I Have Been Young* (London: Victor Gollancz, 1935), pp. 15, 81.

43. Hannah Mitchell, *The Hard Way Up* (London: Faber & Faber, 1968), pp. 42–44. See also Janet Daly, quoted in Jean McCrindle and Sheila Rowbotham, eds., *Dutiful Daughters,* (London: Penguin, 1977), pp. 10–11.

44. Ransome, pp. 38–47; see also, W. F. Bushell, *School Memories* (Liverpool: Philip Son & Nephew, 1962). Regina Gagnier divides public school autobiographies into two types: the "comic" nostalgic and the critical "dissenting," p. 179.

45. Frances Power Cobbe, *The Life of Frances Power Cobbe, as Told by Herself,* vol. 1 (Boston: Houghton, Mifflin, 1894), p. 36; Webb, pp. 49–61; Poynder, in Thea Thompson, p. 225. Deborah Gorham, *The Victorian Girl and the Feminine Ideal* (Bloomington: Indiana University Press, 1982).

46. Peck, *A Little Learning,* p. 12.

47. Russell, p. 29.

48. Vera Brittain, *Testament of Youth* (1933; London: Virago, 1978), chap. 2; Swanwick, chap. 5; Peck, chap. 10. See also Bentley, chap. 4.

49. Phil Gardner, *The Lost Elementary Schools of Victorian England* (London: Croom Helm, 1984); Thomas Laqueur, *Religion and Respectability: Sunday Schools and Working-class Culture, 1780–1850* (New Haven: Yale University Press, 1976).

50. Some writers associated Secular and Socialist Sunday schools with family traditions of political belief. See Annie Davison, quoted in McCrindle and Rowbotham, p. 61; Marion Henery, in Cohen and Fagan, *Childhood Memories;* Turner, pp. 47–49.

51. Gipsy Smith attended school for eight weeks at most: *Gipsy Smith, His Life and Work, by Himself* (London: National Council of Evangelical Free Churches, 1902). For unhappy memories of schooling, see Tillet, p. 42; Baldry, p. 85; Henry Fagan, in Cohen and Fagan, *Childhood Memories,* p. 35. James Griffiths [*Pages from Memory* (London: Dent, 1969), pp. 6–8] and Walter Southgate [*That's the Way It Was* (London: New Clarion Press, 1982), p. 58] were grateful to masters who had encouraged them to read.

52. George Hodgkinson, *Sent to Coventry* (London: Robert Maxwell, 1970), p. 7.

53. Gibbs, p. 1; Fraser, p. 30.

54. Clynes, *Memoirs;* Kenney, p. 14; Clifford Hills, in Thea Thompson, chap. 2.

55. Fred Kitchen, *Brother to the Ox* (1940; Sussex: Caliban Books, 1981), pp. 12, 18; Patrick MacGill, *Children of the Dead End* (1914; Berkshire: Caliban Books, 1980), chaps. 5, 8; Mitchell, pp. 48–49.

56. A. L. Rowse, *A Cornish Childhood* (New York: MacMillan, 1947), pp. 125–27; Rodaway, pp. 56, 65, 69, 123–27. The Education Act of 1902 extended government control over secondary and technical schools. In 1907, all grant-aided secondary schools were required to keep a quarter of their places open to pupils from state elementary schools.

57. Acland, p. 144. Gwen Raverat, *Period Piece* (London: Faber & Faber, 1952), pp. 52, 103.

58. Bentley, p. 11; Russell, p. 9; Pethick-Lawrence, chap. 23.

59. Dora Montefiore, *From a Victorian to a Modern* (London: E. Archer, 1927), p. 11; Manning, p. 43.

60. Turner, p. 23; William Martin Haddow, *My Seventy Years* (Glasgow: Robert Gibson & Sons, 1943), p. 77; Alice Rushmer, quoted in Mary Chamberlain, *Fen Women* (London: Virago, 1975), p. 84.

61. Clynes, *Memoirs,* pp. 17, 25–26.

62. Clynes, *When I Remember,* Macmillan War Pamphlets # 6 (1940), p. 31.

63. Willis, p. 59; Jeremy Seabrook, *The Unprivileged* (Harmondsworth: Penguin, 1973), p. 147. See also Chorley, pp. 152–53.

64. Gladys Otterspoon, in Chamberlain, p. 33; H. M. Tomlinson, *A Mingled Yarn* (London: Gerald Duckworth, 1953), p. 12. For discussions of nostalgia, see David Lowenthal, *The Past Is a Foreign Country* (Cambridge: Cambridge University Press, 1985); Johnson, *Making Histories.*

65. William Belcher, manuscript (n.d.), and Daisy Cowper, manuscript (1964), Brunel University Library.

66. Baldry, pp. 93, 212.

67. Peck, pp. 11–12; Rhondda, p. 8.

68. Russell, pp. 23–24.

69. Bentley, pp. 34, 44–54.

70. Albert Mansbridge, *The Trodden Road* (London: Dent, 1940), p. 14.

71. Mary Jo Maynes analyzes similar working-class narratives of childhood deprivation in *Taking.* See also Vincent, *Bread,* pp. 87, 91, 107.

72. Lord Snell, *Men, Movements and Myself* (London: Dent, 1936), p. 12; Clynes, Memoirs, p. 28; Emma Smith, *Cornish Waif.* See also Tillet, pp. 22–25; and Rowse, pp. 93, 96.

73. Clynes, *Memoirs,* p. 32; MacGill, chaps. 5, 6; Hymie Fagan, in Cohen and Fagan, *Childhood Memories,* p. 43.

74. Manning; Raverat, pp. 237, 281; Corke, p. 62. For analyses of changing ideas about adolescence, see John Gillis, *Youth and History* (New York: Academy Press, 1974); John Springhall, *Coming of Age: Adolescence in Britain, 1860–1960* (Dublin: Gill & Macmillan, 1986); Carol Dyhouse, *Girls Growing Up in Late Victorian and Edwardian England* (London: Routledge, 1981); and Gorham, chap. 5.

75. Bentley, p. 138, chaps. 14, 15.

76. L. E. Jones, *A Victorian Boyhood* (London: Macmillan, 1955), p. 83.

77. Anthony Powell, *Infants of the Spring* (New York: Holt, Rinehart & Winston, 1976), p. 19; Chorley, p. 12.

78. See Coe, pp. 1–9, 117.

79. A. E. Coppard, *It's Me, O Lord* (London: Methuen, 1957), p. 22.

Chapter Two

1. Sonia Keppel, *Edwardian Daughter* (London: Hamish Hamilton, 1958), p. 14.

2. Michael Denning, *Mechanic Accents* (London: Verso, 1987).

3. Michelle Perrot, ed., *A History of Private Life: From the Fires of the Revolution to the Great War,* vol. iv, trans. Arthur Goldhammer (Cambridge, MA.: Belknap Press, 1990), p. 537. David Vincent, *Literacy and Popular Culture* (Cambridge: Cam-

bridge University Press, 1989); Richard Altick, *The English Common Reader* (Chicago: University of Chicago Press, 1957); John Halverson, "Havelock on Greek Orality and Literacy," *Journal of the History of Ideas,* 53, no. 1 (1992), pp. 148–63; Carl Kaestle, ed., *Literacy in the United States: Readers and Reading Since 1880* (New Haven: Yale University Press, 1991); David Mitch, *The Rise of Popular Literacy in Victorian England* (Philadelphia: University of Pennsylvania Press, 1992). James Goodwin reviews the literacy debate in *Autobiography: The Self Made Text* (New York: Twayne Publishers, 1993).

4. Nellie Priest, *The Island: Life and Death of a East London Community, 1870–1970* (London: Centerprise, 1979). Thanks to Anna Davin for giving me access to this book. Annie Wilson, in Thea Thompson, *Edwardian Childhoods* (London: Routledge, 1981), pp. 91–92. Winifred Peck, *A Little Learning, or A Victorian Childhood* (London: Faber & Faber, 1952), p. 20. See also Jeffrey Brooks, *When Russia Learned to Read* (Princeton: Princeton University Press, 1985).

5. Bob Stewart, *Breaking the Fetters* (London: Lawrence & Wishart, 1967), p. 14; Thomas Bell, *Pioneering Days* (London: Lawrence & Wishart, 1941), pp. 15–16; Katherine Chorley, *Manchester Made Them* (London: Faber & Faber, 1950), p. 62. See also Margaret Cohen, Marion and Hymie Fagan, eds., *Childhood Memories, Recorded by Some Socialist Men and Women in Their Later Years* (London: n.p., n.d.), p. 27; Hannah Mitchell, *The Hard Way Up* (London: Faber & Faber, 1968), p. 27; A. E. Coppard, *It's Me, O Lord* (London: Methuen, 1957), p. 50; H. M. Tomlinson, *A Mingled Yarn* (London: Gerald Duckworth, 1953), p. 11. David Vincent discusses the "emotional language" autobiographers use to write about reading in *Literacy,* p. 196.

6. Fred Kitchen, *Brother to the Ox* (1940; Sussex: Caliban Books, 1981), pp. 16–17; Beatrice Webb, *My Apprenticeship* (London: Longmans, Green & Co., 1926), p. 58; Peck, *A Little Learning,* pp. 44–45; Frank Steel, *Ditcher's Row* (London: Sidgwick & Jackson, 1939), pp. 45–46.

7. Graham Greene, *A Sort of Life* (New York: Simon & Schuster, 1971), p. 18; Dorothy Scannell, *Mother Knew Best* (London: Macmillan, 1974), pp. 109–11.

8. William Bowyer, *Brought Out in Evidence* (London: Faber & Faber, 1941), p. 66. In *The Camels Must Go* (London: Faber & Faber, 1961), p. 22, Sir Reader Bullard remembered his aunt's house as a place without books.

9. Patrick MacGill, *Children of the Dead End* (1914; Berkshire: Caliban Books, 1980), p. 40.

10. Lillian Faithfull, *In the House of My Pilgrimage* (London: Chatto & Windus, 1925), p. 34; Bullard, p. 28. Claudia Nelson, *Boys Will Be Girls: The Feminine Ethic and British Children's Fiction* (New Brunswick: Rutgers University Press, 1991).

11. George Meek, *George Meek Bath Chair Man* (London: Constable, 1910), pp. 50–51; J. R. Clynes, *Memoirs* (London: Hutchinson, 1937), pp. 30–32.

12. See Thomas Okey, *A Basketful of Memories* (London: J. M. Dent & Sons, 1930), pp. 17–21; Jeremy Seabrook, *The Unprivileged* (Harmondsworth: Penguin, 1973), pp. 31–32; Lord Snell, *Men, Movements and Myself* (London: J. M. Dent & Sons, 1936), p. 15.

13. Jonas Frykman and Orvar Lofgren, *Culture Builders, An Historical Anthropology of Middle Class Life,* trans. Alan Crozier (New Brunswick: Rutgers University Press, 1987); Perrot, p. 263.

14. Agnes Cowper, *A Backward Glance on Merseyside* (Birkenhead: Wilmer Bros., 1948, 1952), p. 49; Minnie Bowles, in Cohen and Fagan, *Childhood Memories,* p. 6; William Haddow, *My Seventy Years* (Glasgow: Robert Gibson & Sons, 1943), pp. 11–12. See also Annie Kenney, *Memories of a Militant* (London: Edward Arnold, 1924), pp. 6–7.

15. Howard Spring, *Heaven Lies Above Us* (London: Constable, 1939), pp. 11, 50–51.

16. Greene, p. 18.

17. Faithfull, p. 34.

18. Robert Blatchford, *A Book About Books* (London: Clarion Press, 1903), p. 102; Arthur Ransome, *The Autobiography of Arthur Ransome* (London: Jonathan Cape, 1976), pp. 35–37; J. M. Barrie, *Margaret Ogilvy* (New York, Scribner's, 1901), pp. 47–50; Steel, pp. 39–40.

19. Katherine Chorley, *Manchester Made Them* (London: Faber & Faber, 1950), pp. 16–17, 152–53.

20. Philip Inman, *No Going Back* (London: Williams & Norgate, 1952), p. 25; Mitchell, p. 50.

21. Minnie Bowles, in Cohen and Fagan, *Childhood Memories,* p. 6.

22. Robert Roberts, *A Ragged Schooling* (London: Fontana, 1982), pp. 31, 154; Beatrice Webb, *My Apprenticeship* (London: Longmans, Green & Co., 1926), chap. 1.

23. Vera Brittain, *Testament of Youth* (1933; U.S.A.: Wideview Books, 1980), pp. 23–25.

24. See Geoffrey Brady, in Thea Thompson, *Edwardian,* pp. 131–32.

25. Terry Eagleton, *The Function of Criticism* (London: Verso, 1984).

26. Meek, p. 45; Steel, p. 111; Rev. J. H. Howard, *Winding Lanes* (Caernarvon: The Calvinistic Methodist Printing Works, 1938), pp. 27–30; Beryl Lee Booker, *Yesterday's Child* (London: J. Long, 1937), p. 43.

27. Grace Fulford and Frank Benson, quoted in Paul Thompson, *The Edwardians* (London: Weidenfeld & Nicolson, 1975), pp. 92, 130; Walter Southgate, *That's The Way It Was* (London: New Clarion Press, 1982), p. 57.

28. Helena M. Swanwick, *I Have Been Young* (London: Victor Gollancz, 1935), pp. 82–83; Chorley, p. 202; Leah Manning, *A Life for Education* (London: Victor Gollancz, 1970),p. 17; Webb, p. 10.

29. Raymond Firth, *Symbols, Public and Private* (Ithaca: Cornell University Press, 1973); John R. Gillis, *A World of Their Own Making: Myth, Ritual, and the Quest for Family Values* (New York: Basic Books, 1996), chap. 4.

30. Ransome, p. 37.

31. See A. L. Rowse, *A Cornish Childhood* (New York: Macmillan, 1947), p. 201.

32. See M. K. Ashby, *Joseph Ashby of Tysoe* (Cambridge: Cambridge University Press, 1961), p. 207; Flora Thompson, *Lark Rise to Candleford* (London: Oxford University Press, 1939), p. 31.

33. Mitchell, pp. 44, 49.

34. The Bethnal Green Museum of Childhood houses a wonderful picture of a Board school student standing proudly next to a table piled high with her prize books and certificates of merit.

35. Edward Brown, manuscript, Brunel University Library, n.d., p. 38; Bowyer, p. 93.

36. MacGill, p. 138; Scannell, pp. 109–10; Angela Rodaway, *A London Childhood* (1960; London: Virago, 1985), p. 60.

37. J. Millot Severn, *The Life Story and Experiences of a Phrenologist* (Brighton: J. M. Severn, 1929), pp. 47–48; Clynes, *Memoirs,* p. 36; William Collison, *The Apostle of Free Labour* (London: Hurst & Blackett, 1913), p. 42.

38. See Okey, pp. 18–19.

39. Scannell, pp. 83, 104–11; Mitchell, pp. 42–52; William Lovett, *The Life and Struggles of William Lovett* (1876; New York: Garland Publishers, 1984), p. 21; Hymie Fagan, in Cohen and Fagan, *Childhood Memories,* pp. 27, 39–41.

40. Ben Turner, *About Myself* (London: Cayme Press, 1930), p. 27.

41. Howard, p. 29; Inman, p. 12; Kerrigan, in Cohen and Fagan, *Childhood Memories,* p. 75.

42. Mary Jo Maynes, *Taking the Hard Road* (Chapel Hill: University of North Carolina Press, 1995), chap. 1.

43. Clynes, *Memoirs,* pp. 32–34; Fagan, in Cohen and Fagan, *Childhood Memories,* p. 43.

44. George Hodgkinson, *Sent to Coventry* (London: Robert Maxwell, 1970), p. 24.

45. Snell, p. 43.

46. MacGill, p. 136; Ben Tillet, *Memories and Reflections* (London: John Long, 1931), pp. 76, 81.

47. Snell, p. 55. See also David Vincent, *Bread, Knowledge and Freedom: A Study of Working-class Autobiography,* (London: Europa, 1981), chap. 2; and Stephen Yeo, "A New Life: The Religion of Socialism in Britain, 1883–1896," *History Workshop* 4 (Autumn 1977): 5–56.

48. Gipsy Smith, *Gipsy Smith, His Life and Work by Himself* (London: National Council of the Evangelical Free Churches, 1902), p. 75.

49. Margaret Bondfield, *A Life's Work* (London: Hutchinson, 1949), p. 29; James Griffiths, *Pages from Memory* (London: J. M. Dent, 1969), pp. 11–14. See also John Wilson, *Memories of a Labour Leader* (London: T. Fisher Unwin, 1910).

50. Okey, *Basketful;* A. L. Rowse made a similar journey into academic life. Kitchen, pp. 73–74. In *Sixty Years in Uniform* (London: Stanley Paul, 1939), John Fraser describes beginning to read seriously in the company of two fellow soldiers in India. J. Millot Severn's self-education led to a career in phrenology.

51. Margaret Llewelyn Davis, ed., *Life as We Have Known It* (1931; New York: W. W. Norton, 1975).

52. Bondfield, pp. 27–28; Clara Grant, *Farthing Bundles* (London: Fern Street Settlement, 1930), p. 43. On the borderline between the working class and the lower middle class, both women's families sent them to private schools for portions of their educations.

53. Vincent, *Bread,* pp. 120–22; E. P. Thompson, *The Making of the English Working Class* (New York: Vintage Books, 1963).

54. Born in 1895, Philip Inman remembered that his family only switched from candles to oil lamps after he began working: Inman, *No Going Back* (London: Williams & Norgate, 1952), pp. 36–37. Ben Tillet believed that he might have been a writer, instead of a speaker, if he had had more time to study: Tillet, p. 81.

55. Vincent, *Bread,* p. 3.

56. Margaret Rhondda, *This Was My World* (London: Macmillan, 1933), pp. 102–3; Emmeline Pethick-Lawrence, *My Part in a Changing World* (London: Victor Gollancz, 1938), pp. 64–65; Swanwick, chap. 3.

57. Pethick-Lawrence, p. 66; Swanwick, pp. 80–81.

58. Rhondda, pp. 119, 125.

59. Rhondda, pp. 128–29; Swanwick, pp. 183–87; Bondfield, p. 77.

Chapter Three

1. W. T. Stead, "The Maiden Tribute of Modern Babylon," *Pall Mall Gazette,* 4 July 1885, p. 10. My understanding of this series as a melodramatic narrative of sexual identity is indebted to Judith R. Walkowitz's *City of Dreadful Delight: Narratives of Sexual Danger in Late-Victorian London* (Chicago: University of Chicago Press, 1992).

2. Walkowitz, pp. 82, 115.

3. Miss E. Barlee, *Pantomime Waifs, or A Plea for Our City Children* (London: S. W. Partridge, 1884), preface, chap. 7, p. 272.

4. Kimberley Reynolds, *Girls Only? Gender and Popular Children's Fiction in Britain, 1880–1910* (Philadelphia: Temple University Press, 1990), pp. xvi–xix. See also, Michael Denning, *Mechanic Accents: Dime Novels and Working-class Culture in America* (London: Verso, 1987).

5. For discussions of anxieties about racial degeneration, see Deborah Dwork, *War Is Good for Babies and Other Young Children* (London: Tavistock Publications, 1987); Thomas Jordan, *The Degeneracy Crisis and Victorian Youth* (Albany: State University of New York Press, 1993). For the history of nineteenth-century popular culture and upper-class anxieties about it, see Stuart Hall, "The Discovery of Popular Culture," in Raphael Samuel, ed., *People's History and Socialist Theory,* (London: Routledge, 1981); Peter Bailey, *Leisure and Class in Victorian England* (Toronto: University of Toronto Press, 1978); Alan J. Lee, *The Origins of the Popular Press* (London: Croom Helm, 1976).

6. For analyses of the idea of reading as consumption, see Janice Radway, *Reading the Romance* (Chapel Hill: University of North Carolina Press, 1984), p. 6; David Mitch, *The Rise of Popular Literacy in Victorian England* (Philadelphia: University of Pennsylvania Press, 1992); Michel de Certeau, *The Practice of Everyday Life,* trans. Steven F. Rendell (Berkeley: University of California Press, 1984), chap. XII.

7. Ann Ackerman, "Victorian Ideology and British Children's Literature, 1850–1914" Ph.D. diss., University of North Texas, 1984; Gillian Avery, *Childhood's Patterns, A Study of Heroes and Heroines of Children's Fiction* (London: Hodder and

Stoughton, 1975); Mary Cadogan and Patricia Craig, *You're A Brick, Angela* (London: Victor Gollancz, 1976); James Fraser, ed., *Society and Children's Literature* (Boston: David R. Godine, 1978); Mary V. Jackson, *Engines of Instruction, Mischief and Magic* (Lincoln: University of Nebraska Press, 1989), p. xi.

8. Louis James, "Tom Brown's Imperialist Sons," *Victorian Studies* xviii (September 1973): 89–99.

9. For discussions of this "golden age," see Gillian Avery, *Nineteenth Century Children: Heroes and Heroines in English Children's Stories, 1780–1900* (London: Hodder & Stoughton, 1965), chaps. 6–8; Julia Briggs, *A Woman of Passion: The Life of E. Nesbit, 1858–1924* (New York: New Amsterdam Books, 1987), p. 401; Humphrey Carpenter, *Secret Gardens: The Golden Age of Children's Literature* (Boston: Houghton, Mifflin, 1985); Harvey Darton, *Children's Books in England,* rev. ed., Brian Alderson, ed. (Cambridge: Cambridge University Press, 1982), pp. 296–303, 314–18; M. F. Thwaite, *From Primer to Pleasure* (London: The Library Association, 1963), chap. 4. In *The Image of Childhood* (1957; Harmondsworth: Penguin, 1967), Peter Coveney distinguishes early nineteenty-century Romantic depictions of childhood from the sentimentalized children depicted in late nineteenth-century stories for children.

10. Claudia Nelson, *Boys Will Be Girls: The Feminine Ethic and British Children's Fiction, 1857–1917* (New Brunswick: Rutgers University Press, 1991), p. 1.

11. Nelson, pp. 4, 142–43, 148–49.

12. Kirsten Drotner, *English Children and Their Magazines, 1751–1945* (New Haven: Yale University Press, 1988); Zohar Shavit, *The Poetics of Children's Literature* (Athens: University of Georgia Press, 1986); Jane Tompkins, *Sensational Designs: The Cultural Work of American Fiction* (New York: Oxford University Press, 1985).

13. Henry Mayhew had stressed the precocity of the poor children he observed in *London Labour and the London Poor,* vol. 1 (reprint; New York: Augustus Kelley, 1967), pp. 61–68.

14. See Deborah Gorham, "'The Maiden Tribute of Modern Babylon' Reexamined: Child Prostitution and the Idea of Childhood in Late Victorian England," *Victorian Studies* (Spring 1978): 353–79.

15. E. M. Field, *The Child and His Book,* 2nd ed. (London: Wells, Gardner, Darton, 1895), p. 8; Alfred Ainger, "The Children's Books of a Hundred Years Ago," *Lectures and Essays* (1895), reprinted in Lance Salway, ed., *A Peculiar Gift* (Harmondsworth: Penguin, 1976), p. 74. See Jacqueline Rose, *The Case of Peter Pan, or The Impossibility of Children's Fiction* (London: Macmillan, 1984).

16. Joshua Meyrowitz, "The Adultlike Child and the Childlike Adult: Socialization in an Electronic Age," *Daedalus* 113, no. 3 (Summer 1984): 19–47. For discussions of how the construction of childhood was about the formation of adult identities, see Reynolds, *Girls Only?;* Rose, *The Case of Peter Pan;* Carolyn Steedman, *Strange Dislocations: Childhood and the Idea of Human Interiority, 1780–1930* (Cambridge: Harvard University Press, 1995).

17. Gaye Tuchman and Nina E. Fortin, *Edging Women Out: Victorian Novelists, Publishers, and Social Change* (New Haven: Yale University Press, 1989).

18. Raymond Williams, *Culture and Society: 1750–1950* (1958; New York: Columbia University Press, 1983). Robert Colls and Philip Dodd, eds., *Englishness, Politics and Culture, 1880–1920* (London: Croom Helm, 1986).

19. Terry Eagleton, *The Function of Criticism* (London: Verso, 1984), pp. 45–46; Marjory Lang, "Childhood's Champions: Mid-Victorian Children's Periodicals and the Critics," *Victorian Periodicals Review,* vol. 13 (1980): 17–31; Reynolds, p. 23.

20. "Children's Literature," *London Quarterly Review* (1860), reprinted in Salway.

21. Edward Salmon, *Juvenile Literature As It Is* (London: Henry Drake, 1888), p. 154. See also John Hepburn Millar, "On Some Books for Boys and Girls," *Blackwood's Magazine* (1896); Eveline C. Godley, "A Century of Children's Books," *The National Review* (1906); both are reprinted in Salway.

22. "Children's Literature," in Salway, p. 302.

23. Robert Blatchford, *A Book About Books* (London: Clarion Press, 1903), pp. 184–90.

24. J. Newby Hetherington, "The Use of Fairy Tales in the Education of the Young," *The Journal of Education,* XIX (1897), in Salway, p. 148; Salmon, p. 225.

25. See Rose, pp. 8–9.

26. John Ruskin, "Fairy Stories" (1868), in Salway, pp. 127–32; Hetherington, in Salway, p. 147.

27. Field, p. 257; Salmon, p. 227. See also, R. E. D. Sketchley, "Some Children's Book Illustrators," *The Library* (October 1902), in Salway, pp. 260–80.

28. Marjory Lang, p. 30.

29. "Juvenile Literature," *British Quarterly Review* XLVII (1868), quoted in Marjory Lang, p. 20; Field, p. 8.

30. Charles Dickens, "Frauds on the Fairies," *Household Words* (1853), in Salway, p. 111; Ruskin, in Salway, p. 129; Salmon, pp. 207–8; Walter Crane, Cantor Lecture (1879), quoted in Field, pp. 312–13.

31. Hetherington, in Salway, pp. 148–49.

32. Hetherington, in Salway, p. 149; "Children's Literature," in Salway, p. 311; E. Nesbit, *Wings and the Child* (London: Hodder & Stoughton, 1913), p. 72.

33. Field, p. 202.

34. Andrew Lang, *Adventures Among Books* (London: Longmans, 1905), pp. 7, 11.

35. Hetherington, in Salway, pp. 150–51; Salmon, p. 232.

36. Margaret McMillan, *Early Childhood* (London: Swan Sonnenschein, 1900), pp. 101, 112.

37. Alfred Ainger, "The Children's Books of a Hundred Years Ago," in Salway, p. 75.

38. Field, p. 347.

39. Barlee, p. 12.

40. Salmon, pp. 184, 192–98, 233–38.

41. Salmon, pp. 184, 192–98, 233–38.

42. Molesworth raised her five children alone after separating from her mentally disturbed army officer husband. From 1887, when her youngest son was fourteen,

until 1892, Molesworth wrote as many as eight books a year, and up to three books a year until 1911. See Roger Lancelyn Green, *Mrs. Molesworth* (1961; New York: Henry Z. Walck, 1964), pp. 24, 46–47, 73–80.

43. Alexander Shand, "Children Yesterday and Today," *The Quarterly Review* (1896), reprinted in Salway, p. 90; Salmon, p. 199.

44. Salmon, quoted in Green, *Mrs. Molesworth*, p. 53; and Salmon, *Juvenile*, p. 180. Molesworth wrote "naturally, lightly, and pleasantly," according to literary historian Harvey Darton in *Children's Books in England.* See also Sketchley, in Salway, p. 264.

45. Molesworth, "How I Write My Children's Stories," *Little Folks* (hereafter, *LF*), vol. 40 (1894): 16.

46. Mrs. Molesworth, *Studies and Stories,* reprinted in Salway, p. 199.

47. Molesworth, "On the Art of Writing Fiction for Children," *Atalanta* vi (1893), reprinted in Salway, pp. 340–46; Molesworth, "How I Write My Children's Stories, *LF,* vol. 40 (1894): 18–19.

48. Molesworth, *LF,* vol. 40: 16.

49. Mrs. Molesworth, "The Palace in the Garden," *LF,* vol. 23 (1896).

50. Molesworth, "Sheila's Mystery," *LF,* vol. 39 (1894). Regina Gagnier discusses this "suture" of the character's, author's, and intended reader's viewpoints in *Subjectivities, A History of Self-Representation in Britain, 1832–1920* (New York: Oxford University Press, 1991), pp. 113, 137. See also Michael Denning's analysis of ideology and narrative structure in *Cover Stories* (London: Routledge, 1987).

51. L. T. Meade, "A Madcap," *LF,* vol. 49 (1899). Edward Salmon praised Meade's depictions of "baby ways" and parent-child relations. Salmon, pp. 176–79.

52. During the late 1880s, Wilde also wrote reviews for W. T. Stead's *Pall Mall Gazette.* Richard Ellmann, *Oscar Wilde* (New York: Alfred A. Knopf, 1988), pp. 286, 299.

53. Wilde's letter is quoted in Ackerman, p. 121.

54. Oscar Wilde, *The Works of Oscar Wilde* (New York: Lamb Publishing, 1909), p. 171.

55. Wilde, *Works,* p. 175.

56. Wilde, *Works,* pp. 182–83.

57. Rupert Hart-Davis, ed., *The Letters of Oscar Wilde* (New York: Harcourt, Brace & World, 1962), pp. 218–19.

58. "Books for the Young," *The Athenaeum,* no. 3175 (1888), p. 286.

59. Hart-Davis, p. 219. During his undergraduate days at Oxford, Wilde had been influenced by both Pater and John Ruskin. Ellmann, p. 47

60. Ellmann, pp. 303–25.

61. Wilde wrote to the Editor of the *Pall Mall Gazette* (Stead's successor) that his paper's reviewer been silly to ask whether the book was meant for children. "I had as much intention of pleasing the British child as I had of pleasing the British public. . . . No artist recognizes any standard of beauty but that which is suggested by his own temperament." Quoted in Hart-Davis, pp. 301–2.

62. Nelson suggests that Wilde's fairy tales, like his trial, "cast doubt on the innocence of androgyny," hitherto an ideal in children's literature. Nelson, pp. 164–65.

63. Salmon, pp. 181–83.

64. Regina Gagnier argues that Wilde exacerbated a late nineteenth-century "crisis of the male" by embracing the image of the idle, beauty-loving "dandy" in opposition to a middle-class masculinity based on sober industriousness. Regina Gagnier, *Idylls of the Marketplace: Oscar Wilde and the Victorian Public* (Stanford: Stanford University Press, 1986), see especially pp. 51, 93.

65. W. T. Stead, quoted in Lee, p. 29. The successful series lasted into the 1920s and was later reissued. See Joyce Whalley and Tessa Chester, *A History of Children's Book Illustration* (London: John Murray, 1988), p. 127.

66. W. T. Stead, *Books for the Bairns,* vol. 1, no. 7 (1898), preface.

67. Dora Russell, *The Tamarisk Tree* (London: Elek Books, 1975), p. 27; Leah Manning, *A Life For Education* (London: Victor Gollancz, 1970), p. 17; Phyllis Bentley, *O Dreams, O Destinations* (London: Victor Gollancz, 1962), p. 38.

68. Oscar Wilde, Letter to the Editor of the *Daily Chronicle* 27 May, 1897, in Hart-Davis, *Letters,* pp. 568–74; Ellmann, p. 523.

Chapter Four

1. John Gillis, *Youth and History* (New York: Academic Press, 1974); Kirsten Drotner, *English Children and Their Magazines, 1751–1945* (New Haven: Yale University Press, 1988); Harvey Darton, *Children's Books in England,* rev. ed., Brian Alderson, ed. (Cambridge: Cambridge University Press, 1982), pp. 265–71.

2. See Diana Dixon, "Children and the Press, 1866–1914," in Michael Harris and Alan Lee, eds., *The Press in English Society from the 17th to the 19th Centuries* (Cranbury, N.J.: Associated University Presses, 1986).

3. *Little Folks* (hereafter referred to as *LF*), vol. 1 (1871): 1.

4. *LF,* vol. 3 (1872): 1.

5. Christopher P. Wilson, "The Rhetoric of Consumption: Mass-market Magazines and the Demise of the Gentle Reader, 1880–1920," in Richard Wightman Fox and Jackson Lears, eds., *The Culture of Consumption* (New York: Pantheon Books, 1983); Kathryn Shevelow, "Fathers and Daughters: Women as Readers of the *Tatler,*" in Elizabeth Flynn and Patrocinio Schweickart, eds., *Gender and Reading* (Baltimore: Johns Hopkins University Press, 1986).

6. *LF* editors included Bonavia Hunt, with Clara Matiauz, 1871–75; George Wetherley, 1870–80; Ernest Foster, 1880–94; Sam H. Hamer, 1894–?. See Simon Nowell-Smith, *The House of Cassell,* 1848–1958 (London: Cassell, 1958). In contrast, the even longer running *Children's Own Magazine* (1854–1930s), published by the Anglican Sunday School Union, had several editorial voices, sometimes within a single issue. With its established audience of Sunday scholars, it had less need of a unified editorial persona.

7. *LF,* vol. 1 (1871).

8. *LF,* vol. 3 (1872): 1.

9. *LF,* vol. 8 (1874), final page.

10. *LF,* vol. 41 (1895): p. 61. John Gillis discusses the construction of fathers as gift-givers in "Bringing Up Father: British Paternal Identities, 1750–Present," a

paper presented at the Rutgers Center for Historical Analysis in 1990. See also Raymond Firth, *Symbols, Public and Private* (Ithaca: Cornell University Press, 1973).

11. *LF,* vol. 24 (1886): 380.

12. See *LF,* vol. 41 (1895): 428. Mrs. Molesworth, for example, serialized many of her stories in *LF,* then published them as books, often with Cassell. The fame from her books then made her a bigger draw as a contributor to the magazine.

13. *LF,* vol. 42 (1895): 428.

14. *LF,* vol. 43 (1896): 120.

15. *LF,* vol. 45 (1897): 1–2.

16. Gillis, "Bringing Up Father," pp. 32–34. Dixon, p. 147, sees a general shift in the tone of children's magazines during these years.

17. See for example *LF,* vol. 4 (1872): 151.

18. *LF,* vol. 8 (1874): 1.

19. *LF,* vol. 1, New Series (1875), final page.

20. *LF,* vol. 8, New Series (1878): 63, 127–28.

21. *LF,* vol. 8 (1878): 127–28; the discussion continued in vols. 9 and 10.

22. *LF,* vol. 27 (1888): 68.

23. *LF,* vol. 27 (1888): 215.

24. *LF,* vol. 47 (1897): 135, 148.

25. *Little Folks* was published in London, New York, and Paris.

26. Lady Angela Forbes, *Memories and Base Details* (London: Hutchinson, 1921), p. 132.

27. *LF,* vol. 46 (1897): 132; volume 49 (1899): 158.

28. *LF,* vol. 43 (1896): 156; vol. 46 (1897): 75; vol. 47 (1898): 396; vol. 59 (1904): 316.

29. *LF,* vol. 28 (1888): 143.

30. *LF,* vol. 28 (1888): 69.

31. See Leonore Davidoff and Catherine Hall, *Family Fortunes: Men and Women of the English Middle Class, 1750–1850* (Chicago: University of Chicago Press, 1987), pp. 348–53.

32. *LF,* vol. 28 (1888): 426; vol. 34 (1891): 215; vol. 48 (1898): 475.

33. *LF,* vol. 4 (1876): 416; vol. 15 (1882): 112.

34. *LF,* vol. 47 (1898): 319; vol. 48 (1898): 75. Unfortunately, the Swedish girl who wrote that she would "like to be a boy" did not explain her reasons (vol. 27 (1888): 359).

35. *LF,* vol. 45 (1897): 476.

36. *LF,* vol. 43 (1896): 469; vol. 45 (1897): 398.

37. *LF,* vol. 59 (1904): 65.

38. *LF,* vol. 44 (1896): 154, 473; vol. 45 (1897): 398.

39. *LF,* vol. 42 (1895): 131; vol. 46 (1897): 316.

40. Margaret Rhondda, *This Was My World* (London: Macmillan, 1933), pp. 13, 38.

41. "Little Ones of the Streets," *LF,* vols. 17, 18 (1883). See also "The Lancashire Mill Girl," *LF,* vol. 6 (1873); "Little Toilers," *LF,* vol. 20 (1884); and *LF,* vol. 49 (1899).

42. Deborah Gorham, "'The Maiden Tribute of Modern Babylon' Reexamined: Child Prostitution and the Idea of Childhood in Late Victorian England," *Victorian Studies* (Spring 1978): 353–79.

43. F. K. Prochaska, *Women and Philanthropy in 19th Century England* (New York: Oxford University Press, 1980), chap. 3; Gareth Stedman Jones, *Outcast London* (Oxford: Oxford University Press, 1971), chap. 13.

44. For discussion of other children's magazine charities, see Dixon, p. 143.

45. *LF*, vol. 1, New Series (1875), final page.

46. From 1886 on, the age categories were 9 and under, 10 to 13, and 14 to 16.

47. The editor reported in 1879 (vol. 10: 380) that thousands of painted books had been sent in, and in 1897 (vol. 45: 1) that 100 large parcels had been sent to the hospital.

48. *LF*, New Series, vol. 5 (1877): 250; vol. 7 (1878): 252.

49. *LF*, New Series, vol. 7 (1877): 188.

50. *LF*, vol. 31 (1890): 135; vol. 33 (1891): 134; vol. 39 (1893): 137.

51. *LF*, vol. 11 (1880): 47–49.

52. *LF*, vol. 11 (1880): 123, 375.

53. Jonas Frykman and Orvar Lofgren, *Culture Builders, An Historical Anthropology of Middle Class Life,* trans. Alan Crozier (New Brunswick: Rutgers University Press, 1987); Harriet Ritvo, *The Animal Estate* (Cambridge: Harvard University Press, 1987).

54. *LF*, vol. 15 (1882): 49–50, 118.

55. *LF*, vol. 15 (1882): 184–6, 374; vol. 16 (1882): 52–62; vol. 20 (1884): 373. A thousand new members joined during a membership drive in 1897.

56. *LF*, vol. 13 (1881): 122; vol. 15 (1882): 119, 302; vol. 16 (1882): 47–8, 62.

57. *LF*, vol. 15 (1882): 302; vol. 18 (1883): 246.

58. The essay topic for 1904 was "My Favourite Character in History."

59. *LF*, vol. 59 (1904): 20–6, 125.

60. Davidoff and Hall, pp. 29–30.

61. See John Barr, *Illustrated Children's Books* (London: The British Library, 1986); Joyce Irene Whalley and Tessa Rose Chester, *A History of Children's Book Illustration* (London: John Murray, 1988).

62. Grandpa's Little Darling," *LF*, vol. 1 (New Series, 1875). Vol. 46 (1897) features "Cherubs," by Joshua Reynolds, and a poem describing their "lovely and radiant angel faces."

63. John Ruskin, "Fairy Land: Mrs. Allingham and Kate Greenaway," from *The Art of England: Lectures given in Oxford by John Ruskin* (1884), reprinted in Lance Salway, ed., *A Peculiar Gift* (Harmondsworth: Penguin, 1976), p. 240. For analyses of adults' pleasure in images of childhood, see Jacqueline Rose, *The Case of Peter Pan, or The Impossibility of Children's Fiction* (London: Macmillan, 1984), and James R. Kincaid, *Child-Loving: The Erotic Child and Victorian Culture* (New York: Routledge, 1992).

64. *LF*, vol. 34 (1892); vol. 39 (1894).

65. *LF*, vol. 46 (1897); vol. 60 (1904). Deborah Dwork discusses the concern for feeding babies "pure" food in *War Is Good for Babies and Other Young Children* (London: Tavistock, 1987).

66. Erika Rappaport, "Sherry and Silks: Defining Women's Pleasure in Victorian England," unpublished paper, Rutgers History Department, Spring 1992. In "Notions of Childhood in the London Theatre, 1880–1905 (Ph.D. thesis, Cambridge University, 1981), Brian Crozier argues that upper-class women of this period were incorporating children into their social rituals of conspicuous consumption.

Chapter Five

1. E. Nesbit was her professional name.

2. Mrs. Molesworth, "On the Art of Writing Fiction for Children," *Atalanta,* vi (1893): 583–86, reprinted in Lance Salway, ed., *A Peculiar Gift* (Harmondsworth, Penguin, 1976), p. 341.

3. Julia Briggs, *A Woman of Passion: The Life of E. Nesbit, 1858–1924* (New York: New Amsterdam Books, 1987), p. 401.

4. Frances Hodgson Burnett, for example, began writing for children when her trademark happy endings and explorations of spirituality were no longer marketable as serious adult fiction. See Ann Thwaite, *Waiting for the Party* (New York: Scribners, 1974); Phyllis Bixler, *Frances Hodgson Burnett* (Boston: G.K. Hall, 1984); Claudia Nelson, *Boys Will Be Girls: The Feminine Ethic and British Children's Fiction, 1857–1917* (New Brunswick: Rutgers University Press, 1991).

5. Both were interested in alternative spiritual practices: Nesbit studied Theosophy, and Lang was a founding member of the Society for Psychical Research.

6. Gaye Tuchman and Nina E. Fortin, *Edging Women Out: Victorian Novelists, Publishers, and Social Change* (New Haven: Yale University Press, 1989); Andrew Birkin, *J. M. Barrie and the Lost Boys* (New York: Clarkson N. Potter, 1979); J. M. Barrie, *Margaret Ogilvy* (New York: Scribners, 1901); Richard Ellmann, *Oscar Wilde* (New York: Alfred A. Knopf, 1988).

7. Eleanor De Selms Langstaff, *Andrew Lang* (Boston: Twayne Publishers, 1978).

8. Roger Lancelyn Green, *Andrew Lang* (New York: Henry Z. Walck, 1962), pp. 11–26; Langstaff, pp. 16–36.

9. Lang wrote for the *Daily News, Macmillans, Saturday Review,* the *Illustrated London News, Punch, Fortnightly Review, The Spectator,* several American magazines, and had a column in *Longman's Magazine.* See Langstaff, p. 31; Joseph Weintraub, "Andrew Lang: Critic of Romance," *English Literature in Transition* 18, no. 1 (1975): 5. Aside from his fairy tales, he is perhaps best known for his translations of *The Odyssey* and *The Iliad;* see Langstaff, p. 58.

10. Henrika Kuklick, *The Savage Within: The Social History of Anthropology, 1885–1945* (New York: Cambridge University Press, 1991), p. 5. Kuklick argues that, as part of a developing intellectual class, anthropologists were central to national debates about race, empire, and national progress up until World War I, but were mostly writing for themselves by World War II. George Stocking lays out the debates within anthropology in *Victorian Anthropology* (New York: The Free Press, 1987).

11. Langstaff, pp. 14, 128; Terry Eagleton, *The Function of Criticism* (London: Verso, 1984).

12. Weintraub, p. 10.

13. Richard M. Dorson, *The British Folklorists, A History* (Chicago: University of Chicago Press, 1968); Andrew Lang, *Myth, Ritual and Religion,* rev. ed. (London: Longmans, 1913).

14. From Lang's introduction to *Perrault's Popular Tales* (1888), quoted in Langstaff, p. 136.

15. Lang, *Adventures Among Books* (London: Longmans, 1905), p. 37.

16. Dorson, p. 332.

17. Weintraub describes Lang as the most visible critic of Thomas Hardy and Henry James.

18. Books he praised often sold well, Langstaff, p. 89.

19. Both Weintraub, pp. 6–7, and Langstaff, p. 15, suggest that Lang was uneasy about the spread of democracy. Lang's comments on the French Revolution in prefaces to his *Blue* and *Olive* "Fairy Books" suggest a fear of mob rule.

20. See Lang's essay on William Morris in *Adventures.*

21. Langstaff, pp. 38–39, 92–93.

22. Lang, *Myth, Ritual and Religion,* p. 336; Weintraub, pp. 9, 11.

23. Weintraub, p. 6; Langstaff, p. 104. See also Andrew Lang and 'X' a Working Man, "The Reading Public," *Cornhill Magazine* (1901): 783–95.

24. Despising the "sham sentiment, forced fun," and sermons of modern fairy tales, he preferred the "unobtrusive" morality of older tales. Roger Lancelyn Green, *Tellers of Tales* (Leicester: Edmund Ward, 1953), p. 117.

25. Green, *Andrew Lang,* p. 52; Langstaff, pp. 138–39.

26. *Archives of the House of Longman, 1794–1914* (Cambridge: Chadwyck-Healey, 1977), reel 27, 1889, p. 24; 1899–1900, p. 385.

27. Quoted by Dorothy Lake Gregory in her foreword to *The Orange Fairy Book* (New York: David McKay, 1950), p. ix; Green, *Andrew Lang,* p. 50; Langstaff, pp. 139–45. Kay Vandergrift discusses Leonora Lang's role in "Collecting: Passion with a Purpose," *School Library Journal,* vol. 33, no. 2 (1986): 91–95.

28. Langstaff, p. 139.

29. Lang, *The Green Fairy Book* (1892; New York: David McKay, 1948), p. xii; *The Violet Fairy Book* (1901; New York: David McKay, 1951), p. xi.

30. Lang, *Violet Fairy Book,* p. xii.

31. Lang, *The Blue Fairy Book* (London: Longmans, 1889), pp. xi–xii; *The Pink Fairy Book* (London: Longmans, 1897), p. vii. The former included Norse, Middle Eastern, Scottish, and French tales; the latter included Danish, Swedish, Sicilian, African, Japanese, and French tales.

32. *The Crimson Fairy Book* (1903; New York: David McKay, 1962); *The Pink Fairy Book,* p. viii.

33. Lang, *The Blue Fairy Book,* p. xiii.

34. Lang, *The Yellow Fairy Book* (1894; New York: David McKay, 1962), p. xi; *The Olive Fairy Book* (1907; New York: David McKay, 1950), p. xii; *Green Fairy Book,* p. xi.

35. Lang, *The Blue Fairy Book*, p. xi; "Charles Dickens," *Fortnightly Review*, LXX (1898): 948, quoted in Weintraub, p. 11. See also J. Newby Hetherington, "The Use of Fairy Tales in the Education of the Young," (1897), in Salway, *A Peculiar Gift*; Alexander Francis Chamberlain, *The Child and Childhood in Folk-Thought* (New York: Macmillan, 1896). For analyses of the late nineteenth-century vision of child development as a mirror of evolution, see Dorothy Ross, *G. Stanley Hall, The Psychologist As Prophet* (Chicago: University of Chicago Press, 1972); Jacqueline Rose, *The Case of Peter Pan, or The Impossibility of Children's Fiction* (London: Macmillan, 1984); Carolyn Steedman, *Strange Dislocations: Childhood and the Idea of Human Interiority, 1780–1930* (Cambridge, MA: Harvard University Press, 1995).

36. Quoted in Green, *Andrew Lang*, p. 59.

37. Lang, *Adventures*, p. 53.

38. Lang, *Adventures*; Langstaff, p. 95.

39. Lang, *Adventures*, pp. 4–7.

40. Lang, *Adventures*, pp. 7, 10–11.

41. Lang, *The Green Fairy Book*, p. xii.

42. Judith Walkowitz discusses how the language of science could be used to exclude women in *City of Dreadful Delight: Narratives of Sexual Danger in Late-Victorian London* (Chicago: University of Chicago Press, 1992), chap. 5.

43. Lang, *The Orange Fairy Book*, p. xi; *The Violet Fairy Book*, p. xi.

44. See *The Blue Fairy Book* (1920 edition); Langstaff, p. 144.

45. Briggs, p. xi. Alison Lurie, *New York Review of Books* 31, no. 16 (October 25, 1984): 19–22; Colin Manlove, "Fantasy as Witty Conceit: E. Nesbit," *Mosaic* 10 (1977): 109–30; U. C. Knoepflmacher, "Of Babylands and Babylons: E. Nesbit and the Reclamation of the Fairy-Tale," *Tulsa Studies in Women's Literature* vol. 16, no. 2 (1987): 299–325.

46. Briggs, p. xix. Polly Beals, "Fabian Feminism: Gender, Politics and Culture in London, 1880–1930," Ph.D. diss., Rutgers University, 1989, chaps. 3, 4.

47. Nesbit's poetry included *Ballads and Lyrics of Socialism, 1883–1908* (London: The Fabian Society, 1908) and *Songs of Love and Empire* (London: Archibald Constable, 1898).

48. Doris Langley Moore, rev. ed., *E. Nesbit, A Biography* (Philadelphia: Chilton Books, 1966), pp. 58, 65; Briggs, pp. 9–30, 40. Bland's father, a property-owning commercial clerk, was probably lower middle class.

49. Bland later edited the Socialist magazine *Today* and wrote for the *Daily Chronicle* and the Manchester *Sunday Chronicle*. Briggs, pp. 58, 163–64; Moore, pp. 68–69.

50. Briggs, pp. 64–66; Beals, pp. 55, 227–30.

51. Briggs, pp. 78–105.

52. Letters dated March and April 1884, quoted in Briggs, p. 61. France Hodgson Burnett, also responsible for supporting her family, once described herself as "a kind of pen-driving machine." Quoted in Thwaite, p. 67.

53. Briggs, 61–73, 122.

54. Briggs, p. 349; Moore, pp. 92, 140–46; John Feather, *A History of British Publishing* (London: Croom Helm, 1988), pp. 175–78. Nesbit's profits were often

small, but accumulated over the years. Longmans paid her 20 percent of the profits from one book after the first 500 copies sold. See *Archives of the House of Longman,* reel 30.

55. Harpers paid her 37 pounds per episode and 15 percent of the retail price for the American publication of *The Wouldbegoods: Archives of Harper and Brothers* (Cambridge: Chadwyck-Healey, 1980), reel A10.

56. *The Story of the Treasure Seekers,* first published by T. Fisher Unwin in 1899, had gone through 15 impressions by 1928.

57. Nesbit letter, n.d., Macmillan Archives, Add. mss. 54964, British Library.

58. Nesbit, "My School Days," reprinted as E. Nesbit, *Long Ago When I Was Young* (London: Ronald Whiting & Wheaton, 1966). She discusses this "gulf" between children and adults in *Wings and the Child* (London: Hodder & Stoughton, 1913).

59. Nesbit, *Long Ago,* pp. 99, 109.

60. Letter to Morris Colles, February 7, 1898, Berg Collection, NYPL. In a letter to her mother, Nesbit mentioned the story as one of several projects; Moore, p. 148. She appears to have gauged the market well; the book's third printing sold out.

61. Edward Garnett's reader's reports for T. Fisher Unwin (October 27, 1898; January 30, 1899; June 26, 1899), Berg Collection, NYPL.

62. Briggs, p. 186.

63. Briggs, pp. xix, 244. Kimberly Reynolds discusses Nesbit's celebration of class distinctions in *Girls Only? Gender and Popular Children's Fiction, 1880–1910* (Philadelphia: Temple University Press, 1990), p. 94.

64. Nesbit's recurring themes of absent fathers and restoration of the family unit are discussed in Briggs, pp. 1, 250, and Lurie, p. 22.

65. Briggs, pp. 218, 348.

66. Manlove: 219–21; Lurie: 21.

67. Nesbit, *Five Children and It* (London: T. Fisher Unwin, 1902), p. 22.

68. Briggs, p. 190.

69. When the queen sends her possessions flying out of the British Museum, a newspaper headline reports "Mrs. Besant and Theosophy, Impertinent Miracle at the British Museum." Nesbit, *The Story of the Amulet* (London: T. Fisher Unwin, 1906), pp. 128, 132–37.

70. Nesbit, *The Story of the Amulet,* pp. 203, 212–13.

71. Briggs, pp. 63, 76, 252–53, 290, 309–23.

72. Nesbit, *The Story of the Amulet,* pp. 54, 76, 243–44. Briggs discusses Nesbit's anti-Semitism, p. 292.

73. Nesbit, *Long Ago.*

74. Briggs, pp. 20, 186–88.

75. Nesbit, *The Wouldbegoods,* p. 176.

76. Nesbit, *Five Children and It,* pp. 138, 213–22. See also *The Story of the Amulet,* p. 171.

77. Nesbit, *Five Children and It,* pp. 45, 69, 72, 249.

78. Briggs, p. 402; Reynolds, pp. 152–53.

79. Edward Garnett's reports to T. Fisher Unwin (October 27, 1898; June 29, 1899), Berg Collection, NYPL; Moore, pp. 231–35.

80. From Cole Lesley, *The Life of Noel Coward,* quoted in Briggs, pp. 388, 404.

81. Letters from Rudyard Kipling to E. Nesbit, quoted in Briggs, pp. 254–56.

82. Andrew Lang's undated letters to E. Nesbit are quoted in Moore, pp. 173–74.

83. H.G. Wells to E. Nesbit, December 17, 1904, quoted in Moore, p. 187.

84. Nesbit's letter to Morris Colles, received November 5, 1898, in Berg Collection, NYPL. See Nesbit's letters to agent J.B. Pinker undated, but probably written in March 1904, asking for advances on her work and for commissions for "grown-up stories," Folder 5 of a series of Nesbit's letters to Pinker, Berg Collection, NYPL.

85. Nesbit may have been exhausted; she was also preoccupied with Baconianism, a movement to prove that Francis Bacon was the real author of Shakespeare's works. See Nesbit's letters to her agent A.P. Watt, n.d., Berg Collection, NYPL.

86. This letter to novelist Clemence Dane is quoted in Moore, p. 282. The original is in the Macmillan Archives, British Library, Add. mss. 54964.

Chapter Six

1. John Lawson and Harold Silver, *A Social History of Education in England* (London: Methuen, 1973), p. 318.

2. The following studies do a particularly good job of capturing what Dina Copelman calls the "difficult, politically contested struggle" (p. 57) involved in implementing Board schooling: Dina Copelman, *London's Women Teachers: Gender, Class and Feminism, 1870–1930* (London: Routledge, 1996); David Rubinstein, *School Attendance in London, 1870–1904: A Social History* (Hull: University of Hull Publications, 1969); Harold Silver, *Education as History* (New York: Methuen, 1983); Gillian Sutherland, *Policy-making in Elementary Education, 1870–1895* (Oxford: Oxford University Press, 1973). See also Geoffrey Sherington, *English Education, Social Change and War, 1911–20* (Manchester: Manchester University Press, 1981).

3. Historians of British education are divided between those who consider Board schooling an example of social progress and those who see in it elements of social control. The former includes Alec Ellis, *Educating Our Masters* (Hampshire, England: Gower, 1985), and Nigel Middleton, "The Education Act of 1870 as the Start of the Modern Conception of the Child," *British Journal of Educational Studies* 18 (1970): 166–79. The latter position is taken by J. M. Goldstrom, *The Social Content of Education, 1808–1870* (Shannon, Ireland: Irish University Press, 1972), and E. G. West, *Education and the Industrial Revolution* (New York: Barnes & Noble, 1975). The development of this debate can be traced in these works: Lawrence Stone, "Literacy and Education in England, 1640–1900," *Past and Present,* 42 (1969): 69–139; Philip McCann, ed., *Popular Education and Socialization in the Nineteenth Century* (London: Methuen, 1977); John Hurt, *Elementary Schooling and the Working Classes, 1860–1918* (London: Routledge, 1979); Anne Digby and Peter Searby, *Children, School and Society in Nineteenth Century England* (London: Macmillan, 1981).

4. Regarding the redefinition of British working-class childhood, see Anna Davin, *Growing Up Poor: Home, School and Street in London, 1870–1914* (London: Rivers Oram Press, 1996); Carolyn Steedman, *Childhood, Culture and Class in Britain: Margaret McMillan, 1860–1931* (New Brunswick: Rutgers University Press, 1990); Steedman, *Strange Dislocations: Childhood and the Idea of Human Interiority, 1780–1930* (Cambridge, MA: Harvard University Press, 1995). Stephen Humphries recaptures the voices of working-class youths in *Hooligans or Rebels?* (London: Basil Blackwell, 1981).

5. Goldstrom, *The Social Content of Education;* W. A. C. Stewart and W. P. Mc-Cann, *The Educational Innovators, 1750–1880* (London: Macmillan, 1967).

6. Thomas Laqueur, *Religion and Respectability: Sunday Schools and Working-class Culture, 1780–1850* (New Haven: Yale University Press, 1976); Philip Gardner, *The Lost Elementary Schools of Victorian England* (London: Croom Helm, 1984).

7. Gareth Stedman Jones analyzes middle-class perceptions of the poor in *Outcast London* (Oxford: Oxford University Press, 1971).

8. Brian Simon, *Education and the Labour Movement, 1870–1920* (London: Lawrence & Wishart, 1965).

9. See *Minutes of the Proceedings of the School Board for London* (hereafter SBL *Minutes*), vol. 17, 1882, British Library, p. 463. In 1883, two Board school boys were reported to have made it to Oxford and Cambridge—rare enough events to be noted: SBL *Minutes,* vol. 19, 1883, p. 403. Sidney Webb promoted the "ladder" concept in *London Education* (London: Longmans, 1904).

10. Lawson and Silver, p. 320; Gillian Sutherland, pp. 109–10. There were 2,500 school boards in England and Wales by 1892, although a majority of children continued to attend voluntary schools into the 1890s. When the government eliminated school Boards in 1903, assigning their duties to county councils, opponents viewed it as an attack on Board schools, democracy, and nondenominational education. See Thomas Gautrey, *Lux, Mihi Laus: School Board Memories* (London: Link House, 1937); Rev. A. W. Jephson, *My Work in London* (London: Isaac Pittman, 1910); Simon, *Education.*

11. The first SBL included Elizabeth Garrett, Emily Davies, T. H. Huxley, Benjamin Lucraft, and W. H. Smith; its chairman, Lord Lawrence, was the first of several former colonial administrators to serve on the Board. Annie Besant, Edward Aveling, and Helen Taylor served on later Boards. For firsthand accounts of the SBL, see Gautrey, *Lux, Mihi Laus,* and Thomas Spalding, *The Work of the London School Board* (London: P. S. King & Son, 1900). Women's roles on the Board are discussed in Patricia Hollis, *Ladies Elect: Women in English Local Government, 1865–1914* (Oxford: Clarendon Press, 1987), and Annmarie Turnbull, "'So Extremely like Parliament'" the work of the women members of the London School Board, 1870–1904," in The London Feminist History Group, *The Sexual Dynamics of History* (London: Pluto Press, 1983).

12. SBL *Minutes,* vol. 1, 1871, pp. 5, 17, 51; vol. 2, 1872, p. 182.

13. The first Board had recommended that middle-class women be appointed as visitors because they could be paid less than men and because, the attendance committee reasoned, they could work well with working-class mothers. In fact, visitors were mostly male and from the lower middle and working classes. SBL *Minutes,* vol.

1, 1871, pp. 172–74; David Rubinstein, "Socialization and the London School Board," in McCann, ed., *Popular Education,* p. 232.

14. See SBL *Minutes,* vol. 5, 1875, p. 535; volume 9, 1878, p. 333. The difficulties compulsory attendance caused working-class families are discussed in Ellen Ross, *Love and Toil: Motherhood in Outcast London* (New York: Oxford University Press, 1993), chap. 5, and Davin, chaps. 5, 6.

15. See SBL *Minutes,* vol. 1, 1871, pp. 189, 283; vol. 18, 1883, p. 808; vol. 29, 1888, pp. 173–74.

16. SBL *Minutes,* volume 13, 1880, p. 589. See Ellen Ross's analysis of the power dynamics in working-class homes in "Labour and Love: Rediscovering London's Working-Class Mothers, 1870–1918," in Jane Lewis, ed., *Labour and Love* (Oxford: Basil Blackwell, 1986). Rubinstein discusses SBL strategies for prosecuting cases in *School Attendance,* p. 104.

17. SBL *Minutes,* vol. 17, 1882, p. 458; vol. 21, 1884, p. 393.

18. SBL *Minutes,* vol. 24, 1886, p. 512.

19. SBL *Minutes,* vol. 13, 1880, pp. 782–83; vol. 25, 1886, p. 252. See Gillian Sutherland, p. 158, and Rubinstein, *School Attendance,* pp. 102–3.

20. SBL *Minutes,* vol. 1, 1871, p. 158.

21. See Davin, *Growing Up Poor.*

22. SBL *Minutes,* vol. 10, 1879, p. 387; see also vol. 16, 1881, p. 29.

23. Rubinstein, *School Attendance,* pp. 83–84.

24. SBL *Minutes,* vol. 5, 1875, pp. 1173, 1309, 1384.

25. SBL *Minutes,* vol. 1, 1871, p. 174; and see Jones, chap. 13.

26. SBL *Minutes,* vol. 9, 1878, p. 327. Hollis, in *Ladies Elect,* points out that several women members spent so many hours hearing remissions cases in their very poor districts that they had little time to devote to gaining influence on SBL committees.

27. SBL *Minutes,* vol. 11, 1879, p. 301; vol. 17, 1882, p. 458; vol. 32, 1889–90, pp. 106, 515.

28. SBL *Minutes,* vol. 31, 1889, p. 705.

29. Rubinstein, "Socialization," in McCann, *Popular Education,* pp. 232–33. The SBL used census returns to assess the number of school places needed, and the Births, Deaths and Registration Act of 1874 allowed the Board to ascertain children's ages. Parliament requested information from visitors on the conditions of London's poor, as did Charles Booth when he began his social survey of London in the late 1880s. SBL *Minutes,* vol. 1, 1871; vol. 5, 1875; vol. 10, 1879.

30. SBL *Minutes,* vol. 18, 1882–83, pp. 504–6; *The Times,* 22 February 1884, p. 3, 1 March 1884, p. 6. Williams's contemporary, H. Jephson, argues that his were the first reliable figures on overcrowding in London; see Rubinstein, "Socialization," in McCann, *Popular Education,* pp. 237–39. SBL visitors were later called to testify in Parliamentary investigations of working-class housing conditions; see SBL *Minutes,* vol. 30, 1889, vol. 32, 1890.

31. SBL *Minutes,* vol. 31, 1889, pp. 162–63.

32. SBL *Minutes,* vol. 2, 1872, p. 88. Regarding scandals over mistreatment of children in industrial schools, see SBL *Minutes,* vols. 15–16, 1881–82, and Rubinstein, *School Attendance.*

33. SBL *Minutes,* vol. 3, 1873.

34. Peek renewed the grant in 1882. SBL *Minutes,* vol. 5, 1875, p. 621; vol. 18, 1883, pp. 425, 887; Charles Loch Mowat, *The Charity Organisation Society, 1869–1913* (London: Methuen, 1961).

35. See Ellen Ross, "Hungry Children: Housewives and London Charity, 1870–1918," in Peter Mandler, ed., *The Uses of Charity* (Philadelphia: University of Pennsylvania Press, 1986), chap. 6.

36. Approved in 1861, payment by result drew criticism from the first. Amended in 1883, it was eliminated in the 1890s. In the 1870s, an Infant school teacher could earn a maximum of five shillings for each child who attended eighty times, was at least six years old, and passed the three exams necessary to enter the Junior department; the teacher's pay was cut if the child passed fewer exams. See SBL *Minutes,* vol. 3, 1873, p. 294; Gillian Sutherland, 234–67; Lawson and Silver, pp. 28–29.

37. Scheme of Education Committee Recommendations, SBL *Minutes,* volume 1, 1871.

38. SBL *Minutes,* vol. 23, 1885, pp. 88–99.

39. See Steedman, *Childhood,* and Thomas Jordan, *Victorian Childhood* (Albany: State University of New York Press, 1987).

40. The higher the admission fee, the more respectable the neighborhood was considered to be. See SBL *Minutes,* vol. 22, 1884, p. 203, and the *Report of the School Management Committee,* March 1888, Greater London Record Office [LCC 221/2] pp. xliv–xlvii.

41. SBL *Minutes,* vol. 5, 1875, p. 835.

42. SBL *Minutes,* vol. 8, 1878, p. 118.

43. SBL *Minutes,* vol. 8, 1877, pp. 105–34.

44. SBL *Minutes,* vol. 16, 1881, p. 40.

45. *The Times,* 1 March, 1884, p. 6.

46. SBL *Minutes,* vol. 18, 1883, pp. 504–6. Andrew Mearns's "The Bitter Cry of Outcast London," depicting East London as the repository for the city's poor, was published the same year. *The East London Observer,* on 3 November 1883, responded with a more complicated map of London's economic ills.

47. Scheme of Education Committee Report, SBL *Minutes,* vol. 1, 1871, p. 157.

48. Copelman, pp. 83, 88–90. Women Board members' efforts to restrict use of corporal punishment are discussed in Hollis, chap. 2, and Gillian Sutherland, p. 104.

49. SBL *Minutes,* vol. 5, 1875, p. 621; vol. 6, 1876, pp. 191, 447–48. The Education Department had ruled in 1873 that girls could not participate in military drill.

50. SBL *Minutes,* vol. 6, 1876, pp. 191, 447, 537.

51. One inspector found good discipline in schools that gave plenty of time to drill: SBL *Minutes,* vol. 8, 1877, p. 130.

52. SBL *Minutes,* vol. 19, 1882–83, p. 183. The SBL heard further protests against drill in 1879 and 1885. Pamela Horn discusses military drill's wider use during the Boer War in *The Victorian and Edwardian Schoolchild* (Gloucester: Sutton, 1989), p. 56.

53. SBL *Minutes,* vol. 10, 1878, p. 132.

54. SBL *Minutes,* vol. 19, 1883, p. 905.

55. SBL *Minutes,* vol. 19, 1883, pp. 904–5; vol. 25, 1886, p. 300. Regarding Brabazon's campaign for public parks and physical education, see Digby and Searby, p. 147.

56. SBL *Minutes,* vol. 1, 1871, p. 158. I discuss kindergarten's role in the elementary curriculum more fully in Chapter Eight.

57. SBL *Minutes,* pp. 158–59, 845. For the history of object lessons, invented by Swiss educator Johann Pestalozzi and adapted by Robert Owen, see Stewart and McCann, pp. 68, 88–89, 137–53.

58. The campaign for domestic education intensified in the 1880s and '90s with growing anxiety over high infant mortality rates and the apparent physical deterioration of Britain's poor. Copelman, chaps. 5, 9; Davin, p. 142; Carol Dyhouse, "Good Wives and Little Mothers," *Oxford Review of Education,* vol. 30, no. 1 (1977): 21–35.

59. SBL *Minutes,* vol. 9, 1878, p. 331.

60. SBL *Minutes,* vol. 23, 1885, p. 373.

61. SBL *Minutes,* vol. 4, 1874, p. 762; vol. 20, 1884, p. 1289; vol. 24, 1886, p. 355; vol. 33, 1890, p. 881.

62. See Copelman's analysis, chaps. 5 and 9, of the relationship between women teachers' increased feminist activity in the 1900s and their embrace of a vision of sexual difference that elevated women's roles as mothers.

63. SBL *Minutes,* vol. 19, 1883, pp. 154–55.

Chapter Seven

1. *Minutes of the Proceedings of the School Board for London* (hereafter SBL *Minutes*), vol. 20, 1884, p. 923; vol. 21, 1884, pp. 85–86; *Lloyd's Weekly,* 3 February 1884, 6–7. See also Dina Copelman, *London's Women Teachers: Gender, Class and Feminism, 1870–1930* (London: Routledge, 1996), pp. 96, 109–11; Lionel Rose, *The Erosion of Childhood* (London: Routledge, 1991); Gillian Sutherland, *Policy-making in Elementary Education, 1870–1895* (Oxford: Oxford University Press, 1973).

2. See Anna Davin, "Imperialism and Motherhood," *History Workshop* (Spring 1978): 9–65; Thomas E. Jordan, *The Degeneracy Crisis and Victorian Youth* (Albany: State University of New York Press, 1993); Daniel J. Kevles, *In the Name of Eugenics* (New York: Alfred A. Knopf, 1985).

3. Anson Rabinbach, *The Human Motor: Energy, Fatigue, and the Origins of Modernity* (Berkeley: University of California Press, 1992), pp. 21, 147–48.

4. *British Medical Journal* (hereafter *BMJ*), 9 August 1884, p. 296.

5. Mary Langan and Bill Schwarz, eds., *Crises in the British State, 1880–1930* (London: Hutchinson, 1985), chap. 1.

6. SBL *Minutes,* vol. 20, 1883–84, pp. 206, 357. For the teachers' perspectives on overpressure, see Copelman, chap. 5.

7. *BMJ,* 9 February 1884, pp. 279–80.

8. "Fatal Overwork in a Board School," *Lloyd's Weekly,* 2 March 1884, p. 3; "Death from Overwork in a Board School," *East London Observer,* 5 July 1884, p. 3. *The Times,* 10 January 1885, p. 4, printed the 22 cases of alleged overpressure. Medical reports suggested two possibilities: overpressure had caused the meningitis or brain fever that killed the children or anxiety about schoolwork had brought on a "dormant" disease such as tubercular meningitis.

9. SBL *Minutes,* vol. 19, 1883, pp. 859–60.

10. *BMJ,* 9 February 1884, p. 278.

11. *East London Observer,* 23 February 1884, p. 6; *East London Leader,* 16 February 1884, p. 3. For SBL discussions of needlework and cooking requirements, see SBL *Minutes,* vol. 20, 1884, pp. 309, 357, 897, and Patricia Hollis, *Ladies Elect: Women in English Local Government, 1865–1914* (Oxford: Clarendon Press, 1982), chap. 2.

12. Forbes-Winslow was embroiled in a legal battle with spiritualist Georgina Weldon. He had conspired with her husband to place her in an insane asylum; neither had counted on her ability to use publicity and the law to fight back. See Judith R. Walkowitz, *City of Dreadful Delight: Narratives of Sexual Danger in Late-Victorian London* (Chicago: University of Chicago Press, 1992), chap. 6.

13. *The Times,* 27 March 1884, p. 5.

14. *The Times,* 12 March 1884, p. 6.

15. *The Times,* 1, 8, 16 February 1884; *East London Leader,* 16 February 1884.

16. *Lloyd's Weekly,* 3 February 1884, pp. 5–7.

17. *The Times,* 8 March 1884, p. 12. Mundella, MP for Sheffield, was given oversight of the Education Department when Gladstone's Liberal government took office in 1880.

18. *Lloyd's Weekly,* 16 March 1884, p. 5; *East London Leader,* 22 March 1884, p. 2. Protests over the SBL budget also took place before and after the overpressure controversy.

19. *Lloyd's Weekly,* 16 March 1884, p. 5; *East London Leader,* 16 February 1884, p. 3; *East London Observer,* 23 February 1884, p. 6.

20. *East London Leader,* 20 September 1884, p. 3; *Pall Mall Gazette* (hereafter *PMG*), 17 October 1884, p. 11. Regarding battles over children's attendance, see chap. six above, and David Rubinstein, *School Attendance in London, 1870–1914: A Social History* (Hull: University of Hull, 1969).

21. *East London Leader,* 9 August 1884, p. 3.

22. *The Times,* 28 June 1884, p. 8; *School Guardian,* 15 March 1884, pp. 180–81.

23. James Runciman (a former teacher),"School-Board Idylls," *PMG,* 27 September 1884, p. 1. See Copelman, p. 109.

24. *East London Observer,* 8 November 1884, p. 5.

25. See for example *East London Observer,* 9 June 1883, p. 6; *Lloyd's Weekly,* 27 January 1884, p. 4; *East London Leader,* 1 March 1884, p. 3.

26. *East London Observer,* 13 January 1883, p. 6.

27. *East London Observer,* 3 March 1883, p. 7; 21 July 1883, p. 3; 1 December 1883, p. 7; Walkowitz, chaps. 3, 4.

28. See Lionel Rose's history of the child protection movement in *The Erosion of Childhood.*

29. *East London Observer,* 17 July 1884, p. 6.

30. *East London Leader,* 29 November 1884, p. 2; 21 February 1885, p. 1; 28 February 1884, p. 2.

31. Neither man's career suffered from this publicity. Crichton-Browne (1840–1938) served as president of a number of medical organizations and was knighted in 1886; the *Dictionary of National Biography* credits him as one of the first to recognize the importance of warning symptoms of mental disease. Fitch (1824–1903) was given several special assignments to investigate educational methods after the overpressure crisis. He also served as principal of Borough Road Training College, as inspector of teaching colleges for women, and was knighted in 1896.

32. *The Times,* 8 May 1884, p. 5.

33. *The Times,* 16 June 1884, p. 16.

34. *The Times,* 13 August, p. 2; *School Guardian,* 14 June 1884, pp. 396–97.

35. *The Times,* 21 August 1884, p. 6; *School Guardian,* 30 August 1884, p. 595.

36. *BMJ,* 9 August 1884, p. 296.

37. *Report of Dr. Crichton-Browne to the Education Department upon the Alleged Over-Pressure of Work in Public Elementary Schools,* PP 1884, lxi (293), pp. 3–54.

38. *Memorandum relating to Dr. Crichton-Browne's Report by Mr. J. G. Fitch, one of Her Majesty's Chief Inspectors of Schools,* PP 1884, lxi (297), pp. 55–79.

39. *Memorandum.*

40. *The Times,* 18 September, 1884, p. 10. A second letter on the same page, by Dr. Kerr, defended Crichton-Browne's credentials and argument. This was most likely the same Dr. Kerr who served as medical officer for the Bradford school Board, then, from 1902, for London. See Rubinstein, p. 79.

41. *The Times,* 20 September 1884, p. 6.

42. *The Times,* 8 October 1884, pp. 2–3.

43. *The Times,* 13 October 1884, pp. 2–3.

44. *The Times,* 18 October 1884, p. 12.

45. *Lloyd's Weekly,* 21 September 1884, p. 6.

46. The reactions of various newspapers were summarized in the *PMG,* 16 September 1884, p. 3; its own editorial appeared 13 October 1884, p. 3.

47. *School Guardian,* 15 March 1884, pp. 180–81; 16 August 1884, pp. 572–73; 4 October 1884, p. 675; 15 November 1884, p. 778.

48. *School Guardian,* 5 April 1884, 221–22.

49. *The Times,* 29 January 1884, p. 4, pointed out that outcries against elementary education were timed to coincide with the Education Department's annual reevaluation of the Education Code.

50. *The Times,* 12 March 1884, p. 6.

51. *The Times,* 13 August 1884, p. 2.

52. *The Times,* 16 September 1884, p. 9.

53. *Lancet,* 8 March 1884, pp. 437–38; *BMJ,* 12 April 1884, p. 729.

54. M. Jeanne Peterson, *The Medical Profession in Mid-Victorian London* (Berkeley: University of California Press, 1978); Dorothy Porter and Roy Porter, eds.,

Doctors, Politics and Society: Historical Essays (Amsterdam: Editions Rodopi, 1993); Dorothy Porter, ed., *The History of Public Health and the Modern State* (Amsterdam: Editions Rodopi, 1994).

55. *BMJ,* 9 February 1884, pp. 279–80.

56. *Lancet,* 1 March 1884, p. 401; 22 March 1884, p. 535.

57. *BMJ,* 25 October 1884, p. 833.

58. *BMJ,* 27 September 1884, pp. 621–22; 25 October 1884, pp. 821–22; 1 November 1884, pp. 879–80.

59. See Dr. Kerr's letter to *The Times,* 18 September 1884, p. 10, and Crichton-Browne's introduction to Niels Hertel, *Overpressure in high schools in Denmark,* trans. C. Godfrey Sorenson (London: Macmillan, 1885).

60. *Report of Dr. Crichton-Browne.*

61. *Lancet,* 26 January 1884, p. 176.

62. Crichton-Browne, introduction to Hertel, *Overpressure in High Schools,* p. xii. Eugenicists' and doctors' warnings about the dangers of higher education for women are discussed in Carol Dyhouse, *Girls Growing Up in Late Victorian and Edwardian England* (London: Routledge, 1981); Joan Perkin, *Victorian Women* (New York: New York University Press, 1993); Martha Vicinus, *Independent Women: Work and Community for Single Women, 1850–1920* (Chicago: University of Chicago Press, 1985).

63. *The Times,* 19 August 1884, pp. 2–3.

64. *Lancet,* 14 July 1883, pp. 63–64.

65. *BMJ,* 9 August 1884, p. 296.

66. *BMJ,* 26 April 1884, p. 826.

67. *BMJ,* 27 September 1884, pp. 621–22; 18 October 1884, p. 781.

68. *Lancet,* 8 March 1884, pp. 437–38.

69. *Lancet,* 8 December 1883, p. 1005.

70. *Lancet,* 9 February 1884, p. 262.

71. See SBL chairman's annual statement casting doubt on "allegations of overpressure," reported in *The Times,* 10 October 1884, p. 8. *PMG,* 9 October 1884, p. 3, approved Buxton's determination not to "reduce the level of education to the weakest," but to have teachers "afford relief in individual cases."

72. *The Times,* 17 October 1884, p. 8.

73. *The Times,* 25 October 1884, p. 5.

74. This prompted a letter from Dr. Charles Roberts disputing Crichton-Browne's claim that most of the medical profession supported his views on overpressure. *The Times,* 29 October 1884, p. 10; 4 November 1884, p. 4.

75. *The Times,* 14 November 1884, p. 3.

76. *The Times,* 28 November 1884, p. 6.

77. *Report of the Special Committee on the Question of Overpressure in the Schools,* July 1885 [SBL 1466], Greater London Record Office, pp. 30, 70–72, 172, 222.

78. *Report,* pp. 115–16.

79. *Report,* pp. 39, 83.

80. *Report,* pp. 4, 236.

81. *Report,* pp. xv–xvii.

82. *Report,* pp. iv–v.

83. *The Times,* 15 July 1885, p. 9.

84. The paper approved most of the committee's recommendations, but criticized the SBL's substitution of fixed salaries for payment by result as a "bribe" to teachers to "moderate their educational zeal." *The Times,* 18 July 1885, pp. 11–12.

85. *BMJ,* 25 July 1885, p. 157.

86. *Lancet,* 27 June 1885, p. 1172.

87. M. E. Bulkley, *The Feeding of School Children* (London: G. Bell & Sons, 1914), pp. 8–12. See also Sir Henry Craik, *The State in its Relation to Education,* rev. ed., (London: MacMillan, 1914); Grace M. Paton, *The Child and the Nation* (London: Student Christian Movement, 1915). For analyses of the politics of the report on physical deterioration and subsequent legislation, see Davin, "Imperialism and Motherhood"; Deborah Dwork, *War Is Good for Babies and Other Young Children* (London: Tavistock Publications, 1987); Ellen Ross, *Love and Toil: Motherhood in Outcast London, 1870–1918* (New York: Oxford University Press, 1993), chap. 7.

88. *Annual Report for 1912 of the Chief Medical Officer of the Board of Education,* PP 1914 [cd.7184]; Bulkley, pp. 15–22.

89. For analysis of working-class mothers' inventive and determined use of charity as part of a series of strategies for sustaining their households, see Ellen Ross, "Hungry Children: Housewives and London Charity, 1870–1918," in Peter Mandler, ed., *The Uses of Charity* (Philadelphia: University of Pennsylvania Press, 1986).

90. Thomas Gautrey, *Lux Mihi Laus: School Board Memories* (London: Link House, 1937), p. 121.

Chapter Eight

1. Board of Education (BOE) Circular, 1912, p. 27, quoted in Jacqueline Rose, "State and Language: Peter Pan as Written for the Child," in Carolyn Steedman, Cathy Urwin, and Valerie Walkerdine, eds., *Language, Gender and Childhood* (London: Routledge, 1985), pp. 88–92.

2. Jacqueline Rose, in Steedman et al., *Language, Gender and Childhood,* 94–96.

3. Jacqueline Rose, in Steedman et al., *Language, Gender and Childhood,* p. 99.

4. See Herbert M. Kliebard's analysis of how the American curriculum was forged out of compromises between educators with conflicting agendas: *The Struggle for the American Curriculum, 1893–1958,* 2nd ed. (New York: Routledge, 1995).

5. In 1867, voting rights were extended to urban working-class men (in boroughs); in 1884, household suffrage was extended to men in the rest of the country.

6. *Minutes of the Proceedings of the School Board for London* (hereafter SBL *Minutes*), vol. 2, 1872, British Library, pp. 140–41, 228. The committee had approved 16 series of books in all.

7. SBL *Minutes,* vol. 2, 1872, pp. 247, 332–33, 353. Costs of books and other supplies were estimated per child.

8. SBL *Minutes,* vol. 16, 1882, p. 657; vol. 17, 1882, pp. 90–91.

9. See Matthew Arnold, *Culture and Anarchy* (1869), in R. H. Super, ed., *The Complete Prose Works of Matthew Arnold* (Ann Arbor: University of Michigan Press, 1962); Raymond Williams, *Culture and Society, 1750–1950* (1958; New York: Columbia University Press, 1983), and *Problems in Materialism and Culture* (London: Verso, 1980), p. 308; Terry Eagleton, *The Function of Criticism* (London: Verso, 1984), pp. 60–65. Williams notes in *Problems* that the New Right ignored Arnold's commitment to extending popular education when it appropriated him as a model in the 1960s. But, as Gillian Sutherland points out, in *Arnold on Education* (Harmondsworth: Penguin Books, 1973), he also maintained an elitist vision of education.

10. Matthew Arnold, *Reports on Elementary Schools* (London: Wyman & Sons, 1908), pp. 81–82.

11. Arnold, *Reports,* pp. 155–56, 178.

12. Arnold, *Reports,* pp. 182, 186–88.

13. See Arnold's famous critique of the 1861 Education Code's provision for payment: "The Twice Revised Code" (1862), in R. H. Super, ed., *The Complete Prose Works of Matthew Arnold,* vol. II.

14. SBL *Minutes,* vol. 11, 1879, p. 720.

15. SBL *Minutes,* vol. 28, 1887–88, p. 319.

16. Miss E. Barlee, *Pantomime Waifs, or A Plea for Our City Children* (London: S. W. Partridge, 1884), pp. 128–40.

17. Biblical Knowledge Prize Day became an annual event, held at the Crystal Palace. SBL *Minutes,* vol. 6, 1876, p. 63.

18. SBL *Minutes,* vol. 5, 1875, pp. 841, 845; vol. 13, 1880, pp. 688–90.

19. Dorothy Scannell, *Mother Knew Best* (London: Macmillan, 1974), p. 110.

20. SBL *Minutes,* vol. 5, 1875, p. 845; vol. 6, 1876, pp. 1561, 1582; vol. 16, 1881, p. 38. See David Vincent, *Literacy and Popular Culture* (Cambridge: Cambridge University Press), p. 91.

21. SBL *Minutes,* vol. 20, 1883, p. 192.

22. Clara Grant, *Farthing Bundles* (London: Fern Street Settlement, 1930), pp. 62–63.

23. SBL *Minutes,* vol. 8, 1877, p. 128; vol. 11, 1879, p. 711; vol. 16, 1881, p. 45. See also Henry Cecil Wyld, *The Place of the Mother Tongue in National Education* (London: John Murray, 1906).

24. SBL *Minutes,* vol. 7, 1877, pp. 109–10, 747–48.

25. SBL *Minutes,* vol. 8, 1878, pp. 676–92.

26. SBL *Minutes,* vol. 8, 1878, pp. 676–92.

27. SBL *Minutes,* vol. 10, 1878, pp. 389–91.

28. SBL *Minutes,* vol. 18, 1883, pp. 918–19.

29. SBL *Minutes,* vol. 18, 1883, p. 512.

30. SBL *Minutes,* vol. 6, 1876, pp. 1571–72.

31. See Kliebard, pp. 11–13 and chap. 2; Dorothy Ross, *G. Stanley Hall: The Psychologist as Prophet* (Chicago: University of Chicago Press, 1972); John Lawson and Harold Silver, *A Social History of Education in England* (London: Methuen, 1973), pp. 254–55; W. A. C. Stewart and W. P. McCann, *The Educational Innova-*

tors, 1750–1880 (London: Macmillan, 1967). See also the British Child-Study Association's journal, *The Paidologist,* first published in 1899.

32. SBL *Minutes,* vol. 20, 1884, p. 619.

33. SBL proponents of technical education included Lucraft, Firth, Taylor, and Coxhead. SBL *Minutes,* vol. 11, 1879, pp. 142–300.

34. Thomas Gautrey, *"Lux Mihi Laus": School Board Memories* (London: Link House, 1937), pp. 83–84.

35. SBL *Minutes,* vol. 26, 1887, p. 769.

36. SBL *Minutes,* vol. 28, 1888, pp. 787–92.

37. SBL *Minutes,* vol. 28, 1888, pp. 787–92. Huxley had made these remarks in a speech in 1887.

38. SBL *Minutes,* vol. 28, 1888, pp. 787–92.

39. *Final Report of the Commissioners appointed to inquire into the Elementary Acts,* PP 1888, xxxv [cd.5485], pp. 214–15. In *Ability, Merit and Measurement: Mental Testing and English Education, 1880–1940* (Oxford: Clarendon, 1984), p. 8, Gillian Sutherland links the appointment of this commission to the overpressure crisis. The push for domestic education for girls is reviewed in Chapter Six above, in Dina Copelman, *London's Women Teachers: Gender, Class and Feminism, 1870–1930* (London: Routledge, 1996), and in Anna Davin, *Growing Up Poor: Home, School and Street in London, 1870–1914* (London: Rivers Oram Press, 1996).

40. In 1879, an inspector suggested that girls learn needlework while boys learn geography, since girls took but a "languid interest" in geography while "[i]mperial instincts" moved more freely in boys. SBL *Minutes,* vol. 10, 1879, p. 395

41. SBL *Minutes,* vol. 28, March 1888, pp. 789–92; vol. 29, 1888, pp. 439–41.

42. Gautrey, pp. 85–86.

43. Fitch made these remarks while chairing a talk by Miss E. P. Hughes, "Manual Instruction in Schools," presented at the College of Preceptors, December 12, 1888. This paper is included in a bound series of "Tracts relating to the Slojd system" at the British Library.

44. *Final Report,* PP, 1888, xxxv, pp. 142–51.

45. Smyth is quoted in Brian Simon, *Education and the Labour Movement, 1870–1920* (London: Lawrence & Wishart, 1965), pp. 122–25. Grant, pp. 33–34.

46. *Final Report,* PP 1888, pp. 135–36.

47. SBL *Minutes,* vol. 28, p. 799.

48. *Education Report,* 1898–99, PP 1899, xx [9400], pp. 654–55.

49. Lord Reay, the SBL's final chairman, said as much in 1904. Quoted in Gautrey, pp. 17–18.

50. *Final Report,* PP 1888, xxxv, pp. 145–46.

51. Edmund Holmes, *What Is and What Might Be* (1911; London: Constable, 1917).

52. Grant, pp. 140–47.

53. Joyce M. Morris, "Phonics: From an Unsophisticated Past to a Linguistic-informed Future," in Greg Brooks and A. K. Pugh, eds., *Studies in the History of Reading* (n.p.: University of Reading School of Education, 1984); J. L. Dobson, "English Studies and Popular Literacy in England, 1870–1970," in Greg Brooks, A. K. Pugh,

and Nigel Hall, eds., *Further Studies in the History of Reading* (Cheshire: United Kingdom Reading Association, 1993).

54. Rose, in Steedman et al., *Language, Gender and Childhood* pp. 106–7. Basil Bernstein, 2nd rev. ed., *Class, Codes and Controls* (New York: Schocken Books, 1975). Bernstein, who developed his linguistic theories while teaching working-class adolescents, argued that definitions of "educability," too often characterized in terms of genetics and IQ, must instead account for class-based "communication codes" and access to knowledge.

55. See Louis James, *Fiction for the Working Man, 1830–1850* (London: Oxford University Press, 1963); E. P. Thompson, *The Making of the English Working Class* (New York: Vintage, 1963), esp. chap. 16; Vincent, *Literacy;* Jonathan Rose, "Rereading the English Common Reader: a Preface to a History of Audiences," *Journal of the History of Ideas* 53, no. 1 (1992): 42–70.

56. *The Guardian*'s lead story for 8 May 1996 explained that both parties had declared "The End of the Welfare State."

57. In *The Rise of Popular Literacy in Victorian England* (Philadelphia: University of Pennsylvania Press, 1992), p. xvi, David Mitch points out the similarity between complaints of overpressure under the system of payment by result in the 1880s and complaints about implementation of standardized testing under the Baker Plan of 1988. Following teacher boycotts of the testing, the government scaled back its curriculum and testing goals.

58. *The Independent,* 8 May 1996, pp. 7, 15; *The Guardian,* 9 May 1996, p. 5.

Selected Bibliography

Archival sources

Archives of Harper and Brothers, 1817–1914. Cambridge: Chadwyck-Healey, 1980.

Archives of the House of Longman, 1794–1914. Cambridge: Chadwyck-Healey, 1978.

Archives of Richard Bentley and Sons, 1829–1898. Cambridge: Chadwyck-Healey, 1977.

Macmillan Archives, British Library.

Minutes of the Meeting of the Books and Apparatus Sub-Committee for the School Board of London, 1885 [SBL 681]. Greater London Record Office (GLRO).

Minutes of the Meeting of the Special Committee on the Selection of Schoolbooks, 1899 [SBL 188]. GLRO.

Minutes of the Proceedings of the School Board for London, 1870–1903, British Library.

Nesbit, E., Papers. Berg Collection, New York Public Library.

School Board for London. *Report on Methods of Teaching Reading,* 1877 [SBL 1432], GLRO.

———. *Report of the Special Committee on the Question of Overpressure in the Schools of the Board,* July 1885 [SBL 1466]. GLRO.

Parliamentary Papers

Annual Report for 1912 of the Chief Medical Officer of the Board of Education, PP 1914, xxv [cd. 7184].

Final Report of the Commissioners Appointed to Inquire into the Elementary Education Acts, PP 1888, xxxv [cd. 5485].

Memorandum relating to Dr. Crichton-Browne's Report by Mr. J. G. Fitch, one of Her Majesty's Chief Inspectors of Schools, PP 1884, lxi (293), pp. 55–79.

Report of Dr. Crichton-Browne to the Education Department upon the Alleged Over-Pressure of Work in Public Elementary Schools, PP 1884, lxi (293), pp. 3–54.

Report of the Board of Education for the Year 1911–12, PP 1913 [cd. 6707].

Report of the Committee of Council on Education, 1885–86, PP 1886, xxiv [4849].

Autobiographies

Brunel University Library, Autobiography Collection

Belcher, William. N.d. Manuscript.

Brown, Edward. N.d. Manuscript.

Cowper, Daisy. 1964. Manuscript.

Goffin, Arthur. "A Grey Life." 1933, 1973. Manuscript.

Published Autobiographies and Collections

Acland, Eleanor. *Goodbye for the Present, The Story of Two Childhoods.* London: Hodder & Stoughton, 1935.

Asquith, Margot. *The Autobiography of Margot Asquith.* 1962. London: Methuen, 1985.

Avery, Valerie. *London Morning.* Oxford: Pergamon Press, 1964.

Baldry, George. *The Rabbit Skin Cap.* London: Collins, 1939.

Ballard, Philip. *Things I Cannot Forget.* London: University of London Press, 1937.

Bell, Thomas. *Pioneering Days.* London: Lawrence & Wishart, 1941.

Bentley, Phyllis. *O Dreams, O Destinations.* London: Victor Gollancz, 1962.

Bondfield, Margaret. *A Life's Work.* London: Hutchinson, 1949.

Booker, Beryl Lee. *Yesterday's Child.* London: J. Long, 1937.

Bowyer, William. *Brought Out in Evidence.* London: Faber & Faber, 1941.

Bullard, Sir Reader. *The Camels Must Go.* London: Faber & Faber, 1961.

Burnett, Frances Hodgson. *The One I Knew Best of All.* 1893. New York: Arno Press, 1980.

Bushell, W. F. *School Memories.* Liverpool: Philip Son & Nephew, 1962.

Chorley, Katherine. *Manchester Made Them.* London: Faber & Faber, 1950.

Citrine, Walter. *Men and Work, An Autobiography.* London: Hutchinson, 1964.

Clynes, J. R. *Memoirs.* London: Hutchinson, 1937.

————. *When I Remember.* London: Macmillan War Pamphlets # 6, 1940.

Cobbe, Frances Power. *The Life of Frances Power Cobbe, As told by Herself.* Boston: Houghton Mifflin, 1894.

Cohen, Margaret, Marion and Hymie Fagan, eds. *Childhood Memories, Recorded by Some Socialist Men and Women in Their Later Years.* London: n.p., n.d.

Collison, William. *The Apostle of Free Labour.* London: Hurst & Blackett, 1913.

Coppard, A. E. *It's Me, O Lord.* London: Methuen, 1957.

Corke, Helen. *In Our Infancy, Part I.* Cambridge: Cambridge University Press, 1975.

Cowper, Agnes. *A Backward Glance on Merseyside.* Birkenhead: Wilmer Bros., 1948, 1952.

Davies, Margaret Llewelyn, ed. *Life as We Have Known It.* 1931. New York: W. W. Norton, 1975.

Faithfull, Lillian M. *In the House of My Pilgrimage.* London: Chatto & Windus, 1925.

Farningham, Marianne. *A Working Woman's Life.* London: James Clark, 1907.

Fawcett, Millicent Garrett. *What I Remember.* New York: G. P. Putnam's Sons, 1925.

Forbes, Lady Angela. *Memories and Base Details.* London: Hutchinson, 1921.

Fraser, John. *Sixty Years in Uniform.* London: Stanley Paul, 1939.

Gibbs, Rose. *In Service, Rose Gibbs Remembers.* N.p.: Ellison's Editions, 1981.

Gosling, Harry. *Up and Down Stream.* London: Methuen, 1927.

Grant, Clara. *Farthing Bundles*. London: Fern Street Settlement, 1930.

Greene, Graham. *A Sort of Life*. New York: Simon & Schuster, 1971.

Griffiths, James. *Pages from Memory*. London: Dent, 1969.

Haddow, William. *My Seventy Years*. Glasgow: Robert Gibson & Sons, 1943.

Hawker, Henry. *Notes of My Life*. Stonehouse: W. G. Davis, 1919.

Hobhouse, Stephen. *The Autobiography of Stephen Hobhouse*. Boston: Beacon Press, 1952.

Hodgkinson, George. *Sent to Coventry*. London: Robert Maxwell, 1970.

Howard, Rev. J. H. *Winding Lanes*. Caernarvon: The Calvinistic Methodist Printing Works, 1938.

Hughes, M. V. *A London Girl of the 1880s*. 1943. Oxford: Oxford University Press, 1978.

Hunt, Agnes. *This Is My Life*. 1942. New York: Arno Press, 1980.

Inman, Philip. *No Going Back*. London: Williams & Norgate, 1952.

Jones, L. E. *A Victorian Boyhood*. London: Macmillan, 1955.

Kenney, Annie. *Memories of a Militant*. London: Edward Arnold, 1924.

Keppel, Sonia. *Edwardian Daughter*. London: Hamish Hamilton, 1958.

Kitchen, Fred. *Brother to the Ox*. 1940. Sussex: Caliban Books, 1981.

Lovett, William. *The Life and Struggles of William Lovett*. 1876. New York: Garland Publishers, 1984.

MacGill, Patrick. *Children of the Dead End*. 1914. Berkshire: Caliban Books, 1980.

Manning, Leah. *A Life for Education*. London: Victor Gollancz, 1970.

Mansbridge, Albert. *The Trodden Road*. London: Dent, 1940.

Margrie, William. *The Invincible Smile*. London: Watts, 1924.

Meek, George. *George Meek Bath Chair Man*. London: Constable, 1910.

Mitchell, Hannah. *The Hard Way Up*. London: Faber & Faber, 1968.

Montefiore, Dora. *From a Victorian to a Modern*. London: E. Archer, 1927.

Nesbit, Edith. *Long Ago When I Was Young*. London: Ronald Whiting & Wheaton, 1966.

Okey, Thomas. *A Basketful of Memories*. London: J. M. Dent & Sons, 1930.

Peck, Winifred. *A Little Learning, or A Victorian Childhood*. London: Faber & Faber, 1952.

————. *Home for the Holidays*. London: Faber & Faber, 1955.

Powell, Anthony. *Infants of the Spring*. New York: Holt, Rinehart & Winston, 1976.

Ransome, Arthur. *The Autobiography of Arthur Ransome*. London: Jonathan Cape, 1976.

Ratcliffe, George. *Sixty Years of It*. London: A. Brown, 1935.

Raverat, Gwen. *Period Piece*. London: Faber & Faber, 1952.

Rhondda, Margaret. *This Was My World*. London: Macmillan, 1933.

Roberts, Robert. *A Ragged Schooling*. London: Fontana, 1982.

Rodaway, Angela. *A London Childhood*. 1960. London: Virago, 1985.

Rowse, A. L. *A Cornish Childhood*. New York: Macmillan, 1947.

Russell, Dora. *The Tamarisk Tree*. London: Elek Books, 1975.

Scannell, Dorothy. *Mother Knew Best*. London: Macmillan, 1974.

Seabrook, Jeremy. *The Unprivileged*. Harmondsworth: Penguin, 1973.

Severn, J. Millot. *The Life Story and Experiences of a Phrenologist.* Brighton: J. M. Severn, 1929.

Smith, Emma (pseud.). *A Cornish Waif's Story.* New York: E. P. Dutton, 1956.

Smith, Gipsy. *Gipsy Smith, His Life and Work by Himself.* London: National Council of the Evangelical Free Churches, 1902.

Snell, Lord. *Men, Movements and Myself.* London: J. M. Dent & Sons, 1936.

Southgate, Walter. *That's the Way It Was.* London: New Clarion Press, 1982.

Spring, Howard. *Heaven Lies Above Us.* London: Constable, 1939.

Steel, Frank. *Ditcher's Row.* London: Sidgwick & Jackson, 1939.

Stewart, Bob. *Breaking the Fetters.* London: Lawrence & Wishart, 1967.

Swanwick, Helena M. *I Have Been Young.* London: Victor Gollancz, 1935.

Thompson, Flora. *Lark Rise to Candleford.* London: Oxford University Press, 1939.

Tillet, Ben. *Memories and Reflections.* London: John Long, 1931.

Tomlinson, H. M. *A Mingled Yarn.* London: Gerald Duckworth, 1953.

Turner, Ben. *About Myself.* London: Cayme Press, 1930.

Webb, Beatrice. *My Apprenticeship.* London: Longmans, Green & Co., 1926.

Wellock, Wilfred. *Off the Beaten Track.* India: Bhargava Bhushan Press, 1963.

Willis, Frederick. *Peace and Dripping Toast.* London: Phoenix House, 1950.

Wilson, John. *Memories of a Labour Leader.* London: T. Fisher Unwin, 1910.

Woodward, Kathleen. *Jipping Street.* London: Virago, 1983.

Newspapers and Periodicals (Before 1915)

British Medical Journal (BMJ)
Children's Own Magazine
Cornhill Magazine
East London Leader
East London Observer
Independent Review
Lancet
Lloyd's Weekly Newspaper
Nineteenth Century
The Paidologist
Pall Mall Gazette (PMG)
Punch
School Guardian
The Times

Primary Sources: Books

Arnold, Matthew. *The Complete Prose Works of Matthew Arnold,* ed. R. H. Super, Vol. 2. Ann Arbor: University of Michigan Press, 1962.

———. *Reports on Elementary Schools.* London: Wyman & Sons, 1908.

Barlee, E. *Pantomime Waifs, or A Plea for Our City Children.* London: S. W. Partridge, 1884.

Blatchford, Robert. *A Book About Books.* London: Clarion Press, 1903.

Chamberlain, Alexander. *The Child and Childhood in Folk-Thought.* New York: Macmillan, 1896.

Collar, G. and C. W. Crook. *School Management and Methods of Instruction.* London: Macmillan, 1900.

Cooper, E. H. *The Twentieth Century Child.* London: John Lane, 1905.

Craik, Henry. *The State in Its Relation to Education.* Rev. ed. London: Macmillan, 1914.

Crichton-Browne, James. *Delusions in Diet.* London: Funk & Wagnalls, 1910.

———. *Training of the Hand.* London: Thomas Laurie, 1890.

Crowley, Ralph. *The Need, Objects and Methods of the Medical Inspection of Primary Schools.* London: Churchill, 1906.

Coulton, G. A. *Public Schools and Public Needs.* London: Simpkin, Marshall, Hamilton, Kent, 1901.

Dyer, Henry. *Education and Work.* Dumferline, Scotland: A. Romanes & Sons, 1906.

Field, E. M. *The Child and His Book.* 2nd ed. London: Wells Gardner, Darton, 1895.

Gautrey, Thomas. *"Lux Mihi Laus": School Board Memories.* London: Link House, 1937.

Groser, W. H. *A Hundred Years' Work for the Children.* London: Sunday School Union, 1903.

Hodgson, W. B. "Exaggerated Estimates of Reading and Writing," *Transactions of the National Association for the Promotion of Social Science.* N.p.: 1867.

Holmes, Edmund. *In Quest of an Ideal.* London: Richard Cobden-Sanderson, 1920.

———. *What Is and What Might Be.* 1911. London: Constable, 1917.

Jephson, Rev. A. W. *My Work in London.* London: Isaac Pittman, 1910.

Lang, Andrew. *Adventures Among Books.* London: Longmans, 1905.

———. *The Colour Fairy Book Series.* London: Longmans, 1889–1910.

———. *Myth, Ritual and Religion.* Rev. ed. 2 vols. London: Longmans, 1913.

Laurie, J. S. *First Steps to Reading.* London, 1862.

McCabe, Joseph. *A Hundred Years of Education Controversy.* London: Watts, 1907.

McMillan, Margaret. *Early Childhood.* London: Swan Sonnenschein, 1900.

Mearns, Andrew. *The Bitter Cry of Outcast London,* ed. Anthony Wohl. New York: Humanities Press, 1970.

National Society's Annotated Edition of the Education Bill, 1906. N.p.: 1906.

Nesbit, E. *The Story of the Amulet.* London: T. Fisher Unwin, 1906.

———. *These Little Ones.* London: George Allen & Sons, 1909.

———. *Wings and the Child.* London: Hodder & Stoughton, 1913.

———. *The Wouldbegoods.* London: T. Fisher Unwin, 1901.

Paton, Grace. *The Child and the Nation.* London: Student Christian Movement, 1915.

Radford, George. *The Faculty of Reading.* Cambridge: Cambridge University Press, 1910.

Reports of the Debates of the School Board for London. London: Church and Voluntary Schools Defence Union, 1895.

Salmon, Edward. *Juvenile Literature as It Is.* London: Henry Drake, 1888.

Sherard, Robert. *Child Slaves in Britain.* London: Hurst and Blackett, 1905.

Spalding, Thomas. *The Work of the London School Board.* London: P. S. King & Son, 1900.

Spencer, Frederick. *An Inspector's Testament.* London: English Universities Press, 1938.

Webb, Sidney. *London Education.* London: Longmans, 1904.

Wilson, Richard. *Macmillan's Sentence Building.* London: Macmillan, 1914.

Wyld, Henry Cecil. *The Teaching of Reading in Training Colleges.* London: John Murray, 1908.

————. *The Place of the Mother Tongue in National Education.* London: John Murray, 1906.

Yong, Charlotte. *What Books to Lend and What to Give.* 1886.

Secondary Sources

Ackerman, Ann. "Victorian Ideology and British Children's Literature." Ph.D. Diss., University of North Texas, 1984.

Altick, Richard. *The English Common Reader.* Chicago: University of Chicago Press, 1957.

Anderson, R. D. *Education and Opportunity in Victorian Scotland.* Oxford: Clarendon, 1983.

Avery, Gillian. *Childhood's Patterns, A study of Heroes and Heroines of Children's Fiction.* London: Hodder & Stoughton, 1975.

————. *Nineteenth Century Children: Heroes and Heroines in English Children's Stories, 1780–1900.* London: Hodder & Stoughton, 1965.

Bailey, Peter. *Leisure and Class in Victorian England.* Toronto: University of Toronto Press, 1978.

Barr, John. *Illustrated Children's Books.* London: The British Library, 1986.

Baumann, Gerd, ed. *The Written Word: Literacy in Transition.* Oxford: Clarendon, 1986.

Beals, Polly. "Fabian Feminism: Gender, Politics and Culture in London, 1880–1930." Ph.D. Diss., Rutgers University, 1989.

Behlmer, George. *Child Abuse and Moral Reform in England, 1870–1908.* Stanford: Stanford University Press, 1982.

Bell, Susan Groag and Marilyn Yalom, eds. *Revealing Lives: Autobiography, Biography and Gender.* Albany: State University of New York Press, 1990.

Benstock, Shari. *The Private Self: Theory and Practice of Women's Autobiographical Writings.* Chapel Hill: University of North Carolina Press, 1988.

Bernstein, Basil. *Class, Codes and Control.* New York: Schocken, 1975.

Boas, George. *The Cult of Childhood.* London: The Warburg Institute, 1966.

Bratton, J. S. *The Impact of Victorian Children's Fiction.* London: Croom Helm, 1981.

Briggs, Asa, ed. *Essays in the History of Publishing.* London: Longmans, 1974.

Briggs, Julia. *A Woman of Passion, The Life of E. Nesbit, 1858–1924.* New York: New Amsterdam Books, 1987.

Brodzki, Bella and Celeste Schenk, eds. *Life/Lines: Theorizing Women's Autobiography.* Ithaca: Cornell University Press, 1988.

Brooks, Greg, A. K. Pugh, and Nigel Hall, eds. *Further Studies in the History of Reading.* Chesire: United Kingdom Reading Association, 1993.

Brooks, Jeffrey. *When Russia Learned to Read: Literacy and Popular Literature, 1861–1917.* Princeton: Princeton University Press, 1985.

Burnett, John. *Useful Toil: Autobiographies of Working People from the 1820s to 1920.* London: Allen Lane, 1974.

———. *Destiny Obscure: Autobiographies of Childhood, Education and Family from the 1820s to 1920.* 1982. Harmondsworth: Penguin, reprint, 1984.

Burnett, John, David Vincent, and David Mayall, eds. *The Autobiography of the Working-Class: An Annotated Critical Biography.* Vol. 2. New York: New York University Press, 1987.

Carpenter, Humphrey. *Secret Gardens: The Golden Age of Children's Literature.* Boston: Houghton, Mifflin, 1985.

Carpenter, Kevin. *Penny Dreadfuls and Comics: English Periodicals for Children from Victorian Times to the Present Day.* London: Victoria and Albert Museum, 1983.

Chamberlain, Mary. *Fen Women.* London: Virago, 1975.

Coe, Richard. *When the Grass Was Taller.* New Haven: Yale University Press, 1984.

Colls, Robert and Philip Dodd, eds. *Englishness, Politics and Culture, 1880–1920.* London: Croom Helm, 1986.

Copelman, Dina. *London's Women Teachers: Gender, Class and Feminism, 1870–1930.* London: Routledge, 1996.

Corrigan, Philip and Derek Sayers. *The Great Arch.* New York: Basic Blackwell, 1985.

Cott, Jonathan, ed. *Victorian Color Picture Books.* New York: Stonehill Communications, 1983.

Coveney, Peter. *The Image of Childhood.* 1957. Harmondsworth: Penguin, 1967.

Craig, John E. "The Expansion of Education." *Review of Research in Education* 9 (1981): 151–213.

Crozier, Brian. "Notions of Childhood in the London Theatre, 1880–1905." Ph.D. thesis, Cambridge University, 1981.

Cunningham, Hugh. *The Children of the Poor.* Oxford: Blackwell, 1991.

Cunningham, Peter. "Educational History and Educational Change: The Past Decade of English Historiography," *History of Education Quarterly* 29, no. 1 (1989): 77–94.

Darton, Harvey. *Children's Books in England.* Rev. ed., Brian Alderson. Cambridge: Cambridge University Press, 1982.

Davidoff, Leonore and Catherine Hall. *Family Fortunes: Men and Women of the English Middle Class, 1750–1850.* Chicago: University of Chicago Press, 1987.

Davies, Tony. "Transports of Pleasure: Fiction and Its Audiences in the Later Nineteenth Century." *Formations of Pleasure,* ed. Frederic Jameson. London: Routledge, 1983.

Davin, Anna. *Growing Up Poor: Home, School and Street in London, 1870–1914.* London: Rivers Oram Press, 1996.

Denning, Michael. *Mechanic Accents: Dime Novels and Working-class Culture in America.* London: Verso, 1987.

Digby, Anne, and Peter Searby. *Children, School and Society in Nineteenth Century England.* London: Macmillan, 1981.

Dixon, Diana. "Children and the Press, 1866–1914." *The Press in English Society from the 17th to the 19th Centuries,* eds. Michael Harris and Alan Lee. Cranbury, N.J.: Associated University Presses, 1986.

Dorson, Richard M. *The British Folklorists, A History.* Chicago: University of Chicago Press, 1968.

Drotner, Kirsten. *English Children and Their Magazines, 1751–1945.* New Haven: Yale University Press, 1988.

Dwork, Deborah, *War Is Good for Babies and Other Young Children.* London: Tavistock, 1987.

Dyhouse, Carol. *Girls Growing Up in Late Victorian and Edwardian England.* London: Routledge, 1981.

———. "Good Wives and Little Mothers: Social Anxieties and the Schoolgirl's Curriculum, 1880–1920." *Oxford Review of Education* 3, no. 1 (1977): 21–35.

Eagleton, Terry. *The Function of Criticism.* London: Verso, 1984.

Eakin, John Paul. *Fictions in Autobiography: Studies in the Art of Self-invention.* Princeton: Princeton University Press, 1985.

Ellis, Alec. *Educating Our Masters.* Hampshire, England: Gower, 1985.

———. *A History of Children's Reading and Literature.* Oxford: Pergamon Press, 1968.

Ellman, Richard. *Oscar Wilde.* New York: Alfred A. Knopf, 1988.

Fishman, Sterling. "The History of Childhood and the History of Education," *History of Education Quarterly* 29 (1989): 109–114.

Flynn, Elizabeth and Patrocinio Schweickart, eds. *Gender and Reading.* Baltimore: Johns Hopkins University Press, 1986.

Folkenflik, Robert, ed. *The Culture of Autobiography: Constructions of Self-Representation.* Stanford: Stanford University Press, 1993.

Fraser, James, ed. *Society and Children's Literature.* Boston: David R. Godine, 1978.

Frykman, Jonas, and Orvar Lofgren. *Culture Builders, An Historical Anthropology of Middle Class Life.* Translated by Alan Crozier. New Brunswick: Rutgers University Press, 1987.

Gagnier, Regina. *Subjectivities: A History of Self-Representation in Britain, 1832–1920.* New York: Oxford University Press, 1991.

Gardner, Philip. *The Lost Elementary Schools of Victorian England.* London: Croom Helm, 1984.

Gillis, John. *A World of Their Own Making: Myth, Ritual, and the Quest for Family Values.* New York: Basic Books, 1996.

———. *Youth and History.* New York: Academic Press, 1974.

Goldstrom, J. M. *The Social Content of Education, 1808–1870.* Shannon, Ireland: Irish University Press, 1972.

Goodwin, James. *Autobiography: The Self Made Text.* New York: Twayne Publishers, 1993.

Goody, Jack, ed. *Literacy in Traditional Society.* Cambridge: Cambridge University Press, 1968.

Gorham, Deborah. "'The Maiden Tribute of Modern Babylon' Re-examined: Child Prostitution and the Idea of Childhood in Late Victorian England." *Victorian Studies* (Spring 1978): 353–79.

———. *The Victorian Girl and the Feminine Ideal.* Bloomington: Indiana University Press, 1982.

Graff, Harvey. *Literacy in History.* New York: Garland Publishing, 1981.

———. *The Literacy Myth.* New York: Academic Press, 1979.

Green, Roger Lancelyn. *Andrew Lang.* New York: Henry Z. Walck, 1962.

———. *Mrs. Molesworth.* 1961. New York: Henry Z. Walck, 1964.

Hackett, Nan. *Nineteenth Century British Working-Class Autobiographies: An Annotated Bibliography.* New York: AMS Press, 1985.

Halverson, John. "Havelock on Greek Orality and Literacy." *Journal of the History of Ideas,* 53, no. 1 (1992): 148–63.

Hobsbawm, Eric and Terence Ranger, eds. *The Invention of Tradition.* Cambridge: Cambridge University Press, 1983.

Hoggart, Richard. *The Uses of Literacy.* 1957. New York: Oxford University Press, 1970.

Hollis, Patricia. *Ladies Elect: Women in English Local Government, 1865–1914.* Oxford: Clarendon Press, 1987.

Humphreys, Anne. "G. W. M. Reynolds: Popular Literature and Popular Politics." *Innovators and Preachers: The Role of the Editor in Victorian England,* ed. Joel Wiener. Westport: Greenwood Press, 1985.

Humphries, Stephen. *Hooligans or Rebels?* Oxford: Basil Blackwell, 1981.

Hunt, Felicity, ed. *Lessons for Life.* Oxford: Basil Blackwell, 1987.

Hurt, John. *Elementary Schooling and the Working Classes, 1860–1918.* London: Routledge, 1979.

Jackson, Mary V. *Engines of Instruction, Mischief and Magic.* Lincoln: University of Nebraska Press, 1989.

Jelinek, Estelle, ed. *Women's Autobiography: Essays in Criticism.* Bloomington: Indiana University Press, 1980.

Johnson, Richard et al., eds. *Making Histories: Studies in History-writing and Politics.* London: Hutchinson, 1982.

Jordan, Thomas. *Victorian Childhood.* Albany: State University of New York Press, 1987.

Kaestle, Carl et al. *Literacy in the United States: Readers and Reading Since 1880.* New Haven: Yale University Press, 1991.

Kincaid, James. *Child-Loving: The Erotic Child and Victorian Culture.* New York: Routledge, 1992.

King, Michael, ed. *Childhood Welfare and Justice.* London: Batsford, 1981.

Kliebard, Herbert. *The Struggle for the American Curriculum, 1893–1958.* 2nd ed. New York: Routledge, 1995.

Knoepflmacher, U. C. "Of Babylands and Babylons: E. Nesbit and the Reclamation of the Fairy-Tale." *Tulsa Studies in Women's Literature* vol. 16, no. 2 (1987): 299–325.

Kuklick, Henrika. *The Savage Within: The Social History of Anthropology, 1885–1945.* New York: Cambridge University Press, 1991.

Lang, Marjory. "Childhood's Champions: Mid-Victorian Children's Periodicals and the Critics." *Victorian Periodicals Review* 13 (1980): 17–31.

Langan, Mary and Bill Schwarz, eds. *Crisis in the British State, 1880–1930.* London: Hutchinson, 1985.

Langstaff, Eleanor De Selms. *Andrew Lang.* Boston: Twayne, 1978.

Laqueur, Thomas. "Literacy and Social Mobility in the Industrial Revolution in England" and "A Rejoinder" by Michael Sanderson. *Past and Present* 64 (1975): 97–112.

———. *Religion and Respectability: Sunday Schools and Working-class Culture, 1780–1850.* New Haven: Yale University Press, 1976.

Lawson, John, and Harold Silver. *A Social History of Education in England.* London: Methuen, 1973.

Lears, Jackson. *No Place of Grace.* New York: Pantheon, 1981.

Lejeune, Philippe. *On Autobiography,* ed. Paul John Eakin. Translated by Katherine Leary. Minneapolis: University of Minnesota Press, 1989.

Lewis, Jane. *The Politics of Motherhood.* London: Croom Helm, 1980.

Lowenthal, David. *The Past Is a Foreign Country.* Cambridge: Cambridge University Press, 1985.

McCann, Phillip, ed. *Popular Education and Socialization in the Nineteenth Century.* London: Methuen, 1977.

McCrindle, Jean and Sheila Rowbotham, eds. *Dutiful Daughters.* London: Penguin, 1977.

Meyrowitz, Joshua. "The Adultlike Child and the Childlike Adult: Socialization in an Electronic Age." *Daedalus* 113, no. 3 (Summer 1984): 19–47.

Mitch, David. *The Rise of Popular Literacy in Victorian England.* Philadelphia: University of Pennsylvania Press, 1992.

Moore, Doris Langley. Rev. ed. *E. Nesbit, A Biography.* Philadelphia: Chilton Books, 1966.

Myers, Robin, and Michael Harris, eds. *The Development of the English Book Trade, 1700–1899.* Oxford: Oxford Polytechnic Press, 1981.

Nelson, Claudia. *Boys Will Be Girls: The Feminine Ethic and British Children's Fiction, 1857–1917.* New Brunswick: Rutgers University Press, 1991.

Nord, Deborah. *The Apprenticeship of Beatrice Webb.* Amherst: University of Massachusetts Press, 1985.

Ong, Walter. *Orality and Literacy.* New York: Methuen, 1982.

Opie, Iona and Peter. *Children's Games in Street and Playground.* Oxford: Oxford University Press, 1984.

Pattison, Robert. *The Child Figure in English Literature.* Athens: University of Georgia Press, 1978.

Perrot, Michelle, ed. *A History of Private Life: From the Fires of the Revolution to the Great War.* Vol. iv. Translated by Arthur Goldhammer. Cambridge, MA: Belknap Press, 1990.

Personal Narratives Group. *Interpreting Women's Lives: Feminist Theory and Personal Narratives.* Bloomington: Indiana University Press, 1989.

Peterson, Linda. *Victorian Autobiography.* New Haven: Yale University Press, 1986.

Pinchbeck, Ivy, and Margaret Hewitt. *Children in English Society.* Vol. 2. London: Routledge, 1973.

Rabinbach, Anson. *The Human Motor: Energy, Fatigue, and the Origins of Modernity.* Berkeley: University of California Press, 1992.

Radway, Janice. *Reading the Romance.* Chapel Hill: University of North Carolina Press, 1984.

Rappaport, Erika. "Sherry and Silks: Defining Women's Pleasure in Victorian England." Unpublished paper, Rutgers University History Department, Spring 1992.

Resnick, Daniel, ed. *Literacy in Historical Perspective.* Washington D.C.: Library of Congress, 1983.

Reynolds, Kimberley. *Girls Only? Gender and Popular Children's Fiction in Britain, 1880–1910.* Philadelphia: Temple University Press, 1990.

Ritvo, Harriet. *The Animal Estate.* Cambridge: Harvard University Press, 1987.

Jacqueline Rose, *The Case of Peter Pan, or The Impossibility of Children's Fiction.* London: Macmillan, 1984.

Rose, Jonathan. "Rereading the English Common Reader: A Preface to a History of Audiences." *Journal of the History of Ideas* 53, no. 1 (1992): 47–70.

Ross, Dorothy. *G. Stanley Hall: The Psychologist as Prophet.* Chicago: University of Chicago Press, 1972

Ross, Ellen. *Love and Toil: Motherhood in Outcast London, 1870–1918.* New York: Oxford University Press, 1993.

Rubenstein, David. *School Attendance in London, 1870–1904: A Social History.* Hull: University of Hull, 1969.

Salway, Lance, ed. *A Peculiar Gift.* Harmondsworth: Penguin, 1976.

Samuel, Raphael and Paul Thompson, eds. *The Myths We Live By.* New York: Routledge, 1990.

Sherington, Geoffrey. *English Education, Social Change and War, 1911–20.* Manchester: Manchester University Press, 1981.

Silver, Harold. *Education as History.* London: Methuen, 1983.

Simon, Brian. *Education and the Labour Movement, 1870–1920.* London: Lawrence and Wishart, 1965.

Springhall, John. *Coming of Age: Adolescence in Britain, 1860–1960.* Dublin: Gill & Macmillan, 1986.

Steedman, Carolyn. *Childhood, Culture and Class in Britain: Margaret McMillan, 1860–1931.* New Brunswick: Rutgers University Press, 1990.

———. *The Radical Soldier's Tale.* London: Routledge, 1988.

———. *Strange Dislocations: Childhood and the Idea of Human Interiority, 1780–1930.* Cambridge, MA: Harvard University Press, 1995.

Steedman, Carolyn, Cathy Urwin, Valerie Walkerdine, eds. *Language, Gender and Childhood.* London: Routledge, 1985.

Stephens, W. B. *Education, Literacy and Society, 1830–70.* Manchester: Manchester University Press, 1987.

Stocking, George. *Victorian Anthropology.* New York: The Free Press, 1987.

Stone, Lawrence. "Literacy and Education in England, 1640–1900." *Past and Present* 42 (1969): 69–139.

Sutherland, Gillian. *Policy-making in Elementary Education, 1870–1895.* Oxford: Oxford University Press, 1973.

Sutherland, J. A. *Victorian Novelists and Publishers.* Chicago: University of Chicago Press, 1976.

Thane, Pat. *The Foundations of the Welfare State.* London: Longman, 1982.

Thompson, Paul. *The Edwardians.* London: Weidenfield & Nicolson, 1975.

Thompson, Thea. *Edwardian Childhoods.* London: Routledge, 1981.

Tuchman, Gaye and Nina E. Fortin. *Edging Women Out: Victorian Novelists, Publishers, and Social Change.* New Haven: Yale University Press, 1989.

Vann, Richard T. "The Youth of *Centuries of Childhood.*" *History and Theory* 21 (1982): 279–92.

Vincent, David. *Bread, Knowledge and Freedom: A Study of Working-class Autobiography.* London: Europa, 1981.

———. *Literacy and Popular Culture.* Cambridge: Cambridge University Press, 1989.

Walkowitz, Judith R. *City of Dreadful Delight: Narratives of Sexual Danger in Late-Victorian London.* Chicago: University of Chicago Press, 1992.

Walvin, James. *A Child's World: A Social History of English Childhood, 1800–1914.* Harmondsworth: Penguin, 1982.

Webb, R. K. *The British Working Class Reader, 1790–1848.* London: George Allen and Unwin, 1955.

Whalley, Joyce and Tessa Rose Chester. *A History of Children's Book Illustration.* London: John Murray, 1988.

Williams, Raymond. *Culture and Society, 1750–1950.* 1958. New York: Columbia University Press, 1983

———. *Problems in Materialism and Culture.* London: Verso, 1980.

Wilson, Christopher P. "The Rhetoric of Consumption: Mass-market Magazines and the Demise of the Gentle Reader, 1880–1920" in Richard Wightman Fox and Jackson Lears, eds., *The Culture of Consumption.* New York: Pantheon Books, 1983.

Yeo, Stephen. "A New Life: The Religion of Socialism in Britain, 1883–1896," *History Workshop Journal* 4 (1977): 5–56.

Zelizer, Viviana. *Pricing the Priceless Child.* New York: Basic Books, 1985.

Index